The Parting of the Ways

How Esoteric Judaism and Christianity Influenced the Psychoanalytic Theories of Sigmund Freud and Carl Jung

The **Psychoanalysis and Jewish Life** book series has been established to promote scholarship, research, and a wide range of theoretical, textural, and clinical studies on the multiple interconnections between and mutual influence of Judaism and contemporary psychoanalysis. Its aim is broad, spanning a wide variety of subject areas: from the origins of psychoanalysis in Jewish circles in turn-of-the-century Vienna to clinical studies illuminating contemporary facets of Jewish identity and self-understanding; from explorations of psychological aspects of Jewish theology to psychoanalytic investigations of anti-Semitism; from studies of Jewish religious ritual to analyses of Hasidic mysticism and folklore; from psychoanalytic studies of pre-World War II Yiddish theater to the clinical practice of psychoanalysis in modern-day Tel Aviv. The Psychoanalysis and Jewish Life book series provides a home for fresh and intellectually challenging contributions across the spectrum of this interdisciplinary area of scholarship.

ACADEMIC STUDIES PRESS

The Parting of the Ways

How Esoteric Judaism and Christianity Influenced the Psychoanalytic Theories of Sigmund Freud and Carl Jung

RICHARD KRADIN

Boston
2016

Library of Congress Cataloging-in-Publication Data:
A catalog record for this title is available
from the Library of Congress.

ISBN 978-1-61811-422-8 (cloth)

ISBN 978-1-61811-423-5 (electronic)

On the cover: "Prima facie," by Siobhan Cashman.

Published by Academic Studies Press in 2016
28 Montfern Avenue
Brighton, MA 02135, USA
press@academicstudiespress.com
www.academicstudiespress.com

Table of Contents

Acknowledgements

This book is the culmination of my years of training in both psychoanalysis and religion. I wish to thank all of my teachers of Freudian and Jungian psychoanalysis, especially Robert Bosnak and the late Ann Alonso for their interest in my ideas during training and beyond. I wish to acknowledge my Harvard University thesis advisor Paul Hanson for his help in integrating ideas from early Judaic and Christian history. I acknowledge my heartfelt appreciation for Rev. Michael Domba, z"l, who taught me how to approach a Talmudic text. My thanks to R. Nehemiah Polen, R. Ebn Leader, Barry Mesch, and R. Arthur Green of Hebrew College for their teachings and wisdom. My appreciation is extended to my various teachers in the Chabad Hasidic movement, Rabbis Yossel Polter, Shmuel Posner, Yosef Zaklos, and Yosef Goldberg, who live the lives that some of us merely write about. My thanks extend to my editor, Lew Aron, for giving me the opportunity to author this text and sufficient license to express some controversial ideas. And of course to family and friends—you know how I feel about you. *Shalom*/Peace.

Preface

Like Sigmund Freud and Carl Jung, I am a physician. I chose to pursue my interests in psychoanalysis after having first established a career as both a pulmonologist and pathologist at the Massachusetts General Hospital (MGH), where I continue to practice in all of these areas. I trained in Freudian psychoanalytical psychotherapy at the Boston Institute of Psychotherapies and at the MGH, and served in the MGH Psychopharmacology Clinic where I gained a firm footing in biological psychiatry. I subsequently trained at the C. G. Jung Institute in Boston and received my diploma as a Jungian analyst.

However, I found myself often at odds with my Jungian colleagues. Some had little or no background in clinical psychology or psychiatry, and had received a classical Jungian training in Zurich. Their mode of analysis was focused on dream interpretation and active imagination, which, although fascinating, was in my opinion questionably effective in dealing with the neurotic problems of many patients. Many of my Jungian colleagues expressed little interest in developmental psychopathology, and there appeared to be few mutually agreed upon rules concerning how to conduct the treatment of patients, and a notable resistance towards instituting any.

This was antithetical to my Freudian training. If anything, I had found my Freudian colleagues overly focused on maintaining boundaries and on the analysis of Oedipal issues. Their approach to patients at times seemed formulaic and constrained. I began to suspect that the differences between my Freudian and Jungian approaches had identifiable roots in the tenets of Judaism and Christianity.

I was born into a family of first-generation American Jews and raised in a secular home, but one with strong ties to observant Judaism. My parents were not strictly kosher, although my mother only purchased meat from a kosher butcher, and the idea of mixing meat with dairy at the dinner table was anathema. Unleavened foodstuff (*chametz*) was inadmissible to our house during Passover, yet we celebrated no family Seder. The major religious holidays of Sukkot and Shavuot were ignored, yet our home assumed an aura of scrupulous religiosity during the High Holy Days. We did not observe the Sabbath. In retrospect, I cannot explain why certain tenets of Judaism were firmly held while others were ignored by my family, except to say that the desire to assimilate into American culture and the atrocities of World War II had left traditional Judaism in disarray and in search of new directions.

I was educated in the Conservative synagogue, and taught to read Hebrew, but with little understanding of what I was reading. Like many of my peers, I did not adhere to my religion after my Bar Mitzvah, but neither did I abandon it. When my mother died in 1983, I began to say *kaddish*, the traditional prayer for the dead, and attended the synagogue service twice each day for eleven months. I read voraciously about Judaism but frankly found its legalisms arid. When I asked my teacher, Rev. Michael Domba, a survivor of the Holocaust who had been a student at the Slobodka yeshiva in Lithuania before the war, whether it would be possible to study the Kabbalah, the mystical writings and practices of Judaism, his answer was that it was an area best avoided. I was curious about his reply, and as to why Judaism needed to be limited to Talmudic study and ritual observance.

According to family lore, we were related to the Gaon of Vilna, the great Lithuanian scholar who had opposed the burgeoning Hasidic movement in the eighteenth century. As a physician and medical scientist, I had little inclination to associate with a sect whose members dressed like they were still living in the eighteenth century and who lived in a "world apart" from others. However, one day I decided to attend a Sabbath service at a local branch of Chabad, a Hasidic sect that welcomes Jews of all levels of observance. It was there that I found the spiritual underpinnings of Judaism that I had been searching for.

In order to explore the religious roots of psychoanalysis, I attended Harvard University and graduated with a master's degree in religion. My thesis explored Jesus' healing practices in the New Testament. I subsequently attended the Hebrew College in Newton, Massachusetts, where I studied the Kabbalah and Hasidic thought, writing a master's thesis on the influence of Jewish mysticism on psychoanalysis. Through my journeys into psychoanalysis and religion, I have become convinced that Freudian analysis is in many respects a secular reworking of the tenets of Rabbinic Judaism, with Jungian analysis comparably indebted to Christianity. The present text is an effort to elucidate this thesis.

Introduction

Revolutions are a resolute and conscious
attempt . . . to break with the past
—**Alexis de Tocqueville**

In the early twentieth century, Sigmund Freud and Carl Jung developed two distinct theories of psychoanalysis based on their differing conceptions of the unconscious mind. Their schools of psychoanalysis remain active today, although they have witnessed substantial modifications. As secular psychological approaches, neither is based directly on religious tradition. Freud specifically rejected any link between psychoanalysis and religion, whereas Jung viewed his mode of analytical psychology as within the tradition of ancient religious healing practices.

The history of ideas includes an examination of conceptual borrowings. Secular thought did not spring de novo from the enlightened mind; instead, it emerged out of two millennia of religious tradition in the West. It would be naive to presume that this lengthy heritage has not contributed to how modern minds see the world. This is particularly evident in the field of psychology, where values and modes of thought can be traced back to once-prevalent religious ideas.

The discovery of the unconscious (Ellenberger 1970) has in fact been a process, not an event. It has been nothing less than the slow unfolding of ideas, some of which have gained the light of day only to sink back again into a barely perceptible darkness. As will be discussed below, the Judeo-Christian ethic continues to inform our modern conceptions, and often without our awareness. This extends to the modes of psychoanalysis developed by Freud and Jung, whose debt to religious ideas has never been fully acknowledged.

Scholars have referred to the partitioning of Judaism and Christianity as the "parting of the ways" (Boyarin 2006). This was a process that took place over centuries, and was determined by mutual positive and negative influences, which tended to polarize the positions of the rival religions. It will be demonstrated here that a comparable process has sculpted, and in many respects also distorted, the positions taken by Freud and Jung. Following their final rift in 1912, Freud's writings were for a brief time aimed at refuting Jung's unorthodox ideas concerning the psyche. Jung, in turn, continued to take exception to Freud's notions concerning the unconscious, and he abandoned the domain of personal psychology in order to focus on the collective features of the psyche. While there are indications that each man kept abreast of the other's work, in their later years they rarely referred to each other. This has been the legacy for their intellectual heirs, as well. Unfortunately, such purposeful neglect has tended to limit the scope of their respective approaches.

PSYCHOANALYSIS AND THE ENLIGHTENMENT

Secular thought tends to obscure dependence on religious ideas by clothing them in the language of scientific empiricism. In order to discern the religious motifs that inform secular thought, this veil must be penetrated. Claims that new ideas arise de novo must be dismissed as incorrect, as they emerge necessarily from older ones, and continue to carry the latter's indelible impressions. According to the philosopher Amos Funkenstein:

> The "new" often consists not in the invention of categories or figures of thought, but rather in a surprising employment of existing ones. Of the variety of ways in which a new theory can be said to have been prepared by an older one, two ideal modes are particularly pertinent . . . the dialectical anticipation of a new theory by an older, even adverse one . . . and the transplantation of existing categories to a new domain. (Funkenstein 1986, 14)

This conclusion applies also to the debt that psychoanalysis owes religion. But identifying the religious underpinnings of psychoanalysis is complicated by a paucity of direct acknowledgements of the latter's borrowings, especially in Freud's writings, which convey a distinctly negative attitude towards religion. However, as will be demonstrated, this belies Freud's reliance on religious ideas, so that one must look carefully past Freud's manifest narratives in order to identify the latent motifs of religion. For Freud, religion, and specifically Judaism, is the unconscious element that must be defended against, yet manifests in much of his thought.

CURE OF THE SOUL

Until relatively recent times, religious practice was the dominant mode of countering psychological disturbances. The religious "cure of the soul" was the dominant mode of psychotherapy. Carl Jung acknowledged the therapeutic role of religion as follows:

> What are religions? Religions are psychotherapeutic systems. What are we doing, we psychotherapists? We are trying to heal the suffering of the human mind, of the human psyche or the human soul, and religions deal with the same problem. Therefore, our Lord is a healer; he is a doctor. He heals the sick and he deals with the trouble of the soul, and that is exactly what we call psychotherapy. (*Collected Works*, vol. 18, para. 181)

In his *Eight Chapters* (*Pirke Shemoneh*) the twelfth-century Jewish scholar and physician Maimonides (R. Moshe ben Maimon) (Figure 1) outlines how psychologically troubled individuals should be approached, offering prescriptions that read like modern cognitive-behavioral therapy (Bakan et al. 2009). Maimonides opines, like Aristotle, that actions are virtuous when they achieve a "middle path" between extremes. Accordingly, an individual who has become mentally unsound is encouraged to practice the extreme opposite of his undesirable behavior until the fault had been remedied. For example, if a man

Figure 1. Moses ben Maimon or Maimonides was a twelfth-century rabbinic scholar and Jewish philosopher who compiled the *Mishneh Torah* and authored *Guide of the Perplexed*. His standing as a sage is essentially unrivaled.

is a miser, he is encouraged to spend extravagantly until his niggardliness has been extinguished. Only then can he be persuaded to be generous in moderation. Maimonides' approach is active, directive, symptom-based, and highlights the importance of behavioral change in the cure of the soul.

RELIGION AND PSYCHOANALYSIS

Other scholars have previously examined the influence of religion on psychoanalysis. During Freud's own lifetime, A. A. Roback argued that psychoanalysis was peculiar to the make-up of the Jewish mind (1929), a suggestion that Freud rejected.[1] The historian David Bakan opined that mystical Judaism had played a role in the development of psychoanalysis and that Freud had been a crypto-Sabbatean, i.e., a member of a messianic sect that secretly followed the banned teachings of Sabbatai Tzvi, although this claim has been rejected by most scholars (Bakan et al. 2009). The psychoanalyst Ana-Maria Rizzuto addressed Freud's ambivalent relationship to God, arguing that unresolved Oedipal issues with his father's Judaism were the primary cause of Freud's atheism (1998).

1. For detailed readings on this topic, see Lew Aron and Karen Starr, *A Psychotherapy for the People* (London: Routledge, 2013) and Stephen Frosch, *Hate and the Jewish Science* (London: Palgrave MacMillan, 2009).

The psychologist Sanford Drob has examined the role of the Kabbalah in both Freudian and Jungian analysis (2000), and more recently Karen Starr (2008) and Michael Eigen (2012) have addressed parallels between mystical Judaism and psychoanalysis. Many of these ideas are revisited in the present text. Whereas several neo-Freudian psychoanalysts, including Steven Frosh (2009) and Lew Aron and Karen Starr (2013), agree that Freud's Judaism influenced the directions of his thought, they are wary about labeling psychoanalysis a "Jewish science," as they are justifiably concerned that this might fuel anti-Semitic prejudice. Others have addressed the influence of Christianity on Jung's ideas, and in this regard the works of the Jungian analysts Edward Edinger (1976) and Murray Stein (2012) are noteworthy.

The present text demonstrates that the religious underpinnings of psychoanalysis are both more specific and extensive than have been previously entertained, and that the distinct tenets and practices of traditional Judaism and Christianity account in large measure for the differences that emerged respectively in the theories and practices of Freud and Jung.

RELIGION AND PSYCHOLOGY

Jung, a onetime disciple and colleague of Freud,[2] suggested that all aspects of human experience, including religious ones, are "psychological," and should be considered as such: "Everything to do with religion, everything it is and asserts, touches the human soul so closely that psychology least of all can afford to overlook it" (*CW* 11, para. 172). Jung's notion that religion is psychological raises few objections; however, the converse invariably raises many. This in part results from Freud's having viewed religion as steeped in superstition and

2. Many modern Jungian analysts take issue with the idea of Jung as a disciple of Freud's. They claim that Jung was already an established psychiatrist with his own theories concerning the psyche before encountering Freud. I do not tend to agree with this assessment, and it share similarities with the discomfort that early Christians had with the idea of Jesus being baptized by John the Baptist. As the Jesuit priest and scholar J. P. Meir argues in his magisterial opus *A Marginal Jew* (1991), stories in the New Testament that run counter to the dogma of the church likely reflect actual historical situations. In the same vein, there can be little doubt that Jung was a disciple of Freud's and espoused his doctrines at least for a limited time.

metaphysics, whereas psychoanalysis was, in his opinion, necessarily scientific and devoid of metaphysical underpinnings. Jung's stance on religion, to the contrary, was generally benevolent, and he agreed that religious ideas informed psychoanalysis. But neither man chose to address how their own religious beliefs influenced their theories of psychoanalysis, and this is the aim of the present text.

Whereas the Judeo-Christian ethic has contributed to modern psychotherapeutic thought, it must be acknowledged that Judaism and Christianity are complete soteriologies in their own right,[3] and they continue to compete with psychotherapy. There are large numbers of devotees of each tradition, who, as a result of the salutary effects of confession and ritual expurgation, rarely seek the assistance of a psychotherapist.[4] For them, religion is by itself a source of healing. Indeed, it may be argued that religions, when optimally practiced, may offer more opportunities for psychological healing than do modern secularized modes of psychotherapy, for reasons that will be addressed.

HEALING AND RELIGION

Healing is a rubric for a set of innate processes that antagonize the signs and symptoms of "dys-ease." The concept of healing remains ambiguous, in part, because it derives from a pre-scientific era when body and soul were still experienced as interdependent and interpenetrating. Whereas healing can be fostered by drugs, surgeries, and psychological interventions, it cannot succeed without the innate activities of the body.

Healing occurs beyond consciousness (Kradin 2011); one cannot consciously will oneself to be well. For those who profess deep religious beliefs, healing is attributed to divine intervention, whereas for the secular individual, it is credited to biological processes. However, these ideas are not necessarily mutually exclusive, as many modern theologians

3. One of the most detailed religious psychologies can be found in Theravada Buddhism, although it does not adhere to the notion of a soul. Nevertheless, it clearly has therapeutic and soteriological aims.
4. One can arrive at the same conclusion for any of the major religious systems, all of which offer modes of psychological healing together with the larger goal of salvation.

would agree that God acts through the natural laws of creation (Sacks 2011). Indeed, prominent scientists (e.g., Newton and Einstein), have historically held strong metaphysical beliefs. Nevertheless, a modern-day atheist and God-fearing religionist would likely disagree on this issue based on their distinct weltanschauungs.[5]

Healing must be distinguished from curing. "To heal," from the Old English *haelen*, means to restore to health or "to make whole." Health may be defined as a state of psychophysical well-being, in which mind and body are experienced as working harmoniously together (Kradin 2004). But words do not adequately convey the experience of wholeness. "Cure" is derived from the Latin *curare*, which means "to take care of." A second meaning refers to the treatment of flesh in order to remove undesirable elements, as, for example, in the "curing" of beef. In medical parlance, it is the latter that is most often implied, as it is possible to be "cured" of a disease yet remain in poor health.

In the realm of mental pathology and healing, it may be too optimistic to speak of health. Patients suffering from psychological ills may be cured of their symptoms (e.g., depression), without achieving enduring mental health. Indeed extensive arguments have been raised over the years as to whether symptomatic and goal-oriented cures may have advantages over efforts at reconstructing the psyche towards a state of ill-defined health.[6]

The history of healing is too extensive to rehearse here. As Guido Majno addresses in *Healing and Disease* (1975), *homo medicamentosa* is also *homo religiosus*, and virtually all religions include approaches to the diagnosis and treatment of disease (Eliade 1964). While it is easy with hindsight to dismiss ancient treatments as naive, there is little doubt that pre-scientific modes of therapy were often effective for reasons that modern science cannot explain. Historical perspective also dictates

5. Joseph Ratzinger, the former Pope Benedict XVI, in his *Introduction to Christianity*, makes the interesting argument that both religionists and atheists show an unusual interest in religion, pointing to how most atheists are not in the least impartial with respects to their strongly held antithetical beliefs in a God, and that "the Lady doth protest too much."
6. This controversy is reviewed by Aron and Starr, and the reader is encouraged to evaluate their arguments (2013).

that the currently accepted scientific approaches to disease will in some instances be in the future also be viewed as outmoded and naive.

Modern placebo-controlled clinical trials have repeatedly demonstrated that rational approaches to disease are by no means a guarantee of efficacy, whereas approaches that appear irrational can yield salutary outcomes (Kradin 2011). As the medical anthropologist Craig Moerman has suggested, the healing process includes mental structures of meaning that do not necessarily follow rational ideas (2002).

JUDAISM AND HEALING

Judaism is an ancient religious tradition that addresses ailments that afflict both mind and body (Biale 2002). The Torah (the Five Books of Moses, or Pentateuch) is the textual foundation of Judaism; however, healing plays a relatively minor role in its narratives. The Torah includes a single brief prayer by Moses in Numbers 12:13, which petitions YHWH to heal his sister Miriam of *tzaraat*. "Please God, heal her." This disorder, invariably mistranslated as "leprosy," in fact resembles no disease known to modern medicine, as it also "afflicts" articles of clothing and the walls of houses. *Tzaraat* was attributed to the sin of having spoken ill of others (*lashon ha ra*). It appears that the single example of healing in the Torah pertains to a metaphysical disorder.

Later rabbinic commentaries include numerous references to actual physical (*guf*) and mental (*nefesh*) disorders, and the modern Jewish liturgy is replete with supplications for healing. As a monotheistic religion, Judaism attributes disease and healing to divine intervention, and it was only in the apocryphal *Wisdom of Ben Sirah* (Skehan and DiLella 1995), authored in the third century BCE, that the beneficial role of the physician was first given credence.[7]

7. The *Wisdom of Ben Sirach* is frequently cited in the Talmud. It was originally authored in Hebrew and translated by the author's grandson into Greek. While apocryphal to the Masoretic text of the Hebrew Bible, it is included within the Greek Septuagint.

In the Hebrew Bible, the cause of disease was judged to be either sin (moral impurity), or ritual impurity left unattended (Klawans 2004). The most common Hebrew word for sin, *cheyt*, is an archery term that means "to miss the mark"—that is, a failure to observe the Law properly. Observance of the Mosaic Law with its 613 precepts—248 positive[8] and 365 negative—is the cardinal tenet of Rabbinic Judaism, and even rote observance of these precepts fulfills one's legal religious obligations, although concomitant proper intentionality in is considered optimal.

However, few individuals can consistently achieve righteous discipline in their observance, and as the intentions of others cannot be evaluated, objective action has traditionally been prioritized in Judaism, so that it is commonly viewed as a system of orthopraxy (right action) rather than orthodoxy (right belief). But the motivation to observe the Law is meritorious, as obligations, if approached with proper intention, offer frequent opportunities to sacralize the mundane world.[9] When practiced with the right attitude, rather than constituting a burden, the observance of Jewish Law can imbue meaning to personal, family, and community life. But if the Law is observed merely by rote, its rituals begin to resemble an obsessional neurosis, as Freud noted (Freud 1907).

Proverbs 9:10 states that, "The beginning of wisdom is fear of God." The Law with its commandments and proscriptions conjures notions of responsibility, culpability and punishment. While fear of God is viewed by some as an unduly harsh concept and one that is irreconcilable with a loving God, acceptance of the awesome effects of divine action is a cardinal tenet of Judaism. This is famously addressed in the dialogical arguments of the Book of Job concerning theodicy (Kradin 2014).

8. The 248 positive commandments correspond with the 248 "members" of the body. This emphasizes the requirement of the body in performing these positive commandments.
9. This text is largely based on this critical difference between Judaism and Christianity. Once again, without being properly and deeply understood, the Law quickly becomes burdensome, as it did for the early Christians and others throughout the history of Judaism.

SIN AND DISEASE

Evil is a poorly defined term that is linked conceptually with sin. One explanation within the Judeo-Christian tradition for how evil first entered the world is via Adam's original sin. Man's failure to obey the divine injunction of not eating from the Tree of Good and Bad was the first example of his failure to fear God.[10] The punishment for this disobedience included work, the pain of childbirth, and awareness of one's eventual death.

In the fourth century, the church father Augustine introduced the notion of original sin as the inherited predilection of Adam's descendants to disobey divine will. Man is born tainted by sin, according to Augustine, and lacks wholeness. But according to rabbinic interpretation, sin is not inherited, despite certain references in the Torah that suggest otherwise (e.g., Exodus 20:6), but rather attributable to man's hedonistic psychological inclination, the *yetzer*, which Freud later re-imagined as a pleasure-seeking drive in the unconscious (Rotenberg 1997). The rabbis in late antiquity postulated opposing mental impulses: one, the *yetzer ha tov*, or good impulse, attuned to the proper fulfillment of divine will; the other, the *yetzer ha ra*, or bad impulse, which seeks personal satisfaction in opposition to it. The rabbis had in fact developed a psychodynamic system, one based on contradictory impulses, and comparable to Freud's modern notion of mental conflict.

The idea of competing metaphysical forces of good and evil likely entered Jewish thought via Zoroastrianism during the Babylonian Exile of the late sixth century BCE. Adherence to a belief in radical duality has been identified by scholars within the writings of certain sects of Second Temple Judaisms. One of these sects, Christianity, viewed sin as having its origins as a metaphysical force that eternally opposes the will of God (Pagels 1995). The Gospel authors imagined Satan as the

10. Christianity takes a relatively negative view of this act and Augustine refers to it as the source of the original sin that was transmitted to all subsequent generations. Rabbinic Judaism is more ambivalent concerning the infraction. At one level, it is viewed as the first sinful behavior, on the other, its effects are recognized to have contributed to man's proper place in the world vis-à-vis knowledge and choice.

serpent in the Garden, who tempted Eve to transgress God's command not to eat of the fruit of the Tree of Knowledge but failed to lure Jesus to sin while in the desert immediately following his baptism. Psychologically speaking, Satan acts effectively by introducing doubt; the Devil (from the Sanskrit *dva* meaning "double" or "dishonest") undermines man's undivided faith in God.

Ha Satan first appears in the canonical Job, where he is portrayed as a prosecutorial angel, who questions God's judgment but is obedient to God's will. Rabbinic Judaism eschewed radical duality as it undermines the ideal integrity of monotheism. The second-century rabbis were heirs to a fiercely monotheistic Deuteronomic tradition, which envisioned an unchallenged God who was responsible for all of creation, including what man might interpret from his limited perspective as a good and evil. As the Jewish prophet Isaiah (45:7) states in the name of YHWH,[11] "I form the light, and create darkness: I do the good, *and* the bad; I, YWHW, do all these things."

Yet the rabbis also embraced the idea that man was invested with free will and ultimately responsible for his choices. This idea was expressed by R. Akiva in the *Ethics of the Fathers* (*Pirke Avot*) 3:15, writing that, "All is fated, but free will is given." This idea shares features with modern deterministic chaos theory, which has been used to mathematically model complex systems, including the mind (Eigen 2013). According to chaos theory, the broad outlines of mental activity are determined, comparable to fate, yet sensitive to minor perturbations, analogous to individual choice.

The ancient Israelite religion addressed sin in a highly ritualized manner. Healing required first recognizing one's sin, confessing it to a priest, expressing genuine repentance (*t'shuva*)—which means returning to God—and then bringing an expiatory sacrifice to the Temple. As Maimonides notes in his *Mishneh Torah*, since the destruction of the Temple, confession and repentance have replaced sacrificial offerings (1990).

11. The acronym YHWH is referred to as the Tetragammaton and represents the ineffable name of God, which may be either unpointed or pointed as the word *Adonai*, which means "my Lord."

In the ancient Israelite sacrificial ritual, one discerns a parallel with the Freudian idea of "working through," in which initial cognitive awareness of motive deepens with time, until genuine change is realized. An ancient Israelite who believed that he had committed a transgression of the Law "in error" (*shogeg*), was required to bring a guilt offering in order to repent. But if upon further introspection, he recognized that what he had initially thought to be due to error had in fact been motivated by desire, then bringing a second appropriate sin offering was necessary.

The logistical confluence of the confessed sinner, the priest, the sacrifice, and God was required if the ritual was to be efficacious. During the sacrifice, man and God were imagined as drawn together in at-one-ment. One can only speculate as to whether modern psychological modes of expiation are as effective as the dramatic act of sacrificing the life of an animal in order to be cleansed of sin.

But after the Second Temple was destroyed, it was no longer possible to atone for sin through sacrifice, and alternative approaches were necessary (Neusner 1978). These had already developed following the destruction of the First Temple in 586 BCE, and while the Jews were in exile in Babylonia. There is a passage in an early biblical commentary, in which R. Yochanan ben Zakkai, who is credited with having instituted the earliest practices of Rabbinic Judaism in 70 CE, was asked by a student how sin would be forgiven in the absence of the Temple:

> Once as Rabbi Yochanan Ben Zakkai was coming forth from Jerusalem, Rabbi Joshua followed him and beheld the Temple in ruins. "Woe unto us," Rabbi Joshua cried, "that this place where the iniquities of Israel were atoned for is laid to waste!" "My son," Rabbi Yochanan said to him, "be not grieved. We have atonement as effective as this. And what is it? It is acts of loving-kindness, as it is said, 'For I desire mercy and not sacrifice.' [Hosea 6:6]" *Avot de Rabbi Nathan*, chapter 6 (quoted in Goldin 1990, 34)

Centuries before the destruction of First Temple, the ancient Israelite prophets had warned that the sacrificial penitential ritual had become rote and insincere. The prophets argued that God wanted sinners to raise their ethical standards by showing appropriate concern for the oppressed within society, traditionally the widow, the orphan, and the stranger, who were rarely able to support themselves. The rabbis looked to the prophetic ideas that charity, the performance of good deeds, and prayer were of greater importance than animal sacrifice. In a novel mode of accounting, the rabbis suggested that deeds of "loving-kindness" could be weighed in the balance against previous sins. The penitent sinner was virtually assured of forgiveness and redemption. As Maimonides notes:

> *T'shuva* atones for all sins. Even a person who was wicked his whole life and repented in his final moments will not be reminded of any aspect of his wickedness as [Ezekiel 33:12] states "The wickedness of the evil one will not cause him to stumble on the day he repents his wickedness." (*Mishneh Torah*, *halacha* 3)

But *T'shuva*, as Maimonides defines it, is not a simple process. It requires the in-depth purging of sin, both mentally and behaviorally, in order to be effective. One must forego the impulse to sin again, not in the abstract, but when faced with identical enticements. The penitential system of Judaism insists on genuine transformation, which includes verifiable behavioral change.

MAGICO-THEURGIC HEALING

Apotropaic (i.e., the use of symbols and rituals to ward off evil) and theurgic practices were popularly practiced in parallel to the sacrificial cult by the ancient Israelites. This is evident from the polemics of the biblical prophets who repeatedly exhorted the Israelites to desist from adopting the practices of neighboring nations, including soothsaying, necromancy, divination, etc. The practices of the Canaanite cults of

Asherah and Astarte were widely held to be effective in warding off maternal and fetal deaths during childbirth, and in warding off childhood illnesses (Kaufmann 1972).

It is difficult to differentiate religious from magical healing, as one man's religion may be another man's magic, and for this reason scholars prefer the term "magico-theurgic" healing. Although both appeal to supramundane forces, prayers are supplications, whereas magic endeavors to manipulate divine powers through spells, incantations, and rituals.[12] Perhaps most widely recognized are the miraculous healings and exorcisms attributed to Jesus within the New Testament Gospels (Kradin 2010). The biblical scholar Morton Smith suggested that Jesus was in fact a first-century magician (Smith 1981), and he cites examples of comparable feats in the pagan Greco-Roman world, notably those credited to Apollonius of Tyana, whose story closely parallels Jesus'. Confusion between healers with claims to divine powers and magicians was a common trope in the ancient world. In modern times, charisma has also been attributed to the healing powers of the psychoanalyst, in the form of "transference cures" (Kakar 1991).

HEALING AND THE SCIENTIFIC REVOLUTION

From antiquity and through the Middle Ages, Jews and Christians were immersed in a pervasive milieu of religious belief, and the idea of a secular world with limited religious observance—what we today refer to as religion—was unknown. In his treatise, *A Secular Age*, the philosopher Charles Taylor opines that a progressive "disenchantment" of the world has occurred over the last five centuries (2007). Medieval man, according to Taylor, was permeable to metaphysical forces (e.g.,

12. In a curious side note, a recent study by H. Benson and colleagues, "Study of the Therapeutic Effects of Intercessory Prayer (STEP) in Cardiac Bypass Patients: A Multicenter Randomized Trial of Uncertainty and Certainty of Receiving Intercessory Prayer," *American Heart Journal* 151 (2006): 934–42, showed that patients with cardiac diseases who were told that they were being prayed for actually had *worse* outcomes than those who were not. The reason for this is uncertain but may reflect the so-called nocebo response, in which individuals actually do worse when given what would a priori be expected to have either a positive or neutral response. I explore reasons for this in my text, *The Placebo Response: The Power of Unconscious Healing* (London: Routledge, 2008).

angels and demons), and the concept of the individual as independent of the spirit realm was unknown (Taylor 1989). The social historian Brad Gregory argues that secularism and science were unexpected by-products of the European Reformation, and that today only a dim awareness remains that man's perception of the world is still swayed by dimly perceived metaphysical notions (2012).

By the seventeenth century, the Enlightenment had infused the European mind with new heady possibilities of objectivity and intellectual freedom (Berlin 2013). For the first time, man was capable of imagining himself as no longer subject to divine whim, nor as a passive object buffeted by forces beyond his control; instead, he was now an active observer and participant within a world ruled by physical laws that could be expressed in mathematical terms and with predictable results. Man was now able to ponder the possibility of controlling his fate and environment without preconceived divine limitations.

The philosopher René Descartes posited that human cognition allowed one to separate oneself from nature for the purpose of observing it dispassionately (1988). This idea was instrumental in the decline of theological explanations and in the ascent of empirical observation. As the cosmos was disenchanted, God's role in creation also became increasingly difficult to define, and man's belief in mystery waned.

The Jewish philosopher Baruch Spinoza, in the seventeenth century, declared that God and his creation were in fact isomorphic (i.e., superimposable), which is the definition of pantheism (Garrett 1996). Spinoza did not deny God's existence, but neither did he recognize him as the creator. Instead, Spinoza saw God as present in all of creation but not outside of it. Like Maimonides, Spinoza opined that the highest form of religious achievement could only be attained through pure reason, but his ideas led to his excommunication.[13]

13. The State of Israel publically reclaimed Spinoza as the first secular Jew. However, it is not at all clear from his behavior in life that he would have welcomed being reinstated into the Jewish fold. His stance clearly was a rebuke of organized religion. D. Schwartz, *The First Modern Jew: Spinoza and the History of an Image* (Princeton: Princeton University Press, 2012).

By the nineteenth century, the supremacy of science had reached the point that the philosopher Henri Laplace was sufficiently comfortable to respond to Napoleon's inquiry as to why he had not mentioned God in a discourse on the planetary orbits by saying, "Sire, I have no need for that hypothesis!" (Bartlett 1992, 351). Rejecting a requirement for a first cause permits pantheism to merge with atheism, as it had for Laplace.

For the eighteenth-century deists, God continued to serve a role as demiurge, but one who subsequently retired from creation, allowing it to function via the natural laws with which it had been imbued. This position countered the nominalist stance of the medieval scholastics who believed that God could, if he so wished, suspend the rules of nature at any point, as he had when the sun stood still for Joshua while conquering Jericho (Funkenstein 1986). Deists, including Thomas Jefferson and Benjamin Franklin, played an important role in the founding of the United States, so that the credo "In God We Trust" is perhaps more an affirmation of natural law than of Divine Providence. This post-Enlightenment idea had already been prefigured by the story of the Oven of Akhnai in *Baba Metzia* 59b, in which the rabbis argue that the Law, once given to man, was no longer "in the heavens," but must be decided by a majority of men without divine interference.

The new European zeitgeist in which individuals were free to express anti-clerical and even atheistic beliefs with impunity was transported in the early nineteenth century by Napoleon to Eastern Europe, and eventually reached the traditional Jewish enclaves of the Polish Pale. According to the historian Ada Rapoport-Albert, Hasidism, a movement that sought to reform Rabbinic Judaism, also desired to counter the effects of the Jewish Enlightenment or *Haskalah* (Rapoport-Albert 1996). The founder of Chabad Hasidism, R. Schneur Zalman of Lyadi, in spite of repeated imprisonment by the anti-Semitic Czarist government, feared that the new Napoleonic freedoms posed a far greater threat to Judaism's survival than Russian persecution.

Science, the handmaiden of the Enlightenment, began to encroach on the healing practices of Judaism. Ritualized prayer healing and amulets written by traditional Jewish healers, or *B'aalei Ha Shem*, increasingly took a back seat to modern medicine (Rosman 1996). But whereas medical science was rooted in the rigors of anatomy and physiology, the therapeutic approach to disorders of the mind still has not achieved the status of a physical science. Secular psychotherapies adopted religious ideas and rituals but disguised them as science. Freud's psychoanalysis attempted to fill the gap between science and religion but in so doing never achieved the rigor of the former or the depth of therapeutic feeling that may accompany the latter. It is from this perspective, (i.e. of psychoanalysis as a liminal endeavor), that it must rightly be examined.

THE EMERGENCE OF PSYCHOLOGY

As Jung notes, what were considered metaphysical disorders of the soul have, in a secular world, been reconceived as "mental illnesses." In antiquity, depression was generally attributed to sin, as in the case of King Saul's melancholia in 1 Samuel, and, until recently, psychoses were viewed as the result of demonic possession, a prime biblical example being Jesus' exorcisms of the demoniacs.

Following the witch craze that extended for several centuries and cost the lives of thousands in Europe and the American colonies—most of them women—scientific rationalism increasingly rejected the notion of demonic possession and instead postulated non-metaphysical biological causes of severe mental illness (Kradin 2012). Freud wrote in "A Neurosis of Demoniacal Possession in the Seventeenth Century" that:

> What in those days were thought to be evil spirits to us are base and evil wishes, the derivatives of impulses that have been rejected and repressed. In one respect only do we not subscribe to the explanation of these phenomena current in medieval times; we have abandoned the projection of these into the outer world, attributing their origin instead to the inner life of the patient in whom they manifest themselves. (*Standard Edition* 1923, 72)

In the late nineteenth century, the majority of patients seen in medical practice suffered from psychosomatic disorders, which were theoretically attributed to inherited vulnerabilities of the nervous system that were incurable (Shorter 1993). In part due to the clinical experiments of Martin Charcot, a French neurologist at the *fin de siècle*, it became apparent that the symptoms of hysteria, the most common nervous disorder in the nineteenth century, were in fact both reproducible and curable by "suggestion," suggesting that it was in fact a mental disorder.

Early psychoanalytical treatment was, like hypnosis, aimed at the relief of symptoms. This was true for Anna O. in Breuer and Freud's 1895 "Case of Hysteria," in which the "talking cure" was first reported, although the technique was, in fact, discovered by the patient.[14] But Freud soon found that symptomatic cures rarely restore patients to health, as new symptoms invariably emerged with time. For this reason, psychoanalysis began to focus less on achieving symptom relief and more on the root of the problem, which was judged to be the need to transform character, although the latter approach is invariably lengthy and carries no guarantee of success (Eysenck 1994). Freud viewed his new ideas on neuroses as scientific. But as will be seen, they were instead deeply rooted in his Jewish milieu.

14. Anna O. was later revealed to be Bertha Pappenheim who went on to have her own illustrious career as a founder of the social work movement.

CHAPTER 1

Sigmund Freud: "Godless Jew"

There may be a reason that the founder of psychoanalysis is a Jew.

—Sigmund Freud

William James, a philosopher and the first experimental psychologist at Harvard University, expressed a strong interest in mysticism. He recognized the mystical experience as an unusual but normal psychological activity, and elucidated his thoughts on the topic in the classic text *Varieties of Religious Experience* (1902). A devout Christian and philosophical pragmatist, James warned against attempts at reducing religious experience to psychopathology, reasoning that this might undermine the former's practical psychological benefits.[1]

1. Wolfgang von Goethe took up this point in his eighteenth-century polemic against Newton's *Opticks*, the former arguing that the phenomenon of vision was not reducible to the mathematics of spectral light. Indeed, all efforts to reconcile science with metaphysical experience are ultimately doomed to fail, although that does not appear to impede the near endless flow of articles and texts that attempt to harmonize these two subjects.
   Like Freud, I am also a firm believer in psychopathology. However, as pathology is defined in most cases as "morbid anatomy," it may be said that at this stage in our understanding of the mind there is no basis for an anatomical psychopathology. Some psychiatrists, most notably Thomas Szasz, *The Myth of Mental Illness* (San Francisco: Harper, 1974) have argued adamantly that there is no basis for mental illness. While I do not agree, there is room for substantial disagreement as to what

Figure 2. Sigmund Freud on his fifty-sixth birthday. Freud was a neuroscientist who went on to develop psychoanalysis.

However, not all of the early psychologists were as appreciative of religion as James. Sigmund Freud was a self-described "godless Jew" (Gay 1987), who referred to religion as misguided illusion, and to mysticism as superstitious occultism. Trained as a neuropathologist, Freud's psychoanalysis was, by his own claim, devoted to both the pathogenesis and treatment of psychopathology (Figure 2). When, early in his career, Freud turned his attention to the psychological disorder then termed hysteria, he insisted that any approach to its treatment must be based on unbiased scientific observation. Freud was keen to establish psychoanalysis as a science. He saw religion as a potential threat to psychoanalysis and was desirous of eradicating any persistent ideas that religious thought might have anything positive to offer in the approach to mental disorders. But as the psychoanalyst Ana-Maria Rizzuto suggests in *Why Did Freud Reject God?* (1998):

> Freud generalized into universal principles his personal religious evolution. He firmly believed that his personal stance must be normative. By losing perspective about his own personal suffering, he became blind to the "variety of religious

constitutes mental pathology. The Harvard psychologist Richard McNally addresses this ambiguous topic in his text *What is Mental Illness?* (Cambridge: Harvard, 2012), which is highly recommended.

> experiences" that William James, his contemporary, described so well. (269)

By the late nineteenth century, the physical sciences (e.g., physics, chemistry, and biology) had become well entrenched in materialism and objective observation. Within the academy, the notion of vitalism as a determinant factor in biology had been rejected in favor of the materialist ideas of biochemistry and physiology. Prior to developing what would become the epistemology of psychoanalysis, Freud had made considerable efforts at explaining psychology quantitatively based on the excitations of the nervous system, only to grow frustrated with his inability to develop a neurologically based explanatory model. He reticently abandoned his project for a scientific psychology, conceding that psychoanalysis was not yet ready to be explained as a material science.

Undoubtedly, Freud recognized that in doing so, the place of psychoanalysis in the academy might be placed in jeopardy. Nevertheless, he remained undeterred in his wish to position psychoanalysis within the world of science, despite knowing that its methods were hermeneutical. Freud's approach drew criticisms from a variety of directions and for various reasons. Scientists recognized that psychoanalysis lacked quantitative rigor. It was based on anecdotal observations and innovative theories. Although he was a skilled observer of his fellow man, Freud never adopted the scientific method that includes experimentation under controlled conditions. Instead, more like medieval religious scholars, his theories tended to be grand and explanatory, and locked the slow empirical and atheoretical advances of a physical science. At best, psychoanalysis was what we today refer to as social science. It included axiomatic beliefs, such as the sexual theory, which runs counter to the defining features of science (Borch-Jacobsen and Shamdasani 2012).

James, who had performed early experimentation in psychology, openly wondered how Freud could choose which aspect of a patient's narrative to analyze without bias. Others were disturbed by Freud's emphasis on sexuality, especially the sexuality of children. Finally,

Freud was a Jew and therefore subject to the aspersions that accompanied the widespread anti-Semitism of Christian European society at all levels (Goldhagen 2009).

Like many scientists in the late nineteenth century, Freud's thought had been shaped by Darwinism (Sulloway 1979). He envisioned the human mind as an evolutionary advance, adapted to achieve the survival of the fittest. Those with selective procreative advantage, reasoned Freud, stood an increased chance of being naturally selected. For this reason, sexuality was considered to be the dominant driving force of the psyche, and this dogma, according to Freud, could not be abandoned, lest psychology lapse back into the metaphysical realm of religion from which it had emerged (Sulloway 1979).

However, Freud's psychoanalysis shared features with a religious cult, whose founder's claims to revealed truth were deemed infallible by his supporters, at least during his lifetime. While there have been significant modifications in the theory and practice of Freudian psychoanalysis over the last century, these were rarely welcomed during Freud's lifetime. Instead the early years of psychoanalysis saw the ideas of Adler, Jung, Rank, and others dismissed as heresies, and these innovators were ridiculed and purged from the movement.

Unable to raise psychoanalysis legitimately to the level of science, Freud instead adopted a hostile stance concerning religion, which he apparently viewed as a continuing threat to psychoanalysis. In his *Future of an Illusion*, he attempts to explain away religion as superstition, and as a childlike distortion of reality:

> The scientific spirit brings about a particular attitude towards worldly matters; before religious matters it pauses for a little, hesitates, and finally there crosses the threshold. In this process, there is no stopping; the greater the number of men to whom the treasures of knowledge become accessible, the more widespread is the falling away from religious belief—at first only from its obsolete and objectionable trappings, but later from its fundamental postulates as well. (1927, 38)

As the psychoanalyst Ana-Maria Rizzuto suggests, Freud's polemics against religion display his personal investment in the topic. In *Totem and Taboo* and *Moses and Monotheism*, his two major treatises on the origins of religion, he conflates the idea of the personal father with that of God. Freud displays little sophisticated appreciation for the transcendent God of the philosophers. Instead, he clings to a naive anthropomorphic notion of God. This prejudice, according to Rizzuto, is perhaps best explained by his strong contempt for his father and the latter's simple religious beliefs, which he refers to in his correspondence with Fliess (Freud and Fliess 1985).

Freud demonstrated substantial ambivalence concerning his Judaism. On the one hand, he was openly proud of being a Jew and closely identified with Jewish culture; on the other, he was rabidly disdainful of Jewish religious practices, and openly contemptuous of the *shtetl* Jews from Eastern Europe, who may have uncomfortably reminded him of his own Moravian roots. In *Moses and Monotheism*, Freud suggests in his description of the Christian myth that oedipally driven patricide led to deicide, and in this vein it appears to have been Freud's own wish to expunge the influence of God from his personal life, psychoanalysis, and the modern world. But as Joseph Cardinal Ratzinger, the former Pope Benedict XVI, notes, such ardent advocacy of atheism is simply another way of confessing one's negative relationship to God; the relationship is not abandoned, rather it necessarily persists (Ratzinger 1969).

In autobiographical statements, Freud frequently denied having had the benefit of a Jewish religious education, despite considerable documentary evidence to the contrary (Yerushalmi 1991). Despite the fact that Freud's education was primarily based on ethical, humanistic, and universalistic post-Enlightenment ideals, vestiges of traditional Judaism can easily be demonstrated in Freud's life and thought.

Freud's family of origin remained connected to traditional Judaism, despite his denial (Gay 1987). Consider Jakob Freud's dedication of the family Philippsohn Bible to his son Sigmund on the occasion of the latter's thirty-fifth birthday, written in his own hand in grammatically correct Hebrew:

> My dear son Schlomo:
> In the seventh year of your life the spirit of the Lord began to move you (Judges 13:2) and said to you: Go read in my Book that I have written, and there will be opened to you the sources of wisdom, knowledge, and understanding. See the Book of Books from which the wise men dug out their wisdom and the lawmakers learned law and justice (Numbers 21:18). You have looked upon the face of the Almighty (Numbers 24:4), have heard and striven to climb upwards, and you flew upon the wings of the Spirit (Psalms 18:10) For a long time this book has been hidden for the day on which you have completed your thirty-fifth year. I have had it covered with a new leather binding and given it the name "Spring up, O well." Sing ye unto it (Numbers 21:17) and I offer it to you for a remembrance and memorial of love.
> From you father who loves you with unending love,
> Jacob, Son of Rabbi Schlomo Freud (Rizzuto 1998, 68–70)

As Yerushalmi notes, this is a *melitzah* (i.e., a compilation of biblical verses), with whose verses Freud would almost certainly have been acquainted. Would a father communicate something to his son that was totally incomprehensible! The phrase "wisdom, knowledge, and understanding" (*chochmah*, *binah*, and *daat*) is a reference to Proverbs 2:6, but it is also the acronym for Chabad Hasidism (Drob 2000). Jakob Freud had been raised in a Hasidic family and although he was no longer a strictly observant Jew by the time that his youngest son Sigismund (Freud Germanized it to Sigmund) was born, there can be no doubt that Jakob Freud was versed in the Hebrew language, the Hebrew Bible, and the verses of the daily prayer book, which constituted a standard level of education for an observant Jewish layman in his day. However, Freud insisted that he had learned virtually nothing of his father's Judaism

> It may interest you to know that my father did indeed come from a Chassidic background. He was 41 when I was born and

> had been estranged from his native environment for almost 20 years. My education was so un-Jewish that today I cannot even read your dedication, which is evidently written in Hebrew. In later life I have often regretted this lack in my education. (Freud quoted in Frosh 2009, 14)

In Jakob Freud's dedication, one perceives the concern of a traditional Jewish father for a son who has strayed far from his religious roots. Freud's wife, Martha Bernays, herself the product of an observant rabbinic family, also chafed at her husband's refusal to allow her to light Sabbath candles in their home (Gay 1987). Whatever Freud's attitudes may have been toward Judaism, there can be no doubt that he knew first-hand far more about it than he wished to acknowledge.[2]

Ambivalence towards Judaism was not uncommon among Jews in Austria at the *fin de siècle* (Scholem 2012). Anti-Semitism reached its zenith during Freud's lifetime, and, like many other accomplished European Jews, he faced real obstacles in obtaining a successful position in Viennese society. Bakan notes that Freud's academic mentors had told him "tactfully" that there would be no role for him as a Jew in the academic medical establishment (Bakan 1971). Many of his colleagues and other professionals abandoned their Judaism and converted to Christianity in order to promote their social status. But despite his outspoken negativity concerning Jewish religious practices, Freud was adamantly opposed to cutting his cultural ties to Judaism. Objections raised to Freud's psychoanalysis as a "Jewish

2. Retrospective psychoanalysis of historical figures is fraught with problems, but others have concluded that Sigmund Freud's Oedipal issues with his father were substantial and almost certainly account for his strong negative reaction to traditional Jewish religion. See Sander Gilman, *Freud, Race, and Gender* (Princeton: Princeton University Press, 1993). If there are indeed blind spots in Freud's self-analysis it can be safely concluded that this may be one of them. It took Jung, who was also struggling with his own father complex to redeem the idea of religion in psychology, in part in reaction to Freud's refusal to see it as anything other than the "black mud of occultism." See Jung's autobiography, Carl Jung and Aniela Jaffe, *Memories, Dreams, Reflections* (New York: Vintage, 1989).

science" were primarily irrational and rooted in the widespread anti-Semitism of Christian Europe. As Aron and Starr suggest:

> Psychoanalysis is not alone in being haunted by the memory traces of Nazi categorization. In addition to psychoanalysis, Einstein's physics, anthropology, and Communism were all "Jewish sciences." The Nazis attacked Einstein's physics as a Jewish science of relativity. Anthropologist Franz Boas' books were burned because his anthropology challenged racist assumptions (2013, 332)

Freud was unapologetic about his cultural ties to Judaism. In an address to the B'nai B'rith in 1924, he acknowledged this indebtedness:

> What bound me to Jewry was (I am ashamed to admit) neither faith nor national pride. . . . But plenty of other things remained over to make the attraction of Jewry and Jews irresistible—many obscure emotional forces, which were the more powerful the less they could be expressed in words, as well as the clear consciousness of inner identity, the safe privacy of a common mental construction. . . . Because I was a Jew I found myself free from many prejudices which restricted others in the use of their intellect, and as a Jew, I was prepared to join the Opposition and to do without agreement with the "compact majority." (*Standard Edition*, vol. 20, 9)[3]

Freud credits Judaism with having influenced his own inquisitiveness, and one can justifiably assume that this attribution must apply to his ideas concerning psychoanalysis. As Yerushalmi notes:

> The Psychological Jew was born before Freud . . . Psychological Jews tend to insist on inalienable Jewish traits.

3. I take Freud at his word here. There are a variety of hints that Freud was in part ashamed of his Jewishness, despite obvious elements of pride in his ethnic background. See Sander Gilman, *Freud, Race, and Gender*.

> Intellectuality and independence of mind, the highest ethical standards, concern for social justice, tenacity in the face of persecution—these are among the qualities that they will claim, if called upon as quintessentially Jewish. (1990, 10)

But whereas anti-Semitism reflects an irrational hatred of Jews, it does not exclude the possibility that Freud's psychoanalytical ideas might in fact have had a greater resonance for the Jewish psyche. While acknowledging the sensibilities of our post-Holocaust world, political correctness must not dissuade scholars from exploring whether this idea has an evidential basis.

Freud was able to acknowledge his debt to the independence of his Jewish mentality, but resisted crediting the contributions of Jewish religious thought to his ideas concerning psychoanalysis.

PSYCHOANALYSIS: A JEWISH SCIENCE?

In an incisive analysis of Freud's Judaism, the historian Sander Gilman explains how anti-Semitism raised critical concerns for Freud about the future of psychoanalysis (1993). Gilman notes that the Enlightenment heralded a modern retreat from the time-honored Augustinian dogma that viewed Jews as the errant ancestors of Christianity, who would eventually embrace the divinity of Jesus. The Augustinian doctrine tolerated Jews but prohibited their social elevation to the status of Christians. This doctrine was generally honored until the eleventh-century crusades, when marauding bands of pilgrim warriors on their way to fight the Muslims in the Holy Land chose to decimate the Jewish populations of the Rhineland in their path.

Later in the fifteenth century, following the Reconquista of the Iberian Peninsula from Islamic control, the Jews of Spain were given the uncomfortable choice either to convert or be expelled from the country in 1492. Many Spanish Jews left for neighboring Portugal, and some migrated to other locations in Europe, North Africa, and the Middle East. However, the established Christian communities of Spain viewed the new Jewish converts (*conversos* or *marranos*) with suspicion (Roth 1992). Rather than regarding the Jews as a religious group, which had until that time traditionally been the case, the Christian communities saw them instead as a distinct race, distinguished not by their religious beliefs but by their physical and ethnic characteristics. Unfortunately the otherness of the Jew did not stop at that. The Jew was no longer merely different; he was demonical the embodiment of everything that Christians needed to avoid or eliminate.

In the late nineteenth and first part of the twentieth century, Germany, which was widely viewed as the seat of high culture and scientific achievement in Europe, increasingly adopted a rabid form of eliminationist anti-Semitism, in which Jews were imagined to be both racially inferior and demonic, as the historian Daniel Goldhagen argues in *Hitler's Willing Executioners* (2009). This troubled period in Jewish history coincides with the lifetimes of Freud and Jung.

Anti-Semitic perspectives colored virtually all aspects of German thought, including ideas about mental illness. It was widely believed that degenerative "illnesses of the nervous system," especially the prevalent conditions of neurasthenia and hysteria, were inheritable and disproportionately represented among Jews (Gilman 1993). The current idea that mental disorders might be acquired in reaction to the squalid conditions that Jews were forced to live under was never considered (Gaw 1993). Ethnic differences dominated psychiatric thought and such ideas were shared by Jewish doctors, including Freud, (Freud and Fliess 1985).

Anti-Semites and purportedly unprejudiced professionals questioned whether Jewish psychoanalysts might not be biased by their own mental disturbances. Consequently, Freud's efforts at generalizing his psychoanalytical observations to non-Jews were staunchly resisted. Pierre Janet, a respected French psychiatrist, whose own theories of hysteria and obsessionality rivaled those of Freud's, openly questioned whether one could accept the "psychoanalysis" coming out of Vienna, a euphemism for its Jewish origins. Even Freud's mentor Jean-Marie Charcot was convinced that Jews, like women, were predisposed to hysteria (Aron and Starr 2013).

Freud was well aware of these opinions and privately shared his concerns with his Jewish colleagues (Freud and Fliess 1985). Yet in public he worked at distancing psychoanalysis from such conclusions, defending it primarily with the assertion that as a "scientific" approach, it must be applicable across religious, ethnic, and racial differences.

Like his anti-Semitic colleagues, Freud was disturbed by the potential adverse effects of the Jewish religion on its practitioners (Patai 1977). In his early writings (Freud 1907) and in his last published work, *Moses and Monotheism* (Freud 1938), he expresses the opinion that the ritual observance of the 613 commandments of Judaism resembles an obsessional neurosis:

> Driven by the need to satisfy this sense of guilt, which was insatiable, and came from sources much deeper, they must make those commandments grow ever stricter, more meticulous and even more trivial. In a fresh rapture of moral asceticism, they posed more and more new instinctual renunciations on themselves, and in that way reached—in doctrine and precept, at least—ethical heights, which had remained inaccessible to the other people of antiquity. Many Jews regard this attainment of ethical heights, as the second main characteristic, and the single great achievement of their religion (the first being the idea of a single God). (134)

On one hand, Freud sees meticulous religious observance as having the potential to become repetitive and devoid of meaning, while at the same time he extols its role in heightening the ethical stance of Jews. Aron and Starr have suggested that Freud harbored the idea that Jews were ethically superior to Christians, who had rid themselves of the obligations of the Law (Aron and Starr 2013).

Freud's closest friends and confidants, who in many instances became the first generation of psychoanalysts, were virtually all Jews.[4] In a letter to Karl Abraham, Freud writes, "May I say that it is our

4. A notable exception was the Englishman Ernest Jones, who was one of Freud's first biographers. Jones had wanted to marry Freud's daughter Anna, but her father discouraged the match. Jones was also noted by many to have made frankly anti-Semitic comments during his time as a psychoanalyst (Gilman 1993).

consanguineous Jewish traits that attract me to you? We understand each other" (Freud and Abraham 2002, 46; italics in original). After passing Abraham up for a position of leadership in the psychoanalytical movement, Freud apologized as follows:

> Please be tolerant and do not forget that it is really easier for you than it is for Jung to follow my ideas, for in the first place you are completely independent, and then you are closer to my intellectual constitution because of racial kinship, while he is a Christian and a pastor's son and finds his way to me against great inner resistances. (Freud and Abraham 2002, 34)

In Abraham's conciliatory reply to Freud, he suggests with keen insight that perhaps it was not simply ethnicity, but *also* Jewish religious thought that contributed to their shared appreciation of psychoanalysis:

> I find it easier to go along with you than with Jung. I too have always felt this intellectual kinship. After all our Talmudic way of thinking cannot disappear just like that. Some days ago a paragraph in *Jokes [and the Unconscious]* strangely attracted me. When I looked at it closely, I found that in its technique of apposition and in its whole structure, it was completely Talmudic. (Freud and Abraham 2002, 34)

Abraham is referring here to the structure of the Talmudic argument or *sugya*, which stylistically begins with a question, followed by a lengthy discussion of different opinions by various sages, and concludes, in most cases, with a legal decision. Freud's oft-lauded literary style, for which he was awarded the Goethe Prize while in the gymnasium, paralleled this Talmudic genre. In a monograph devoted to Freud's literary style, *Healing Fictions*, the Jungian analyst James Hillman points out that Freud's writing is like that of a detective novel, in which clues are dropped, returned to, and then all neatly wrapped up in the end (Hillman 1998). But this is *also* the style of the Talmudic *sugya*.

Freud was acutely aware of the differences between Jews and Christians, but he was, unlike Abraham, unwilling to admit that his religious background had influenced psychoanalysis.

RACE AND ETHNICITY

In Freud's mention of consanguinity when addressing Abraham, he raises the question of a biologically based difference between Jews and others. The idea of Jews as a distinct ethnic group was not a new one in Freud's time. In fact, whether ethnic and racial differences have a genetic basis is still being argued by scientists, to no conclusion (Hart 2011). Modern genetic analysis confirms that many European Jews are the result of many generations of endogamous mating, and in this regard, there is reason to wonder whether they have become to some degree a phenotypically distinct group.

Might Jews exhibit distinct neuro-psychologies from other groups that cannot be explained fully on the basis of environmental differences (Patai 1977)? The answer is uncertain. Differences should not be used to malign any group, but as Goldhagen notes, the human reaction to difference cannot be ignored because it is to some degree adaptive and part of our evolutionary heritage (2013). But with respect to the present argument it is noteworthy that Freud, unlike most post-Darwinian scientists, continued to adhere to a Lamarckian view of inheritance, in which mnemonic elements of memory are transmitted genetically (Sulloway 1979). He argues this point in *Totem and Taboo*, *The Psychopathology of Everyday Life*, and again in *Moses and Monotheism*.

While adamant about refuting Jewish religious traditions, Freud was equally clear concerning his inextricable ties to his fellow Jews. In the introduction to a 1930 Hebrew translation of *Totem and Taboo*, Freud writes:

> No reader of this book will find it easy to put himself in the emotional position of the author who is ignorant of the Holy

> Writ, who is completely estranged from the religion of his fathers—and from every other religion—and who cannot take a share in nationalist ideals, but who has never repudiated his people, who feels that he is in his essential nature a Jew and who has no desire to alter that nature. If the question were put to him: "Since you have abandoned all those common characteristics of your compatriots, what is left to you now that is Jewish?" he would reply, *A very great deal, and probably, its very essence.* He could not now express that essence in words; but some day, no doubt, it will become accessible to the scientific mind. (quoted in Yerushalmi 1991, 14)

Freud viewed Jews as a distinct group, and largely in positive ways. He attributes their bond not to education or religious beliefs, but to kinship and poorly defined inheritable memories.

In his final years, facing death from terminal mouth cancer, while writing *Moses and Monotheism* and being victimized by Nazi anti-Semitism, Freud addressed the Viennese Psychoanalytical Society, prior to going into exile in England following the German Anschluss of Austria:

> After the destruction of the Temple in Jerusalem by Titus, R. Yochanan ben Zakkai asked for permission to open a school at Yavneh for the study of *Torah*. We are going to do the same. We are after all, used to persecution by our history, tradition, and some of us by personal experience. (Frosh 2009, 32)

This statement suggests that Freud not only identified with the collective fate of the Jews, but may also have imagined psychoanalysis as the new Law. Yerushalmi claims that Freud's disavowed aspects of Judaism may have returned *qua* psychoanalysis (1991). The ethical principles that he had attributed to the Jew's observance of the Law would now be incorporated into his secular psychoanalysis.

JUDAISM AND THE LAW

What separates traditional Jews from Christians is not primarily theology but the observance of the Law. As Goldhagen notes in *Anti-Semitism: The Devil that Will Not Die* (2013), the classical position of the church was that if Jews were right in continuing to observe the Law, then Christianity was not valid.

Despite Freud's abandonment of the Law, his psychoanalysis is preoccupied with the dynamic relationship of the super-ego (i.e., internalized law) with the other sectors of the psyche. Indeed, Freud's ideas concerning the development of the super-ego as the result of paternal identification at the end of the Oedipal period, suggest his preoccupation with the patriarchy of Judaism.

But there is no reason necessarily to conclude that Christians or even less concerned Jews would necessarily share Freud's perspectives. One can, with integrity and without anti-Semitic bias, honestly question whether psychoanalysis is the product of Freud's particular psychology and *not* a universally applicable approach. The possibility that psychoanalysis might indeed be *Jewish* science cannot blithely be dismissed, in large measure because Freud privately agreed that it was. As for his assertion that psychoanalysis is *science*, which was his primary claim to its universal applicability, this is unsupported.

In response to his looming fear that psychoanalysis might be dismissed by anti-Semitic prejudice (Gay 1978), Freud attempted to recruit a group of Swiss Christian psychiatrists, including the renowned psychiatrist Eugen Bleuler and his younger but promising colleague Carl Jung, to positions of leadership in the new psychoanalytical movement. Freud bluntly announced to his Jewish colleagues in the Viennese Psychoanalytical Society in 1910:

> Most of you are Jews and therefore incompetent to win friends for the new teaching. Jews must be content with the modest role of preparing the ground. It is absolutely essential that I should form ties in the world of general science. . . . The Swiss will save us. (Gilman 1993, 41)

Freud hoped that the Christian psychiatrists of Switzerland would affirm the universal relevance of psychoanalysis. Unfortunately, that would not prove to be the case, as Swiss psychiatry ultimately abandoned Freud's psychoanalysis. Jung, however, would go on to formulate his own type of psychoanalysis, one steeped in the ideas of his own Christian background.

CHAPTER 2

Carl Gustav Jung: A Preacher's Son

We always think that Christianity consists in a particular confession of faith and in belonging to a Church. No, Christianity is our world. Everything that we think is the fruit of the Middle Ages and indeed of the Christian Middle Ages . . . we are inevitably stamped as Christians.

—Carl Jung

Carl Jung was a psychiatrist, unlike Freud who was a neurologist (Figure 3). Jung was the junior colleague of Eugen Bleuler, famous for having developed the modern criteria for the diagnosis of schizophrenia. As a young medical student, Jung embraced the scientifically disreputable position of vitalism in his *Zofingia Lectures*, claiming that life could not be explained simply by the mechanistic activities of biochemistry but instead had a metaphysical source:

> The vital principle extends far beyond consciousness in that it also maintains the vegetative functions of the body which, as we know, are not under our conscious control. Our consciousness is dependent on the functions of the brain, but these are in turn dependent on the vital principle, and accordingly the vital principle represents a substance, whereas consciousness represents a contingent phenomenon. Or as Schopenhauer

Figure 3. Carl C. Jung was a Swiss Christian psychiatrist who developed his approach to psychoanalysis after breaking with Freud.

> says: "Consciousness is the object of a transcendental idea." Thus, we see that animal and vegetative functions are embraced in a common root, the actual subject. Let us boldly assign to this transcendental subject the name "soul." What do we mean by "soul"? *The soul is an intelligence independent of space and time.* (1895 para. 95; italics in original)

Jung hailed from an old and respected Swiss family. His father was a Swiss Reform Protestant minister who struggled with questions of faith throughout his life. In his autobiography, *Memories, Dreams, Reflections*, Jung attributes his father's crisis of faith to a "dry" theological approach devoid of authentic feeling (Jung and Jaffe 1989).

In his autobiography, Jung describes an early fear of God and the Christian religion. He recounts an obsessive childhood fantasy in which a large piece of excrement falls from underneath the throne of God to crush the dome of the Basel cathedral, an idea that delighted the puerile Jung, for he realized that it was possible to entertain heretical ideas without suffering divine retribution

With some initial reservation, Jung opted to study psychiatry, a field that was still in its infancy at the turn of the nineteenth century. While conducting research on the word association experiment, an exercise in which patients were asked a list of words and monitored both for the latency of their verbal responses and autonomic nervous system activation, Jung discovered that certain patients had reproducible physiological reactions to specific words. He referred to these as "complexes" and theorized about their intrapsychic organization. The idea of the complex plays an important role in Jungian theory and his mode of psychoanalysis is sometimes referred to as "Complex Psychology."

When Freud heard of Jung's results, he viewed them as the objective experimental support that he was seeking for his own theories of the unconscious. This led to a correspondence between Freud and Jung, and eventually to their meeting in Vienna, in which the conversation lasted late into the night. Jung was impressed with Freud's intellect and bearing, and in the elder Freud he may have imagined having identified an idealizable father figure (Jung and Jaffe 1989).

Freud was favorably disposed to Jung's intellect and enthusiasm for psychoanalysis. Motivated by his lingering concerns about future of psychoanalysis, Freud suggested that Jung and his Swiss Christian colleagues join the Jewish membership of the International Psychoanalytical Association. For several years, Jung held leadership positions in the Association, and was regarded as Freud's heir apparent

Recognizing the importance of the Oedipus myth from his own theoretical inquiries into the psyche, Freud encouraged his colleagues to explore the field of mythology. Jung embarked on an exhaustive exploration of comparative myth, which inspired him to consider novel ideas concerning the structure of unconscious. Jung rejected Freud's positions that that the unconscious was primarily the site of elemental sexual drives and repressed mental contents, and that neuroses were invariably the result of Oedipal conflicts. Rather, he concluded that the psyche was a mythopoietic organ and that individuals were unwittingly living out variations of a limited number of archetypal mythological motifs.

JUNG AND TRANSFORMATION

Jung's first independent major work as a psychoanalyst, *Symbols of Transformation* (Jung 1911), included a detailed examination of the role of myth as a motivating psychological factor and did not hold sexuality to be the cause of neuroses. Disturbed by Jung's neglect of what he firmly held was the core drive within the psyche, Freud summarily dismissed Jung's ideas. When Jung insisted on defending them, the relationship between the two men grew strained. They parted ways inimically in 1912 due to what Jung claimed was Freud's intractable authoritarian style, and Freud Jung's adolescent rebellion against "the father."

Following his break with Freud, Jung suffered a severe depression with elements of what has tactfully been described by some as a "creative illness," and by others as a psychosis with schizophreniform features (Shamdasani 2003). Jung admitted in later years to having slept with a gun beneath his pillow and having considered suicide (Jung and Jaffe 1989).

During this time he reported visions and conversations with a series of imaginal characters.[1] He assigned generic roles in the psychic apparatus to the images that he encountered in his active imaginations and dreams. Jung's model of the psyche was experiential and based in the imagination as opposed to Freud's which was abstract and primarily conceptual.

Following Plato, Jung posited that the structuring elements of the mind were archetypes, which he envisioned as the innate ordering capacities of the collective unconscious (i.e., an aspect of unconscious activity shared by all members of the species). Unlike Freud, Jung did not posit Lamarckian inheritance of specific ideas or memories, but the a priori potential of the psyche to create a limited repertoire of images (Jung 1967).

Jung posited a central "supraordinate" archetype, which he termed the "self" (this term is often capitalized as Self in post-Jungian writings), that structured the psyche, including the other archetypes. This notion is akin to the problem put to monotheism of how a singular God becomes the many aspects of creation. The self was, according to Jung, the source of the various God images encountered in world religions, the element that can manifest psychologically as the God image, comparable to James notion of the mystical religious experience. Jung's ideas

1. Although it is difficult and questionable to diagnose Jung's disorder, it seems to me most likely that today it would have been termed "bipolar disease" with psychotic features triggered by loss of self-esteem due to Freud's rejection of his ideas.

about the self were in constant flux, at times he suggested that it was an innate neurobiological capacity of the human brain, at others a metaphysical force akin to the Platonic soul. In this regard, he imagined the archetypes as bipolar and capable of manifesting either in the realm of matter or spirit. He speculated on the immortality of the self, as he states in his introduction to Richard Wilhelm's *Secret of the Golden Flower*:

> As a doctor, I make every effort to strengthen the belief in immortality, especially with older patients when such questions come threateningly close. For, seen in correct psychological perspective, death is not an end but a goal, and life's inclination towards death begins as soon as the meridian is past. (*CW* 13, para. 68)

Jung's ideas and method of analysis tend to be popular with individuals who are seeking spiritual experience rather than a reductive analysis of their neuroses. Jung suggested that his mode of therapy was most helpful for individuals in the second half of life who had already been cured of their childhood neuroses by Freud's approach. But once independent of Freud, Jung showed little interest in relying upon, or referring to, Freud's psychoanalytic methods. The rift in their views widened and their approaches became increasingly polarized, with Freud showing as little interest in spiritual experience as Jung does in childhood sexuality.

Jung views psychological healing as a process of transformation. This idea is reminiscent of the core Christian mythos, with its emphasis on death and resurrection. As John 12:23–27 states:

> . . . And Jesus answered them, saying, "The hour has come for the Son of Man to be glorified. Truly, truly, I say to you, unless a grain of wheat falls into the earth and dies, it remains alone; but if it dies, it bears much fruit. He who loves his life loses it, and he who hates his life in this world will keep it to life eternal."

From his first major work, *Symbols of Transformation* (1916), to his writings on alchemy (1944) and the psychology of the mass (1942), Jung repeatedly emphasizes the central motif of transformation. This is different from Freud's psychotherapeutic approach of working through defenses and resistances with the goal of raising repressed unconscious contents to awareness. The guiding myth of Jungian therapy is one of organic change, in which the ego must experience cycles of death and rebirth, akin to what Sir James Frazer in his *Golden Bough* described as the myth of the dying and resurrected god in agricultural societies (Frazer 1922). This agricultural motif is also the basis of Christianity. Jung's notion of transformation intimates its metaphysical basis, as change occurs in ways that cannot be readily seen, and rather appears to be guided by chthonic activities within the psyche.

Jung's emphasis on archetypes and the collective unconscious displaces the focus of psychology away from the immediate physical life of the individual to a universal and spiritual realm of shared transpersonal psychological activities. Jung ascribed to no theories of psychopathology and he adhered to no specific technique in his approach to patients. His approach is best described as existential and phenomenological.

Jung's writings also make no mention of ego defenses or how to dismantle them, a topic that preoccupied Freud. Instead, nearly all of Jung's advice centers on the symbolic interpretation of dreams, or on active imagination, in which patients are encouraged to engage with imaginal characters while in a self-induced trance. It is not clear that Jung believed in ego defenses at all. Instead, he viewed symbols as mediating both the forward-seeking forces and resistances within the psyche. In practice, many Jungian analysts are forced to seek additional clinical training from non-Jungian therapists, in order to become adept at recognizing and addressing the defenses of the ego. However, there are more than a few classical Jungian analysts who are unconcerned with what neo-Freudians insist is missing in Jung's approach.

JUNG AND PROTOTYPIC PSYCHOLOGY

Jung was competent in classical languages and steeped in the writings of the Greek philosophers, especially those of the Platonists. In his lifelong inquiries into myth, he exhibited an interest in Christian Gnosticism, a radically Hellenized and dualistic form of second-century Christianity that emphasized the primacy of spirit, denigrated the material world, and claimed that esoteric knowledge was necessary in order to achieve salvation. He studied the Church Fathers' references to the Gnostic texts, and following the discoveries of a hidden Gnostic library at Nag Hammadi in 1945 (Robinson 1990), which had been lost for 1,500 years, he managed to acquire one of the precious papyrus Coptic texts for his own collection, the so-called Jung Codex.[2]

In later years, Jung's theoretical interests turned to an intensive study of medieval alchemy (Jung 1980). He pored through ancient alchemical texts, concluding that some of the alchemists had been engaged in a prototype of psychotherapy. According to Jung, the alchemical opus was an effort at achieving spiritual transformation, in which some unwittingly projected their own unconscious imagery onto matter (Jung 1944). Jung adopted alchemical terms and images liberally as explanations of psychological transformation in his subsequent writings, a choice that has proved off-putting for many non-Jungian analysts and modern psychologists. Jung's unabashed interest in the arcane continues to make him a controversial figure.

JUNG ON THE PSYCHOLOGY OF DIFFERENCE

Like Freud, Jung ascribed to the reigning nineteenth-century paradigm that racial and ethnic differences extend to personal psychology.[3] In his

2. After Jung's death, the Jung family donated the Jung Codex to the Cairo Museum, where it is currently exhibited.
3. The charges of Jung's anti-Semitism represent a complex topic. As has been suggested, he was merely participating, like Freud, in his opinions concerning the racial differences between Jews and Aryans. However, Jung appears to have been an opportunist, and although never fully adopting the tenets of the Nazi Party, did little to distance himself from it during its rise. He has succeeded to a position of being largely abhorrent to the culture of the psychoanalytical profession that remains

private correspondence, he responded to an inquiry concerning the "significance of Freud's Jewish descent for the origin, content, and acceptance of psychoanalysis," as follows:

> One would have to take a deep plunge into the history of the Jewish mind. This would carry us beyond Jewish orthodoxy into the subterranean workings of Hasidism . . . and then into the intricacies of the Kabbalah, which still remain unexplored psychologically. (Jung 1975, *Letters*, 358–359)

While still participating in Freud's inner circle, it appears that some of Jung's novel ideas developed during the course of his treating a young Jewish psychiatrist for hysteria at the Burgholzli psychiatric hospital. As John Kerr discusses in *A Most Dangerous Method* (Kerr 1994)—recently made into a Hollywood blockbuster—Sabina Spielrein was an intelligent, highly imaginative young woman suffering from hysteria who collaborated with Jung in exploring the mythico-symbolic elements of the psyche.[4] In a thinly veiled and anti-Semitic suggestion to Spielrein, Jung made reference to her Hasidic background:

> The patient was a Jewish girl. . . . I saw nothing of her father complex but it gave me the idea to ask about the history of her family. Then I found out that she came from a Hasidic family—you know those great mystics. Her grandfather had been a sort of a wonder-rabbi, he had second sight, and her father had broken away from that mystic community, and she was completely skeptical and scientific in her outlook on life. She was highly intelligent *with that murderous kind of intellect that you often find in Jews*. (*CW* 18, para. 635; italics added)

---

largely Jewish. Few psychoanalysts have honestly evaluated the private positions of Freud on Christianity. For a consideration of Jung's anti-Semitism, see Aryeh Maidenbaum and Stephen Martin, *Lingering Shadows* (Boston: Shambhala, 1991).

4. The idea of patient participation in theory-making was already part of the history of psychoanalysis by virtue of Anna O.'s work with Josef Breuer.

Jung makes few references to Judaism in his own theoretical musings on psychology, although he was fond of alluding to Jacob's struggle with the angel in Genesis as a metaphor for how the ego must struggle with the unconscious. Instead, much of his writing is preoccupied with references to Christianity and to the early Christian Gnostics. Late in his career, after being introduced to the Jewish Kabbalah and Hasidic thought, Jung was evidently deeply impressed. He conceded openly that his own psychological theories, especially those expressed in his last major work, the *Mysterium Coniunctionis*, had been prefigured by the psychological ideas of the Jewish mystics, and specifically by Dov Ber, the Maggid of Mezyritch, second-generation mystic and leader of the Hasidic movement (Drob 2000).

As Murray Stein suggests, Jung's psychological approach was in part an attempt to revivify Christianity by focusing on its affective roots within the imagination (Stein 2012). A Protestant, Jung spoke favorably of Roman Catholicism's continued reliance on symbols, rituals, and the use of Latin in its liturgy, maintaining, like William James, that mystery was an essential feature of religious experience. Jung devoted an entire essay to the psychology of the mass, psychologizing the imagined yet real transubstantiation of bread and wine into the body and blood of Christ (Jung 1942).

Although interested in the great Eastern religions—he adopted the notion of the self from the atman of Hinduism as the paradoxical "center and circumference" of the psyche—Jung did not believe that Eastern religions could be integrated by the Western psyche, seeing the latter as too firmly entrenched in the Judeo-Christian ethic. He rejected the Eastern soteriological notion of world renunciation and was drawn to the idea of experiencing the archetypes consciously in the service of individuation (i.e., the goal of self-realization) (Jung 1984).

Jung valued religion in its own right as a psychotherapeutic approach. He encouraged patients, whenever possible, to return to their religion of origin, although he recognized that the symbols of organized religion had lost much of their appeal for the modern psyche. Indeed, the rift between Freud and Jung was as much fostered by the former's generic devaluation of religion as it was by their underlying personal religious differences.

If Freud was suspect of Jung's loyalties to psychoanalysis because he was a Christian, his concerns would be confirmed by statements that Jung made about the Jews during the Nazi years. During the war, Jung assumed a position of political importance in the Nazi-dominated German psychiatric society, and authored several articles that must be interpreted as anti-Semitic (Martin and Maidenbaum 1991). Despite his subsequent denials of this charge, and support by some prominent Jewish leaders including the German Rabbi Leo Baeck, the largely Jewish world of Freudian psychoanalysts was faced with the choice of either dismissing Jung as an anti-Semite who shared sympathies with the Nazis or seeing him as an unethical opportunist (Yerushalmi 1991). Both explanations were adopted.

In his *State of Psychotherapy Today* (1934), Jung addressed the question that is being posed in the present text:

> Freud and Adler have beheld very clearly the shadow that accompanies us all. The Jews have this in common with women; being physically weaker, they have to aim at the chinks of the armor of their adversary. . . . As a member of a race with a three-thousand-year-old civilization, the Jew has a wider area of psychological consciousness than we. Consequently, it is in general less dangerous for the Jew to put a negative value on the unconscious. . . . The Jew who is something of a nomad, has never yet created a cultural form of his own, and as far as we can see, never will, since all of his instincts and talents require a more or less civilized nation to act as a host to their development.
>
> The Jewish race as a whole—at least this is my experience—possesses an unconscious that can be compared with the "Aryan" only with reserve. . . . In my opinion, it has been a grave error in medical psychology up till now to apply Jewish

> categories—which are not even binding on all Jews—to Germanic and Slavic Christendom. (*CW* 10, para. 353)

Such opinions are gratuitous and offensive. They support the prevalent anti-Semitic notion that Jews and women are prone to hysteria due to innate weakness (Aron and Starr 2013). Nevertheless, the argument that the universality of Freud's psychoanalysis should be viewed with skepticism cannot be dismissed. Jung is suggesting that psychoanalysis may not even apply to all Jews, let alone Christians, and this position is echoed in other statements made by Jung, who stressed the importance of differences in psychological types.

The psychoanalyst Heinz Kohut recommended that the curriculum at the Chicago Institute of Psychoanalysis should not be allowed to include Jung (Strozier 2001). To this day, the predominantly Jewish neo-Freudian analytical community remains suspicious of Jung and his psychology, whereas neo-Jungian psychologists are as often antagonistic to Freud's ideas. To my knowledge, Jung is rarely required reading in Freudian training institutes. Although Freud is generally taught in Jungian institutes, his work often receives rudimentary attention, and is studied mostly for historical reasons with his ideas being presented mostly as a foil for Jung's.

It is a fact that a large percentage of Jungian analysts hail either from Christian backgrounds, or have been trained in Christian theology, or were previously members of the Christian clergy. Certainly, Jungian thought appeals to some Jews—there is an active society in Israel founded by Erich Neumann, one of Jung's disciples—as well as to religiously unaffiliated individuals with spiritual inclinations. On the other hand, most individuals who seek Freudian analysis, or train to be Freudian psychoanalysts, are, like Freud, secular Jews (Aron and Starr 2013). These differences are not due to chance.

CHAPTER 3

Anatomy of Psyche, Anatomy of Soul

For thousands of years, the mind of man has worried about the sick soul, perhaps even earlier than it did about the sick body.

—Carl Jung

Establishing a link between religious thought and psychoanalysis requires a consideration of the pre-modern conceptions of the psyche (Goetz and Taliaferro 2011). The term psychoanalysis is derived from the Greek word for soul, *psyche*.[1] Freud repeatedly referred to the soul (*seele*) in his writings, but James Strachey did not adopt this term in translating Freud's collected works from German into English.

THE SOUL

The concept of a soul is encountered in both pagan[2] and monotheistic religions. Until modern times, when vitalism was superseded by biological materialism, the soul was generally held to be the animating force of both man and the cosmos.[3] In the *Republic*, Plato posits a tripartite

1. The term *psyche* in Greek means butterfly but was synonymous with soul.
2. A notable exception is Buddhism. The Buddha argues against the idea of a soul or any distinct animating factor, despite a belief in reincarnation.
3. Hasidism is very clear that all elements in the cosmos are ensouled. Some writers today prefer to refer to the world as enchanted. But the concept of a soul, the *anima mundi*, was well accepted in medieval times.

soul. The Platonic soul is immortal and returns to its supernal source upon the death of the body. As in other ancient philosophies (e.g., Hinduism and Pythagorean thought), the soul is held to pre-exist birth and to be subject to reincarnation.

Plato viewed the soul as imprisoned (*sema*) in a temporally limited body. While sojourning in the body, the soul is continually distracted from its true essence by animal pleasures. But the soul longs to be reunited with its immaterial supernal source. As Plato states in the *Phaedo*:

> I suppose that the soul reasons most beautifully . . . when bidding farewell to the body, she comes to be herself all alone as much as possible, and when doing everything that she can to avoid communing with the body . . . she strives for what is. (1999, 65)

As in other traditions that ascribe to metempsychosis (i.e., the reincarnation of souls), the soul's experience while residing in the body determines the nature of its reincarnation. Those souls that succumb to the pleasures of the flesh or treat others badly during corporeal life can expect to be reincarnated in bestial forms, whereas those who strive for pure intellection are destined for a noble human rebirth.

Each part of the Platonic soul serves a specific function. The appetitive soul represents the animal life force of the human being but is incapable of rational intellection. Intellection is mediated by the rational soul, which seeks ontological truth in the unchanging perfect Ideas. Linking these two elements is the spirited soul. Plato locates these aspects of the soul in different parts of the body. When incarnate, the rational soul resides in the head, the spirited soul in the chest, and the appetitive soul in the abdomen.

It is not clear from Plato's treatment of the subject whether the different parts of the soul act separately or together. As Goetz and Taliaferro note in their *Brief History of the Soul*, a comparable question is currently being pondered by modern neuroscientists as the "binding problem," in other words, how are the different senses integrated within the psychic apparatus to produce a temporally unified experience (Goetz and Taliaferro 2011).

Plato's model of the soul was partially accepted by his pupil Aristotle and would later be adopted with slight modification by Christianity.[4] In *De Anima*, Aristotle posits that all life is ensouled (1984), but he argues that there is a hierarchical structure to the soul that parallels phylogeny. For Aristotle, plants and animals express a vegetative or nutritive soul, but animals are distinguished by a sensitive soul that allows the senses to mediate their environment. Only man is invested with a rational soul capable of apperception and making conscious choices. Behaviors are driven by a combination of desire and rational thought, with the object of desire serving as its "efficient cause."

Unlike Plato, Aristotle viewed the relationship between soul and body as determinative, not contingent. Whereas the Platonic soul acquires and sheds the body with impunity, the Aristotelian soul is inextricably linked to the body, and does not survive its death. The medieval Jewish philosopher Maimonides, following Aristotle, also envisioned the soul as the animating element of the body that died with it. Yet he insisted that the physical resurrection of both body and soul was a fundamental truth of Judaism, thereby intimating a deeper mystery to their interaction.[5]

Interestingly, the soul was never imagined as a unitary entity either in Greek or Jewish thought. Conceptual borrowing may have played a role in this commonality, as medieval Jews living in the Islamic world had access to the writings of Aristotle and to some of the works of Plato. Alternatively, the universal experience of psychological dissociation may account for the imagined variegate nature of the soul.

4. Catholicism closely follows the Platonic model of the tripartite soul. Calvin posited a consciousness that persists after death, whereas Luther imagined that the soul "sleeps" until it is resurrected at the end of days.
5. Leo Strauss in his *Persecution and the Art of Writing* (Chicago: Chicago University Press, 1988), goes to great lengths to try to explicate how Maimonides revealed aspects of secret teachings in ways that would not raise suspicion among Jewish authorities. According to Strauss, one hint includes apparently contradictory statements, (e.g., the denial of reincarnation and the insistence on the resurrection of the dead).

THE SOUL IN JUDAISM

The ancient Israelite religion believed in a soul that survived death but was destined for a murky afterlife in Sheol. This notion is comparable to that seen in Book 11 of Homer's *Odyssey* in the *nekyia*, in which the souls of the dead languish in eternal shadows. The idea of an afterlife with reward and punishment first appears in Judaism in the book of Daniel, written following the Maccabean revolt in the second century BCE, apparently to account for the fate of righteous martyrs (Cohen 2014).

Rabbinic Judaism viewed the soul as modular and its harmonization as the measure of wholeness or health. Tainting of the soul through sin was the primary cause of mental suffering. Rabbinic Judaism refers to a tripartite soul. The *nefesh* is closely associated with the body, whereas *ruach* and *neshamah* exhibit increasingly transcendent features comparable to the Platonic soul. Rabbinic Judaism and the Kabbalah also refer to two more sublime aspects of the soul. These are extra-corporeal but associated with the individual. The *chayah* is associated with a generic life force, while the *yechidah* determines the quintessential particularity of the Jewish soul and is connected directly to its divine source.

R. Schneur Zalman articulates a Hasidic model for the human soul in *Likutei Amarim* or the *Tanya* (2012). In it, he suggests that individuals have two souls that are thoroughly intermingled. Whereas both ultimately derive from God, the *nefesh behamit*, or animal soul, is shared by all living beings. The *nefesh elokhit* is the divine soul. While the *nefesh behamit* interacts with the body and is affected by the outside world, the second soul, the *nefesh elokhit* is immutable, but can be obscured by sins that accrue through the actions of the *nefesh behamit*. This resembles the notion of impurity within the Holy of Holies of the Temple due to the sins of the ancient Israelites, which required cleansing through the atonement rituals of Yom Kippur (Klawans 2004).

According to R. Schneur Zalman only Jews possess the *nefesh elokhit*, and not the remainder of mankind.[6] The *Tanya* suggests, "The

6. Schneur Zalman of Lyadi, the first Admor (*Adoneinu Moreinu v'Rabeinu*, Our Master, Teacher, and Rabbi) of Chabad was questioned by Russian authorities concerning this statement and replied that the lack of a divine soul was in fact

souls of the *nations* of the world emanate from unclean *kelippot* [shells] that contain no good whatsoever. . . . The second soul of the Jew is a true extension of God, as it is written, 'And he breathed into his nostrils the breath of life . . . '" (Zalman 2002, 6).

R. Schneur Zalman and the medieval kabbalists took issue with Aristotle and Maimonides on the question of reincarnation. The Jewish mystics posited the *gilgul* (circle, i.e., a great cycle of rebirth) as a tenet of Judaism. In Hasidic philosophy, *gilgul* allows for the eventual perfectibility of the *nefesh behamit*, so that, similar to the bodhisattva of Mahayana Buddhism, the ideal soul moves inexorably towards the level of a *tzaddik*, one who no longer is motivated to sin.[7]

THE SOUL OF PSYCHOANALYSIS

Freud's psychoanalytical models of the mind are, like those of the soul, multipartite and stratified. In his early topographical model, Freud imagined the most sublime aspect of the mind as consciousness. Descending, one encounters a pre-conscious repository of thoughts and affects that can be retrieved by willful attention (preconscious), whereas the unconscious, which Freud imagined as a seething cauldron of animalistic drives and a repository for repressed thoughts and feelings, the latter inaccessible except through psychoanalytic retrieval, resides at depth. But in 1923, Freud modified the topographical model into a structural model, in an effort to account for the moralizing element of the mind, the super-ego. This tripartite model included the "I" (ego), the super-ego, and the "It" (id) (Figure 4). In this model, the super-ego reflects the acculturated value system of the individual that is potentially in conflict with the hedonistic wishes of the unconscious. The ego becomes the battlefield upon which these two parts of the psychic system play out their competing aims. It is evident that this system closely mimics the rabbinic impulses of the

limited to pagans. However, the traditional view of the divine soul within Chabad is indeed that it is limited to Jews, reflecting the strong impression by the Kabbalists and the Hasidim that Jews were indeed a chosen people. See Nissan Mindel, *Schneur Zalman of Liadi* (New York: Kehot, 2002).

7. One can only become a less-than-fully perfect *tzaddik* by this path of reincarnation. The true *tzaddik* (*tzaddik gamur*) is born only once from a separate soul.

yetzarim that are pitted against each other in their opposing goals with respect to the observance of the Law.

Jung's model of the psyche is more complex than Freud's, but it is also multipartite and stratified with respect to depth (Figure 5). It is based primarily on Jung's experiences with image-symbols encountered in dreams and in active imaginations. It includes no super-ego or moralizing element, which is of paramount importance for Freud's theories of both the pathogenesis of neurosis and the ethical structuring of society. Jung accounts for a self-persecutory element within the psyche by the activities of the negatively valenced contrasexual *anima* in men, or its counterpart, the animus, in women, a notion that can be traced to both Gnosticism and the Kabbalah. These are experienced

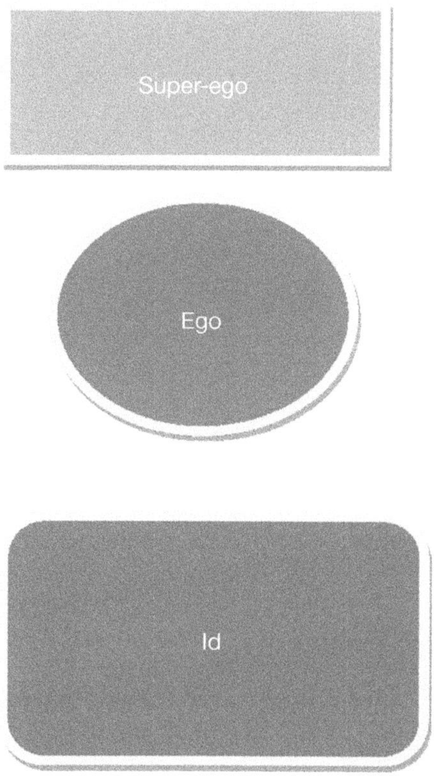

Figure 4. Freud's tripartite structural model of the psyche, which replaced his earlier topographic model, is shown. The dynamic interactions between the parts of the psyche were postulated to determine intrapsychic conflicts.

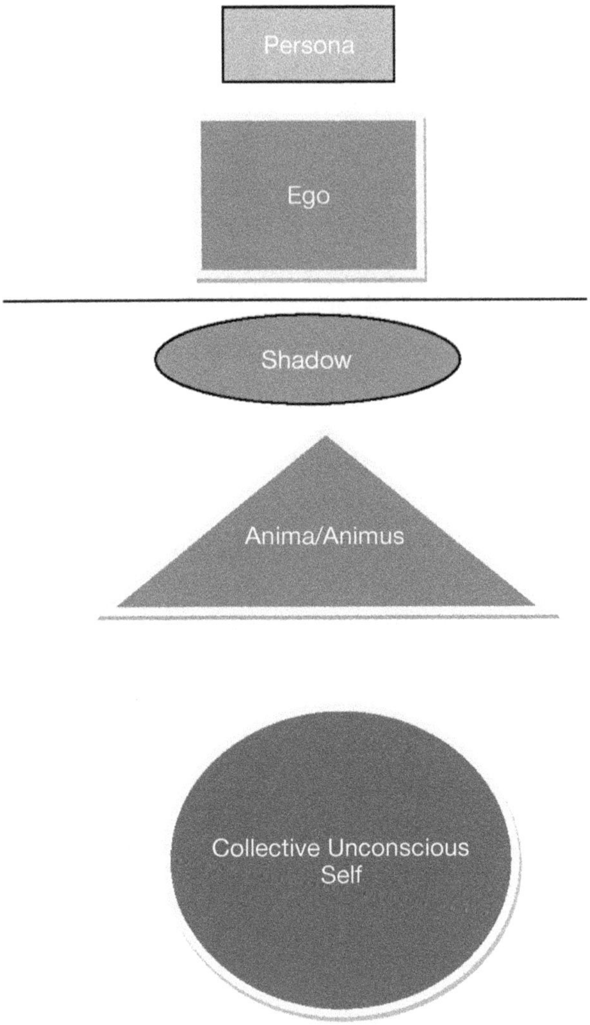

Figure 5. Jung's model of the psyche was based primarily on symbolic imagery and included a collective unconscious that was the source of the archetypes and the God image or self.

imaginally by the ego as harsh and demeaning intrapsychic voices, according to Jung, based on the phenomenology of dreams. Jung's persona accounts for the mode of interaction of the ego with the outer world, but there is nothing in the Jungian model, strictly speaking, that can be likened to a rule-bound conscience.

SIN, EVIL, AND THE METAPHYSICAL REALM

The conflict between opposing impulses within the mind is the basis of Freudian psychodynamics. But what Freud does not explicate, yet nonetheless lurks in the background of his theory as axiomatic, is a moral code of behavior that determines how thoughts and actions are judged as good and bad, right and wrong. Freud implies that these values are imposed by society, and tacitly accepts them as a requisite for normal psychological function. In fact, the moral code in the West for at least two millennia has been based on the so-called Judeo-Christian ethic, although as some suggest, this may be changing in modern times. As Rabbi Lawrence Hoffman notes in an essay on this topic:

> Does anyone still believe in sin? The word seems not just old fashioned but antiquarian. . . . Left to their own devices are people fundamentally good or bad? Trustworthy or devious? Heroes or villains? A wealth of psychological experiments addresses this question but when all is said and done, interpretations of these experiments differ enough to make us doubt whether anything can clinch the argument one way or the other. It eventually comes down to a matter of faith. (2012, 13)

An example of this is the recent acceptance of homosexual behavior as a permissible and moral lifestyle by a sizable part of Western society. Until several decades ago, most psychoanalysts considered homosexuality a psychopathology, undoubtedly, in large measure, based on biblical proscriptions that had been widely accepted as societal norms.[8]

Hoffman suggests that sin can be envisioned as practical (i.e., as common errors in how we treat ourselves and others), psychological

---

8. As I am editing this text for final submission, the once traditionally conservative Catholic country of Ireland has become the first European country to sanction gay marriage. The question of a lack of shared values introduces substantial theoretical issues for the conduct of a treatment. How does one, for instance, define sociopathic features in a patient without reliance on some moral code? This is a question that merits substantial attention by those who practice in the field of mental health.

(i.e., the result of human nature and psychological conflict), or metaphysical (i.e., as the result of spiritual forces beyond our control). Freud's position resembles that of Rabbinic Judaism, which focuses on intra-psychic conflict between good and bad impulses (*yetzarim*). However, Jung argues for the importance of the metaphysical in morality in *Answer to Job*, and elsewhere (Jung and Stein 1996). In this regard, Jung's position more closely resembles the dualism of Christianity:

> The Church has the doctrine of the devil, of an evil principle, which we like to imagine with cloven hoofs, horns, and tail, half man, half beast, a chthonic deity apparently escaped from the rout of Dionysus, the sole surviving champion of the sinful joys of paganism. . . . Probably no one today would be rash enough to assert that the European is a lamblike creature and not possessed by a devil. (*CW* 16, para. 388)

How to understand sin remains an important epistemological issue in psychological therapies, so that it is important to address this question by assessing the influences of the Judeo-Christian ethic on the modern psyche.[9]

9. Goldhagen suggests in *A Moral Reckoning* (New York: Knopf, 2002) that modern anti-Semitism is largely the result of the orthodox dogma of the Catholic Church. However, it is tied deeply to the radical dualism that posits an all-good God and an evil adversary. By not accepting Jesus as their messiah, the Jews were identified with the devil and needed to be suppressed or eliminated. Rabbinic Judaism does not accept this split between good and evil. Jung repeatedly suggests a binary valence for psychological processes.

CHAPTER 4

The Judeo-Christian Ethic

The old ethic of the Judeo-Christian epoch has proved incapable of mastering the destructive forces in man.

—**Erich Neumann**

The Jungian analyst James Hillman opined that the Judeo-Christian ethic is so ingrained in the collective unconscious of our Western civilization that it is virtually impossible to isolate its influence on modern thought (Hillman 2014).[1] In this regard, the psyche can be likened to a fish in water that is unaware of the vital medium that supports it. The idea of a Judeo-Christian ethic is rarely examined in the secular literature. Although Judaism and Christianity are inextricably bound to each other through historical, cultural, and textual underpinnings, the fact is that their relationship has traditionally been an adversarial one, and this must be considered in any effort to explicate the term.

The theologian Albert Schweitzer argued that Christianity began as an apocalyptic sect of Second Temple Judaism (1910). The term apocalyptic, from the Greek *apokalypsis* or revelation (*revelatio*) in Latin, refers to a particular theosophy, as well as to a literary genre that emerged in Judaism during the last centuries BCE. Most apocalyptic

1. According to Jung and Hillman, the Judeo-Christian ethic has formed the ambient cultural milieu in the West for two millennia and its influences are so deeply embedded that it is virtually impossible not to rely upon this matrix for all modern thought.

texts are pseudo-eponymous, a common phenomenon in the ancient world, as originality of authorship was not valued. With the notable exceptions of Daniel and Revelation, all of the ancient apocalyptic texts have been relegated to the Apocrypha, and they are not included within the canons of Judaism or Christianity. However, these apocalyptic texts were popular and widely read into medieval times (Koester 2000).

The apocalyptic text provides a vision of the divine realm as revealed to a man of high spiritual accomplishment. It generally describes an ascent into the heavens, where this man is provided a tour by an angel. There is controversy among scholars as to whether these were imagined narratives or recountings of actual mystical experiences (De Conick 2006).

The mood of the apocalyptic text is foreboding, which is why the modern use of the term apocalypse conveys sinister implications. Typically, they forecast the immanent end of the world, or eschatology, in response to a plethora of human sins that man can no longer atone for. In apocalyptic thought, human choice exerts no influence on future events, as these are wholly dependent on divine will.

Some of these texts have been linked by scholars to Jewish sects that had withdrawn from mainstream life in the days of the Second Temple. They generally refer to perceived societal corruption and breakdown in mainstream religious society from which the sect chose to withdraw. These sects expected the immanent arrival of a divinely instituted new world order, in which they, but not others, would be included, as a result of their faithful clinging to the ways of righteousness.

The authors of these texts also held radically dualistic ideas concerning good and evil. They relied on the astrological dictum "as above, so below," so that the struggles on earth were seen as a microcosm of greater internecine conflicts between forces of light and darkness within the heavens.

One body of apocalyptic literature, dating in some cases from approximately the second century BCE, was discovered among the Dead Sea Scrolls in 1947, and apparently written and studied by an ascetic sect at Qumran (Vermes 2012). These scrolls include the earliest examples of apocalyptic writings, and they predate both the canonical texts of Daniel and Revelation. The apocalyptic books of Enoch expand on the fate of Enoch in Genesis 5:24. The text of Genesis 5:24 states that "Enoch walked faithfully with God and then he was no more," which led early biblical commentators to conclude that he had been taken directly into heaven without suffering a mortal death.[2] The books of Enoch describe his ascent to heaven, and refer to the activities of the fallen angels that are mentioned briefly in Genesis 6:1–4. The Enochian literature suggests that evil entered the world not primarily as the consequence of Adam's sin in the Garden but because of the transgression of the barriers between the sacred heavens and the profane world by a group of renegade angels. These angels introduced technology to man, as Prometheus did in Greek myth, and the texts suggest this as an important factor in the moral deterioration of society.

A fifth book of Enoch, the Similitudes, was not found at Qumran but was discovered in the late nineteenth century preserved in Ethiopic. In it, Enoch ascends to heaven, where he is transformed by fire into the angel Metatron, and then seated at the right hand of God. The theologian Rudolf Otto suggested (1938), and I have also commented (Kradin 2010) that there is reason to believe that the early church was conversant with the Enochian texts, as they appear to suggest that in the first century there were Jews who believed that a man could be elevated to the level of divinity.[3]

Apocalyptic ideology is observed within the Gospels. Jesus' struggle with the worldly powers that be (i.e., the Romans and the Jewish authorities) is paralleled by a metaphysical conflict taking place between the divine Christ and Satan. Like his predecessor

2. The biblical commentaries include a number of noteworthy figures who apparently never died human deaths as we know it. Most notably, Elijah was taken directly into heaven on a fiery chariot. However, this may also include Moses, Jacob, and others; their deaths are recounted in the Hebrew Bible, but commentators suggest they did not actually transpire as we know death.
3. As difficult as this is for the secular modern mind to fathom, the idea of apotheosis was a familiar one in antiquity. The Roman Emperors were thought to become gods upon dying and ancient Egyptian kings were considered to be gods.

John the Baptist, Jesus preaches the immanent end of days and the arrival of the Kingdom of God. Whereas the Gospels include ethical teachings, the extremity of the positions adopted by Jesus is typical apocalyptic.

Jewish apocalyptic ideas, adopted and modified by Hellenizing factions in Palestine and in the Diaspora, gave rise to Christianity. Early Christianity included a devaluation of the physical world, an antinomian stance concerning the Law, as well as an evolving messianic notion of Christ's divinity. These ideas became the primary sources of contention between Rabbinic Jews and the early church. This rift between Christianity's accent on spirituality and Judaism's continued loyalties to the Law and embodied life would two millennia later also mark the differences in the psychological approaches developed by Freud and Jung.

ANTI-JUDAISM AND MATERIALISM

In *Anti-Judaism: The Western Tradition*, the historian David Nirenberg argues that much of the conflict between Judaism and Christianity rests on their differing modes of textual exegesis (2013). Judaism adopts a wide range of textual interpretations, but insists on maintaining its ritual practices based on a literal interpretation of the Law, although there are some notable exceptions. For example, in Exodus 21:24 the Torah calls for justice based on "an eye for an eye, a tooth for a tooth," "which the Rabbis claimed had always been understood as a metaphor for meting out justice proportionately. Another verse repeated three times in the Torah (Exodus 23:19, Exodus 24:26, and Deuteronomy 14:21), which prohibits "seething a kid in its mother's milk," was understood as a prohibition against eating meat with dairy, even within the ancient times. On the other hand, Christian exegesis from its inception tended to dismiss the plain meaning of the biblical text, choosing instead to interpret it allegorically and typologically, as a prediction of Christ's coming. An example from the Gospels is Jesus' comment in Matthew 15:10–12:

> After Jesus called the crowd to Him, He said to them, "Hear and understand. It is not what enters into the mouth that

> defiles the man, but what proceeds out of the mouth, this defiles the man." Then the disciples came and said to Him, "Do you know that the Pharisees were offended when they heard this statement?"

This pericope has often been taken as a proof text for Jesus' rejection of the Jewish laws of *kashrut*, but it is uncertain whether that was Jesus' intention or a polemical effort by the Gospel authors to dismiss the dietary laws of Judaism (Sanders 1985). The Church Fathers insisted that Jewish textual exegesis was errant, and blind to the real spiritualized meaning of the Law. A comparable notion had already achieved popularity among Jewish Hellenizers in the first-century Diaspora. But for at least some of these allegorizing Jews, the simple meaning of the Law was never dismissed.[4]

Differences in exegetical approach, in part, reflect the pervasive influence of Hellenistic philosophy and of Greek language in the Mediterranean world[5] in the first centuries CE. Upon conquering the East in the fourth century BCE, Alexander set the goal of transmitting Greek culture to his new empire. Hellenism was conceived as a political

4. There have been other Jews in history opposed to the Law. The Karaites in the seventh century opposed the rabbinic Oral Law and maintained that only Torah Law was to be observed. In the nineteenth century, the Reform movement all but abandoned the Oral Law, whereas Conservative Judaism has made efforts to retain much of the Law with modifications. Orthodox Judaism has split into two forms: Modern Orthodoxy observes the Law but adopts aspects of modernity, whereas the ultra-Orthodox make efforts to eschew the changes occurring around them in the secular world. Other movements like Reconstructionist Judaism are actively seeking to adopt Judaism into modernity with an emphasis on spirituality. See Raymond Scheindlen, *A Short History of the Jewish People* (Oxford: Oxford University Press, 2000).
5. The New Testament was written entirely in Koine Greek. Its references are to the Septuagint, a third-century-BCE Greek translation of the Hebrew bible. Various arguments that subsequently arose between Jews and Christians in the early centuries of Christianity were focused on what the proper definitions for certain words were. A famous example is the reference in Isaiah 7:14 to an *almah*, which in Hebrew means a young woman, but the term was translated in the Septuagint as *parthenos*, which means virgin. This was adopted as the source of the virgin birth of Mary to the infant Christ in Luke's gospel.

program aimed at elevating foreign cultures out of barbarism,[6] and fostering universal ideals, so as to eliminate the risk that the vast new empire would split politically along lines of ethnic and religious differences. Although the empire was partitioned shortly after Alexander's death, Hellenism remained a pervasive programmatic element. A similar incentive in the fourth century CE would lead Constantine to unify the Roman Empire by establishing Christianity as its dominant religion—one empire, ruled by one emperor, united in one religion.[7]

Jews in Judaea and in the Diaspora had been exposed to Hellenistic influences via the Mediterranean trade routes for years prior to Alexander's conquest (Hengel 1974). Greek was commonly spoken in much of the Greco-Roman world, much as the English language is omnipresent in today's world. In the mid first century, Paul (Saul of Tarsus), a Hellenized Jew writing barely three decades after the death of Jesus, preached a radical new theology in Greek, one based on the salvific effect of the crucifixion and resurrection of the messiah Christ Jesus.[8] Paul asserted that with Christ's death and resurrection man was now living in the *eschaton*. This called for the universal acceptance of the Christian faith, if as many as possible were to be saved. Paul describes the second coming of Christ or the *parousia* in 1 Thessalonians 16–18:

> For the Lord Himself will descend from heaven with a shout, with the voice of the archangel, and with the trumpet of God; and the dead in Christ shall rise first. Then we who are alive and remain shall be caught up together with them in the clouds

6. The word *barbar* is derived from the sounds that Greeks imagined non-civilized Greek speakers to be making (i.e., "bah bah").
7. This approach remains with us today and is in part responsible for much of the global strife that is observed as individual tribal-oriented groups are forced to live inharmoniously within artificial boundaries in the name of progress.
8. Many scholars have questioned whether Paul was in fact a Pharisee or as conversant with the Jewish religion as he claimed. Certainly, despite many efforts to identify a tradition of a crucified messiah in Judaism, there have been no clear precursors for such an idea. See Daniel Boyarin, *A Radical Jew: Paul and the Politics of Identity* (Berkeley: University of California Press, 1997).

> to meet the Lord in the air, and thus we shall always be with the Lord. Therefore comfort one another with these words.

The coming resurrection would not be one of the corporeal body, for as Paul suggests in 1 Corinthians 15:44, the body "is sown a natural body; but it is raised a spiritual body. If there is a natural body, there is also a spiritual body," although one can only speculate as to its form. For Paul, the Law had been superseded by faith in the resurrected Christ, at least for new pagan converts, if not for Jewish Christians as well.[9] Christianity was to be a universal religion, one sown in the spirit of Alexander's vision for Hellenism. According to Paul in his letter to the Galatians 3:28, in Christianity, "There is neither Jew nor Gentile, neither slave nor free, nor is there male and female, for you are all one in Christ Jesus."

In the *First Urban Christians* (2003), Wayne Meeks suggests that it was the conversion of Hellenized Jews and pagan Greeks in urban areas that allowed Christianity to gain a foothold within the empire. This "spiritualized" Judaism adopted features of Greek mystery religion, which appealed to sophisticated pagans who had grown disenchanted with their anthropomorphic gods and were seeking a more meaningful religious experience.[10]

The new religion offered attractive options to pagan converts that Judaism did not. Paul insisted that newly converted Christians were not required to adhere to the Mosaic Law, with its dietary restrictions and ideas of impurity that were foreign to paganism. Nor would male circumcision, a painful procedure when performed on an adult and a ritual widely ridiculed in the Greco-Roman world, be necessary in order to enter the new faith (Cohen 2014). All that was necessary was a

9. Paul is ambiguous on this point, which he discusses in detail in Romans. Whereas it is clear that he opposes new converts from paganism having to take on the yoke of the Jewish Law, it is uncertain whether Jews who accept Jesus as the messiah were also exempt.
10. In this regard, it must be recognized that the Roman Empire under Augustus Caesar esteemed a high level of virtue in which the family and a moral life were emphasized. Caesar was the prime example of the benevolent *pater familias*.

confession of faith in Christ, a short catechism, and a baptism in water.[11] As Jesus says in Matthew 11:30, "My yoke is easy and my burden light."

Due to its Hellenistic roots, early Christianity showed an affinity for Greek philosophical thought, especially Platonic ideas. However, Greek philosophy was in critical respects at odds with the core values of Judaism and the new Christian religion. Efforts at incorporating Greek philosophy into Christianity were viewed by some, according to the historian of Christian mysticism Bernard McGinn, as "miscegenation" (2006, 35). "Athens," a metonym for Greek philosophy, valued a life based on reason, whereas "Jerusalem," a term applied to the Near Eastern religions, tended to value one based on faith.[12]

Despite this, there was a persistent propensity within the early church to philosophize in the Greek style, an impulse that may be one of the earliest precursors of secularism. In his text *De Praescriptione Haereticorum*, the Latin Church Father Tertullian, a one-time Stoic philosopher, addressed the dangers of adopting a rational philosophical approach to Christian belief:

> Writing to the Colossians, he [Paul] says, "See that no one beguiles you through philosophy and vain deceit, after the tradition of men, and contrary to the wisdom of the Holy Ghost." He had been at Athens, and had in his interviews

11. Having said this, the early church also saw baptism as a sealing against sin, which was meant to be a singular event. If one were to sin after being baptized there was no clear path to salvation. For this reason, many chose to be baptized, including Constantine, while on their deathbeds. Today's church has replaced this with infant baptism, confession, and penance.
12. The Great Jewish War discussed in detail by Flavius Josephus culminated in the destruction of the Herodian Temple in Jerusalem. This event postdated the life of the historical Jesus (ca. 4 BCE–30 CE) and the true epistles of the Apostle Paul who is believed to have written in Rome in the early 60s CE. The loss of the Temple cult resulted in a marked transformation in the theology and practices of the Jews, as there was no longer a sacrificial system available for mediating atonement. In this regard, Christianity had already begun to develop in the prior thirty years and its emphasis on Jesus Christ as the final atonement sacrifice left it better prepared to meet the challenges of the loss of the Temple. It is generally agreed that the Gospel writers penned their manuscripts either during or more likely after 70 CE, with Mark the first to appear, as in it Jesus prophesizes the fall of the Temple, an event that Mark may well have already witnessed prior to writing his Gospel.

> become acquainted with that human wisdom which pretends to know the truth, whilst it only corrupts it, and is itself divided into its own manifold heresies, by the variety of its mutually repugnant sects. What indeed has Athens to do with Jerusalem? What concord is there between the Academy and the Church? What between heretics and Christians? Our instruction comes from "the porch of Solomon," who had himself taught that "the Lord should be sought in simplicity of heart." Away with all attempts to produce a mottled Christianity of Stoic, Platonic, and dialectic composition! We want no curious disputation after possessing Christ Jesus, no inquisition after enjoying the gospel! (Book 7)

Tertullian argued, with respect to his mysterious conception of the Trinitarian hypostases of the Godhead, in his *De Carne Christi* that, "it is by all means to be believed, because it is absurd" (*prorsus credibile est, quia ineptum est*). The idea of a paradoxical tripartite yet unitary Godhead was a Christian credo that demanded faith, not rationality. Paul had argued that it was Abraham's faith in God that had led him to sacrifice his own son prior to the Jews having received the Law at Sinai:

> For this reason it is by faith, in order that it may be in accordance with grace, so that the promise will be guaranteed to all the descendants, not only to those who are of the Law, but also to those who are of the faith of Abraham, who is the father of us all. (Romans 4:16)

But Paul ignores the fact that according to the biblical text, Abraham had already accepted the ritual of circumcision prior to the binding of Isaac.

Unlike Judaism, which continued to adhere to the letter of the Law[13] with its observance through the physical mediation of the body, Christians perceived primary ontological value in the immutable archetypal

13. The Law as used in this context refers both to the written Law, the Torah, as well as the Oral Law that was adhered to by the Pharisees in the first century and that

idea, and tended to devalue the material world for its impermanence. The influence of Greek philosophy on Christianity was far greater than on Rabbinic Judaism, as the latter theology had developed prior to Greek influence, and would later mature within the Persian Empire (Cohen 2014). Despite this, Neoplatonic motifs would eventually emerge in both religions.

The devaluation of rabbinic interpretation of the Law and of corporeal concerns is expressed in the polemical positions adopted by the New Testament towards the Pharisees and scribes, who are accused of hypocrisy and failing to recognize the true spiritual meaning of the Law (Sanders 1985). But as the historian of religion Elaine Pagels points out, the Gospels are socio-political, not historical, documents, and it is doubtful that they accurately portray the opinions of the historical Jesus (1995). Rather, they were aimed primarily at delegitimizing Judaism, co-opting its long-standing legal and economic protections by Rome, and ingratiating Christianity to Roman rule (e.g., in portraying the brutish prelate Pontius Pilate as having played a reluctant role in the crucifixion of Jesus).

The near-contemporary rabbinic texts and Flavius Josephus' *History of the Jews* (2003) offer a different picture of the Pharisees; they are described as sages who, while rigorous in their observance of the Law, were also liberal and compassionate in their adjudications.[14]

became increasingly important after 70 CE with the development of Rabbinic Judaism, the Mishnah, and the Talmudic texts.

14. Flavius Josephus or Mattithias Ha Kohen was a Jewish aristocrat who served as governor of the Galilee prior to the Jewish War. See Frederic Raphael, *A Jew Among Romans* (New York: Anchor Books, 2013). He was the leader of the Jewish resistance in the Galilee but then fled from the advancing Roman legions. He found favor with Vespasian's family and served as the official historian of events within Judaism and in the Jewish War. The loyalties of Josephus were clearly ambivalent. On one hand, he served at the pleasure of the Flavian family; on the other, he was proud of his Jewish heritage and wrote a polemical attack against Apion, who had insulted the reputation of the Jews. Most important to historians is that the works of Josephus, written in Greek, represent the bulk of the historical documentation of events in first-century Palestine. At times, Josephus has been proven to be clearly accurate in his historical recollections, whereas at others he is self-serving and evidently considers the political implications of his writings for Roman readers. One must read Josephus with a balanced and informed approach.

Indeed, it is difficult to imagine how Judaism could have survived as a viable religion for millennia in the face of persecution if Christianity's characterization of it as steeped only in legal minutiae and materialism was accurate. As Moses Mendelssohn argued against Judaism's detractors in the eighteenth century, the Law and its ritual performances have always also provided spiritual meaning for the Jews (Batnitzky 2013).

Christianity's devaluation of the material world was not attributable solely to its roots in Platonic philosophy, as this notion was already popular among sects of Judaism in the first century. As Pagels notes in *The Origin of Satan*, the Essenes and the related Dead Sea sect at Qumran also endorsed a radical dualistic philosophy that devalued the body and the material world (1995). The sectarian writings discovered at Qumran suggest that the *Yachad*, as the sect identified itself, imagined themselves as living among the angels in a spiritual milieu, and identified with the "forces of light," while they imagined the Pharisees and the Temple priesthood to be aligned with the materialistic "forces of darkness."[15]

The interpenetrating concepts of radical dualism, mythologization, repugnance for the physical world, and spiritualization of textual interpretations reached a zenith in the writings of the second-century Christian Gnostics (Pagels 1989). Whether Gnosticism was a product of the extreme Hellenization of the early Church (Koester 2000), or, as the historian Gershom Scholem suggested was preceded by a form of Jewish Gnosticism among Hellenizing Jews, is uncertain (Scholem 1969).[16] Some scholars, most notably Karen King, have questioned

15. It is tempting at some level to identify the early Christians with the sect at Qumran, as some scholars have. Nevertheless, the differences between the groups are too great to consider them to be the same. Obviously many religious motifs were circulating in first-century Judaea, and their combination makes it difficult to regard Christianity as clearly part of a pre-existing Jewish sect. In fact, in many respects, it can be postulated that Jesus' teachings are most closely related to those of the Pharisees with whom he appears to be most consistently opposed, which in itself may be a clue to the enmity that breeds, as Freud noted, through "the narcissism of minor difference."

16. Helmut Koester, *Introduction to the New Testament* (Amsterdam: DeGruyter, 1995), has suggested that the writings that preceded the Gospels were collections of sayings that included the virtual document Q, from which Luke and Matthew borrowed, as well as the Gospel of Thomas discovered at Nag Hammadi in 1945.

whether Gnosticism ever existed as a genre, as opposed to a variety of different sects that may have held some notions in common (2005). Nevertheless, what is clear is that the Gnostics were perceived by the church as a threat and roundly condemned by several orthodox church fathers, including Irenaeus and Tertullian.[17]

In some Gnostic myths, the creator of Genesis 1 was portrayed as an ignorant demiurge, a lesser god, who was unaware of the highest deity. The Gnostic Apocryphon of John attributes the creation of the world to a cosmic error due in part to the disobedience of the divine female emanation of wisdom, Sophia (Robinson 1990). This idea of a primordial error in creation reappears in the Lurianic Kabbalah, divested of its anti-materialistic features.

The Gnostic Marcion created a crisis for ecclesiastic authority in claiming that the Hebrew Bible was irrelevant to the teachings of Christianity. Marcion proposed the first Christian canon, and suggested limiting it to an expurgated Gospel of Luke and selected epistles of Paul (Koester 2000). He was excommunicated as a heretic because his ideas proved too challenging for the early church, which based its legitimacy on supersession of Judaism. The physical world, although of diminished ontological importance compared to the spiritual one, could not be abandoned altogether, especially as the Kingdom of God had not yet fully arrived, and the young church refused to declare the world evil in the face of God's biblical pronouncement that it was good.

Nevertheless, maintaining theological ties with Judaism would prove a dilemma for Christianity, because in relying on Judaism as its source while concomitantly rejecting the its legitimacy, the church

The Gospel of Thomas includes several traditional sayings but also shows distinct Gnostic tendencies. In the oft-quoted saying that the "Kingdom of God is within you," the church saw ideas that were both obscure and emphasized the individual's powers of insight, rather than teachings that might be readily grasped by all believers. The question of the provenance of such sayings and whether they in fact reveal a Gnostic tendency in the teachings of Jesus—as the parables in the gospels also imply—is still a matter of debate.

17. Until 1945, most of our knowledge concerning the Gnostic texts came from the writings of the Church Fathers, most notably Irenaeus and Tertullian. The church tended to defame the Gnostics, often accusing them of orgiastic sexual behaviors. The appearance of the primary texts does not support such notions.

was at cross purposes. The question of how to deal with the problem of the Jews was addressed by Augustine, who opined in the fourth century CE that the Jews should be protected but not allowed to prosper in Christian society (Fredricksen 2010). As Augustine writes in the *City of God*: "By evidence of their own scriptures they bear witness to us that we have not fabricated the prophecies about Christ. . . . Hence the prophecy in the book of Psalms, 'Slay them not lest they forget your Law, scatter them by thy might'" (18:46). Augustine's ideas would become dogma for the church, but they also fueled eliminationist anti-Semitism, as there was a fine line between keeping the Jews in a diminished position and exterminating them. As Goldhagen notes (2002), the same bishops who protected the Jews also condemned them from their pulpits every week. This, not surprisingly, led to periodic outbursts of violence from the Christian populace that was not particularly interested in the theological goal that the Church had set for the proper treatment of Jews.

JEWS AND THE MATERIAL WORLD

For Jews, the fulfillment of the Law requires the soul to be embodied within the material world. Judaism views the world as having been created as a place for God to dwell in. It sees its covenental role as sanctifying the world through the observance of the 613 commandments of the Law. The Jews were not a chosen people due to an imagined superiority, but precisely because they were an insignificant nation who accepted the yoke of the Law. God commanded them to serve as a nation of priests set apart from others in a state of ritual purity, setting an ethical example for other nations. However, this idea historically proved problematic, because it did not clearly address how Jews were to disseminate the message of monotheism while avoiding contact with the surrounding pagan world.[18]

18. Both Maimonides and Abraham Ha Rav Kook, the former chief rabbi of Palestine, were critical of Christianity for having abandoned the Law. However, they did concede that it had served an important role in bringing the tenets of monotheism to the pagan world. David Sampson and Tzvi Fishman, *Lights of Orot* (Jerusalem: Eretz Yisroel Publications, 1996).

Observance of the Law, isolation to insure ritual purity, and strict monotheism are the principles that differentiate Judaism from Christianity. For the Jews, Jesus' ministry and death did not signal a messianic end of days, as predicted by the prophets. The world to come is never clearly defined in the traditional texts of Judaism, but the tractate of *Sanhedrin* and Maimonides' *Mishneh Torah* suggest that it will be accompanied by an objective change in the physical world, (e.g., the end of war, the rebuilding of the Temple, etc.), and not limited to one in the spiritual realm.[19]

Judaism posits that healing results from at-one-ment with the divine and cannot be achieved via ritualistic observance. The Jewish mystics claim that every tenet of the Law has a spiritual counterpart that must be identified. But how does one approach the divine in order to be healed? Is it through faith alone, or through faith and adherence to Law? Obviously the answer depends on whether one adopts the core values of Judaism or Christianity. In the next chapter, this question will be considered with respect to how Freud and Jung conceived of how to conduct a psychoanalysis.

19. There is in fact no clear reference to the world to come in the Torah. The idea of resurrection of the dead first appears in the later prophets and in the books of the Maccabees, non-canonical texts in the Hebrew Bible, but included in the New Testament, as well as in the canonical book of Daniel, which modern scholarship dates to the same period, around 165 BCE.

CHAPTER 5

Boundaries: Discerning What Is Holy from What Is Profane

Concepts are coined and negotiable values; images are life.

—Carl Jung

A key notion in Judaism, and one of prime importance in Freud's psychoanalysis, is the notion of boundaries. Both the creation story of Genesis 1 and the priestly texts of Leviticus and Numbers are preoccupied with establishing distinctions between what is holy and what is mundane. As the psychologist of religion James Jones suggests, what makes a place, thing, or time holy, is the wish to idealize it (2002). An interesting example is the Sabbath, which the Fourth Commandment suggests is a holy day. However, nothing per se distinguishes it from any other day, except that one counts every seventh day as idealized time.[1] Valuation requires discernment; and the act of discernment creates boundaries.[2]

1. The Talmud suggests that if one has lost track the Sabbath in a place where there is no way to mark time, e.g., a desert, that one is to count seven days and observe that day as the Sabbath.
2. The first prayer uttered by a traditional Jew upon awakening is a blessing that thanks God for giving the "rooster the wisdom to discern between night and day."

In his paper *On Beginning the Treatment* (1913), Freud sets out his recommendations for how to conduct an analysis. He suggests meeting at a defined time and place, for what is essentially a rented hour, five to six days a week for a determined fee. Any infraction of this framework of rules must be discussed with the patient, as the frame is to be held as inviolable. Like sacred space and time, Freud's notion of the frame distinguishes the treatment hour from other mundane times and places. The structure of the frame furthermore safeguards what is holy; it specifically establishes a set of rules for what is acceptable behavior in therapy, and thereby prevents the analytical treatment from veering out of control, as one cannot be expected to discern at all times potentially hidden motivations for its violations, either on the part of the patient or the analyst. By imposing a frame, Freud, like Judaism, creates an orthopraxy for the analytical treatment, one reliant on the motif of boundaries. There was no precedent for such an idea in the modern practice of medicine in Freud's day, nor is there one today, except in psychotherapies informed by Freud's thought.

In the classic text *Purity and Danger*, Mary Douglas examines how distinguishing categories of purity and impurity creates safety and meaning for a group (2002). A concern of Jewish praxis is to avoid ritual contamination. Exodus 19:6 commands the Israelites to remain apart from others in order to maintain ritual purity in God's presence. The holy spaces of the ancient Israelite religion were safeguarded by the priests, a role that Freud would unwittingly adopt in his stance as analyst.

ANALYST AS PRIEST

Freud's frame fosters the patient's idealization of the analyst, who is unconsciously sacralized. The analyst-as-priest ministers to the patient's unconscious, which he approaches with caution and with the aid of the rituals of the frame. Of course, it is unlikely that most analysts or patients consciously entertain such thoughts, but it may be argued that idealizing transferences emerge in part as a consequence of this archetypal dynamic. As in Judaism, departure from the frame can contaminate what is holy. Consider the following biblical excerpt, in which, following the institution of the priesthood, the sons of Aaron the high priest approach the inner sanctum inappropriately:

> And Nadav and Avihu, the sons of Aaron, took each of them his censer, and put fire therein, and laid incense thereon, and offered strange fire before the Lord, which He had not commanded them. And there came forth fire from before the Lord, and devoured them, and they died before the Lord. (Leviticus 10:1–2)

In this passage, what constitutes "strange fire" is left ambiguous. Some traditional commentators have suggested that the sons of Aaron approached the inner sanctum while intoxicated, others that they incorrectly mixed the incense that was to be offered before the Holy of Holies, or alternatively that they entered the inner sanctum at an inappropriate time. But whatever the nature of the transgression, it exemplifies the general tenet of Judaism that boundaries must be rigorously respected if danger is to be avoided.

The role of the priest was largely lost in Judaism following the destruction of the Second Temple and the permanent cessation of the sacrificial cult. However, the elevated position of the priest is recognized even today. Men who can trace their lineage back to the priests (*kohanim*) are still afforded privileges within the synagogue service, including being called upon to bless the congregation. Their ritual purity is still encouraged, and they are, for example, prohibited from entering a cemetery except for the burial of a close relative, or from marrying divorcees, converts, or women of questionable repute.

While the Temple stood, the priest's primary roles were to conduct the sacrificial service, and to instruct the people with respect to the Law. They were also responsible for diagnosing disorders that rendered the individual ritually impure, receiving confessions, and, in the case of the high priest, for the ritually cleansing the Temple on the Day of Atonement. The important role of the priest can be discerned in the Gospels as well. In a curious narrative in Matthew 8:4, after healing a leper, Jesus instructs him to appear before a priest:

> Jesus stretched out His hand and touched him, saying, "I am willing; be cleansed." And immediately his leprosy was cleansed. And Jesus said to him, "See that you tell no one; but go, show yourself to the priest and present the offering that Moses commanded, as a testimony to them."

Christianity, which emerged several decades prior to the destruction of the Second Temple, retained a mediating role for the priest, who continued to perform the symbolic sacrifice of the mass at the altar. Catholic priests still hear confessions, as they once did in Judaism. Indeed, Jung remarked that psychoanalysis was not popular amongst Roman Catholics, as they used the confession booth as their primary way of resolving psychological conflicts. Jung would often advise his Catholic patients to seek the ministering of a priest:

> If the patient is a practicing Catholic, I invariably advise him to confess and to receive communion in order to protect himself from immediate experience, which might easily prove too much for him. With Protestants, it is usually not so easy, because dogma and ritual have become so pale and faint that they have lost their efficacy to a very great extent. (*CW* 11, para. 76)

How is a psychoanalyst comparable to a priest? Certainly, it is easy to recognize the psychoanalyst in role as confessor. But what may be more difficult to appreciate in today's world is that confessing to an analyst is not simply a matter of mental purgation; rather, it fosters psychological healing in its own right based on an implicit belief that the analyst, like the ancient priest, carries an aura of holiness, and is in a position to mediate divine forgiveness. Indeed, one of the major Pharisaic objections to Jesus was the claim that he could forgive sins, which was a role reserved for God and one mediated by the priest. As it says in Mark 2:3–10:

> Some men came, bringing to him a paralyzed man, carried by four of them. Since they could not get him to Jesus because of

> the crowd, they made an opening in the roof above Jesus by digging through it and then lowered the mat the man was lying on. When Jesus saw their faith, he said to the paralyzed man, "Son, your sins are forgiven." Now some teachers of the Law were sitting there, thinking to themselves, "Why does this fellow talk like that? He's blaspheming! Who can forgive sins but God alone?" Immediately Jesus knew in his spirit that this was what they were thinking in their hearts, and he said to them, "Why are you thinking these things? Which is easier: to say to this paralyzed man, 'Your sins are forgiven,' or to say, 'Get up, take your mat and walk'? But I want you to know that the Son of Man has authority on earth to forgive sins."

The ancient Israelite priest also was responsible for diagnosing states of impurity and for sentencing those suffering from it to live outside the community. This was a weighty decision, as an error held substantial psychological consequences for the exiled member of the community. For this reason, as the traditional Jewish liturgy indicates, the priest also ideally should be a person "who like Aaron, loves and pursues peace" (*shalom*). In the priestly blessing of the congregation (*birkhat kohanim*) in the synagogue, today's "priests" are enjoined to bestow their blessing "with love" (*ahava*). Only a compassionate priest could be trusted to recognize the implications of sentencing an individual to live apart from the community. This same characteristic is optimally required of modern analysts, so that concern for the patient must necessarily transcend whatever he may personally find repugnant in the patient. If the analyst cannot achieve that, then the patient should be referred to another analyst who potentially can.

Patients project a numinous aura onto their analysts; and the importance of such idealization in psychological healing should not be underestimated, as the self psychoanalyst Heinz Kohut recognized (1971). This may be truer for psychoanalysts who are physicians because of the implicit divine expectations that traditionally have been associated with the physician as healer, as described in the Greek myth of Asclepius. Modern egalitarian trends in society tend to demystify the position of those in the helping professions, and this may in fact detract from therapeutic potency (Kradin 2008).

This is the reason that most physician psychoanalysts refer to their "patients" rather than to their "clients," the latter a term frequently preferred by psychologists and other non-medical mental health professionals. But the term "client" implies a business transaction. It was the Latin term adopted by ancient Roman patrons for those who were financially or politically dependent upon them. One is properly termed the client of say an accountant or a lawyer. But those who come to therapy, be it psychotherapy or psychoanalysis, do so in order to have their suffering alleviated. Patients suffer, as the etymology of the term suggests. While the term client may have less pejorative implications for those who object to the medical model of psychotherapy, it also creates a milieu whose meaning potentially limits the unconscious fantasies that promote psychological healing. Modern science also has no claim to psychological healing and scientific approaches that disenchant the world have not enhances the efficacy of psychoanalysis.

JUNG AND SACRED SPACE

Jung referred to analytical treatment as a *temenos* or "sacred space," but he did not specifically examine how ritual contributes to its creation. Jung's concern with the rules that structure an analysis pales by comparison with Freud's. Instead, he focuses on the spiritual effects of what transpires within the sacred space, as opposed to the importance of safeguarding its boundaries. For Jung, as in Christianity, spirit takes precedence over law.

Much of what is commonly accepted in a classical Jungian analysis would be viewed by Freudians as violations of the frame. For example, it is generally accepted in Jungian analysis that the analyst greets the patient by shaking hands. This seemingly benign Western welcoming ritual is specifically avoided in Freudian analysis for fear of contaminating the transference and violating a boundary of not touching the patient. In traditional Judaism, ritual impurity can be transmitted by touch. Whereas most concerns about ritual impurity are no longer applicable in the absence of the Temple cult, the Orthodox rabbinic prohibition of shaking hands with a woman, who may be menstrually "impure," persists. It is quite possible that Freud's rationale for avoiding physical contact was in fact informed unconsciously by his knowledge of Jewish rituals. Just as impurity contaminates the Holy of Holies, which must then be purified, breaches of analytical ritual contaminate the Freudian treatment, which must be cleansed via analysis of the violation, and avoidance of future transgressions. As the historian of religion Jonathan Klawans notes (2004), when ritual impurity is left unaddressed it transforms into moral impurity or sin, which is a more serious transgression. In a similar fashion, repeated boundary violations when not addressed in analysis can lead to premature and unexpected ruptures of the treatment.

The interpersonal boundaries between the analytical couple also share features with the prohibited sexual relationships detailed in Leviticus 17:1–7. This set of laws is positioned in the Hebrew Bible immediately following the detailed description of the service of the high priest on the Day of Atonement, in which the Tabernacle is purified.

Freud recognized that when a man and a woman discuss intimate issues in a secluded space, an erotic attraction, or what he termed the erotic transference, ensues. Indeed, Rabbinic Judaism prescribes strict rules for how men and women are allowed to meet together (*yichud*) in *Kiddushin* 4. Erotic desires are considered potentially so powerful that even the taboos against incest between siblings cannot be relied upon to inhibit prohibited sexual acts.

The early practice of psychoanalysis witnessed many sexual liaisons between psychoanalysts and patients. Jung, for one, was compelled to confess his sexual acting out with the patient Sabina Spielrein to Freud (Kerr 1994). Distressed by this and fearful concerning the potential repercussions on psychoanalysis, Freud warned his colleagues about the damage that can ensue if an erotic transference is acted upon.[3]

3. The list of known transgressors is long, and the list of unknown transgressors likely much longer. Transgressions were attributed to Jung, Ferenzci, Rank, Fromm, etc. See Glen Gabbard and Eva Lester, *Boundary Violation in Psychoanalysis* (New York: Basic Books, 2002). Suffice it to say that managing erotic transference in

Today, the problem of sexual boundary violations is well recognized by Freudian psychoanalysts and the conditions that lead to them have been elucidated (Gabbard and Lester 2002). But the Jungian community has been slow to set rules that forbid them. Indeed, some Jungian analysts have tended to romanticize such relationships in their writings (Haule 1998). While there is no way to ascertain the consequences of sexual transgressions in *all* analyses, the fact that they have the potential to be seriously harmful for the patient should be sufficient cause to prohibit them altogether.

From the above, it is evident that Freud's approach to the treatment shares features with the Jewish religion. As will be seen in the next chapter, Jung tended to ignore the rules that Freud painstakingly developed. The reason may have much to do with the Christian notion of how spirit supersedes law.

---

psychoanalysis can be a slippery slope and even the most virtuous are not immune to its temptations.

CHAPTER 6

Law and Spirit

He has enabled us to be ministers of his new covenant. This is a covenant not of written laws, but of the Spirit. The old written covenant ends in death; but under the new covenant, the Spirit gives life.

—Paul 2 Corinthians 3:6

THE ORAL LAW

The text of the Torah is terse. Without additional guidance, there would be little way for the Jewish devotee to know how to observe the Law properly. For this reason, exegesis of the Law was necessary, and according to Rabbinic Judaism, this was provided by a separate Oral Law, referred to as the *halacha l'Moshe mi Sinai* ("the way given to Moses at Sinai"). Oral tradition was undoubtedly always an element of Judaism, but tenets of the Oral Law were greatly expanded by the Second Temple Pharisees.[1]

The tractate of the Talmud referred to as the *Ethics of the Father* (*Pirke Avot*) delineates the lineage of the transmission of the Oral Law from God to Moses and subsequently down to the rabbis of the

1. Arguments between Jesus and the Pharisees pepper the Gospels. In some cases, as suggested in E. P. Sanders, *Jesus and Judaism* (Minneapolis: Fortress 1985), it appears that certain customs emphasized by the Pharisees (e.g., the washing of hands prior to eating) were not yet universally practiced. Where Jesus stands with respect to other sects of Judaism current at the time is uncertain. His ideas are comparable to the Essenes but differ in some important respects. Indeed, it may well be that Jesus was himself a Pharisee engaged in an ongoing argument concerning several of its practices.

first centuries CE. The Pharisees held that the requirements for how to observe the Law had been imparted at Sinai together with the written Torah. However, the fallaciousness of this idea is suggested in *Berachot* 5a by a famous story in which Moses is given the opportunity by God to listen to the second-century scholar R. Akiva teaching the Oral Law to a group of students. Moses is distressed as he listens, because he recognizes nothing of what is being discussed. However, when the students question R. Akiva as to the source of the Oral Law, he replies that it is the *halacha* given to Moses at Sinai, and Moses is greatly relieved.

R. Akiva reportedly made interpretations based on the tiny crownlets that scribes placed atop the letters of the Torah. However, this is a hyperbolic statement indicating that much of the Oral Law was in fact invented de novo rather than derived by exegesis of the written Law, as it was deemed necessary for the survival of Judaism in response to Roman religious persecution in Palestine (Halivni 1998).

New laws can be derived from textual exegesis. R. Ishmael proposed a set of thirteen rules for how to approach a text in the second century, and these are recited daily as part of the morning liturgy in traditional prayer books:

> Rabbi Yishmael says: Through thirteen rules is the Torah elucidated: 1) through a conclusion inferred from a lenient law to a strict one, and vice versa, 2) through tradition that similar words in different contexts are meant to clarify one another, 3) through a general principle derived from one verse, 4) through a general statement limited by a specification, 5) through a specification broadened by a general statement, etc.

These rules likely strike the modern reader as irrational, e.g., the linking of ideas based on words or phrases used in common in different parts of a text or even totally different texts! But they represent a system of hermeneutics that is standard fare for psychoanalytical interpretation in which phrases, words, and numbers are commonly viewed as having meaning across narratives and time for patients.

Hermeneutics also play a critical role in the esoteric interpretations of Judaism. Approaches to the mystical interpretation of a text include the transformation and recombination (*tzeruf*) of letters within words, as well as the use of letters as numbers in order to bring overtly disparate words into meaningful relationships, techniques referred to as *gematria*, *notarikon*, and *temurah*.

However, following the failed Bar Kokhba revolt (132–135 CE) and the rise of Christianity, the rabbis became justly wary about mysticism, because they viewed it as predisposing to messianism (Scholem 1995a), and the latter historically had had serious negative consequences for the Jews. As the historian of religion Peter Schafer notes:

> Instead of following the old paradigm of "daughter religion" (Christianity) being born from the "mother religion," I prefer to use the term sister religion for Christianity, since ultimately I am arguing that once the idea of the Christian Messiah was put forth—with all of its ramifications—Judaism could not remain the same. (2012, 234)

Christianity is rooted in mysticism. But while it was discouraged under some circumstances (e.g., Paul in 1 Corinthians), it never posed a threat to the survival of Christianity after it became the religion of the Roman Empire in the fourth century. As the Church distanced itself from the Law, there was a parallel withdrawal from mystical practices within Judaism. The spiritual elements of Judaism began a slow process of withering, although they were never lost. The instinct towards mysticism and spirituality persisted, and emerged at various times in efforts at reforming the legalisms of Rabbinic Judaism.

ESOTERICISM

Taylor notes that all religions are invariably faced with the question of how to adapt to the different "speeds" of their religionists (2007). A religious elite tends to emerge spontaneously and is represented by those who are moved to greater degrees of observance. Judaism provides two pathways towards excelling in the service of the divine. One is through the textual study of the Law, this being viewed as the direct revelation of divine will; the other is through mystical practices in which the divine is approached through contemplative practices. But, as every tenet of the Law has its counterpart in the spiritual realm for the Jewish mystic, a complete interpretation of the Law includes an exploration of both its exoteric and esoteric meanings.

However, it was a common view in Rabbinic Judaism that attempting to achieve a mystical relation with the divine was potentially disruptive both to the individual's welfare and to the community, especially if approached incorrectly or without sufficient grounding in the Law.[2] For this reason, esoteric mystical knowledge was permitted to be transmitted only to a small number of elite scholars.

In antiquity, esoteric knowledge was conveyed orally from master to disciple, so that it would not inadvertently fall into the hands of those unprepared to interpret it correctly. Choices to commit oral traditions to writing tend to occur when their transmission is threatened. This occurred in the early third century in Roman Palestine and it resulted in the compilation of the Oral Law or *Mishnah* by Rabbi Judah HaNasi. Although the Oral Law is largely legal in nature and therefore often exoteric, it does also allude to esoteric mysteries concerning the nature of creation, the nature of the Godhead, and sexual taboos, topics that were permitted to be transmitted only verbally by a master to a small number of students, and in the case of the nature of the Godhead, only to a single elite pupil. Others were warned not to entertain these matters.

Christianity began as a sect of esoteric Judaism. As the historian of Christian mysticism Bernard McGinn notes:

> The religious world of late Second Temple Judaism provided a matrix for Christian mysticism in two related ways—through the mystical or at least protomystical ascents to the

2. This notion is in fact not limited to Judaism. Christianity discouraged Gnostic mysticism as it diminished concern for community. Buddhism also emphasizes the importance of *sila* or ethical practices as a prerequisite to achieving enlightened states.

> vision of God found in the apocalypses and through the movement towards the establishment of a canon of sacred texts and the creation of tools and techniques to render it alive for the believing community. . . . To neglect the Jewish roots of Christian mysticism and to see it instead, as many have done, as a purely Greek phenomenon is to risk misconstruing an important part of history. (2006, 22)

However, the role of esoteric interpretations in Christianity is complicated. A basic Christian *kerygma* or program of instruction is already identifiable in the New Testament, as the early Christians thought it important to reach as many believers as possible before the Second Coming or *parousia* of Christ. But controversy still looms, for example, around Morton Smith's discovery of a Secret Gospel of Mark, a text that suggests that the ministry of Jesus included the transmission of secret knowledge and rituals that were lost to the church (Smith 1973).[3] Moreover, the sayings of the Gnostic Gospel of Thomas may include early esoteric teachings potentially attributable, according to historian of Christianity Helmut Koester, to the historical Jesus (Koester and Lambdin 1996). It is evident from several references made in the Gospels that Jesus' deepest message was not meant for everyone.

The oral transmission of secrets has parallels with psychoanalytic practice and training, as much of what takes place in training analyses and supervisions is maintained in secrecy. There is the understandable desire to protect the identity of patients, but the motivations for secrecy run deeper. The symbolic work of psychoanalysis fosters esotericism. Symbols are Janus-faced, as they connote more than a single level of meaning at a time. Readers of the Gospels will be acquainted with Jesus' use of parables to transmit

3. Smith was a prodigious scholar but quite controversial. His discovery of the Secret Gospel of Mark was challenged as perhaps one of the most skilled forgeries and attributed to Smith himself. However, some continue to believe that this text is not a forgery and includes a lost esoteric tradition of the early Church.

the hidden meanings of his sermons to his apostles that he did not wish to share with the masses. Consider Matthew 13:10:

> And the disciples came and said to Him, "Why do you speak to them (the crowds) in parables?" Jesus answered them, "To you it has been granted to know the mysteries of the Kingdom of Heaven, but to them it has not been granted . . ."

Discerning the meaning of a parable requires the ability to think symbolically and to identify references that may escape a non-abstract thinker. This is comparable to the psychoanalyst who listens for transference references and for the symbolic implications of dream narratives. Thinking symbolically is a capacity that can be honed, but some individuals are innately more adept at it than others, while others are frankly impaired. Listening with a "third ear" recalls Jesus' statement in Luke 8:8 in the parable of the sower:

> "Still other seed fell on good soil. It came up and yielded a crop, a hundred times more than was sown." When he said this, he called out, "Whoever has ears to hear, let them hear."

Indeed the notion that *anybody* can train effectively to be a psychoanalyst is a palpable fiction, as no amount of training will reconfigure an innately tin ear, and this should be honestly considered and discussed within psychoanalytical institutes during the admission process and while candidates are in training.

As in religious training, psychoanalysts are considered an educated elite, responsible for passing on the esoteric knowledge to a few designated pupils. This purposeful obscurity constitutes a problem for patients seeking psychological counseling, as many are at a loss as to how to choose a therapist or how to gauge the quality of an analyst's work. The fact is that not even analysts are in a position to assess the work of their colleagues behind closed doors, as public lectures, written papers, and erudite texts are often poor indicators of how analysts actually behave with patients in private. I have known of several analysts whose writings express great empathy for patients, only to hear strikingly different descriptions of how they actually practice from their disgruntled patients.

MEDIEVAL ESOTERIC JUDAISM

For Jews, the mystical secrets of the religion, generically termed the "Kabbalah," which means received knowledge, were jealously guarded until medieval times. In the midst of Muslim persecution in Spain and North Africa in the eleventh century, Maimonides attempted to convey esoteric wisdom in written form to a single pupil living at a distance, justifying this transgression of tradition by concern that these teachings were no longer being transmitted and were in danger of being lost. The fact that his intended audience was a single elite student suggests that the topic of concern was the nature of the Godhead.

Maimonides did so in a lengthy text *The Guide of the Perplexed* (*Moreh Nevuchim*), and in a purposefully disguised manner, via the accepted use of chapter headings. He alludes to his approach in the text's introduction, but the secrets of the text have remained a source of argument among scholars for nearly a millennium (Maimonides 1974). As the political philosopher Leo Strauss explains in *Persecution and the Art of Writing*, the transmission of esoteric knowledge in certain political climates is dangerous:

> Persecution, then, gives rise to a peculiar technique of writing, and therewith to a peculiar type of literature, in which the truth about crucial things is presented exclusively between the lines. The truth is addressed, not to all readers, but to the trustworthy and intelligent readers only. It has all the advantages of private communication without having its greatest disadvantage—that it reaches only the writer's acquaintances. It has all the advantages of public communication without having its greatest disadvantage—capital punishment for its author. (Strauss 1988, 25)

For such communication to be effective it must be sufficiently transparent to convey the desired message, while at the same time adequately opaque not to be understood by an unintended audience. In *The Interpretation of Dreams* (1900), Freud suggests that the dream is constructed by an unconscious dream "censor." According to Freud, the meaning of the manifest dream is obscure to the dreaming ego, and it must be interpreted by one who can grasp its secret meaning, which meant by Freud or someone trained in his system of dream analysis. This approach is a "paranoid" hermeneutic, as it suggests that the unconscious is attempting to convey a message (paranoia) around the dreamer.

Influenced by Aristotle and the Islamic schools of philosophy that flourished in the medieval world, Maimonides' *Guide* focuses on the perfection of intellection as the path toward prophecy, which is equated with intimating the mind of God or, as Aristotle referred to it, the Active Intellect. Despite the opaque construction of the *Guide*, whose message borders on impenetrability, Maimonides was still roundly criticized by many of his contemporaries for having publically revealed closely guarded secrets, as well as for placing inordinate emphasis on the importance of philosophy and the natural sciences as prerequisites for perceiving the mind of God (Green 2003).

Maimonides was a renowned scholar in his time. By the age of twenty-six, he had codified the entire Jewish Law in the *Mishneh Torah*. But his *Guide* was a very different text, as it offered philosophical arguments that did not jibe with his interpretations of the Law. Maimonides appeared to be arguing that the Godhead was unapproachable except through pure intellection, and sufficiently removed to not be concerned about individuals. To some it appeared that he was hypocritically obliging his fellow Jews to pray to a God who might not be listening.[4] Yet prayer, according to Maimonides, was divinely commanded, and he insisted that the Law must be strictly observed.

4. In this regard, Maimonides in *The Guide of the Perplexed* was following the idea of Aristotle who posited a Prime Mover who was not engaged at the level of sublunar activities, which would have included the affairs of men.

Maimonides was not the first to try to meld Greek philosophy with Judaic Law. In the first century, Philo of Alexandria had attempted a line-by-line allegorical exegesis of the Torah. Apparently exclusively versed in Greek, he used the Greek translation of the Hebrew Bible, the Septuagint, which would also be the scriptural source for all of the New Testament authors (Philo 1993). But unlike Maimonides, Philo's inspiration was Plato, not Aristotle, and these two great Greek philosophers offered distinct perspectives on the world. As the historian Arthur Herman notes:

> One path—Plato's path—sees the world through the eyes of the religious mystic as well as the artist. It finds its strength in the realm of contemplation and speculation and seeks to unleash the power of human beings' dreams and desires. The path of Aristotle, by contrast, observes reality through the sober eyes of science and reveals the power of logic and analysis as tools of human freedom. "The fact is our starting point," and he meant it. Over the centuries, Plato's and Aristotle's ideas have managed to pull and tug Western civilization in conflicting directions. (Herman 2014, xx)

Some Hellenized first-century Jews chose to adopt Philo's allegorical interpretations in an effort to free themselves from their obligations to observe the letter of the Law. Hellenists tended to view Jewish Law with disdain. Hellenizing Jews, wishing to assimilate for the purposes of economic gain, social status, intermarriage, etc., saw the literal interpretation of the Law as an impediment. Yet Philo insisted that despite the possibility of interpreting the Law allegorically, its plain sense still needed to be observed in practice. Philo's writings, which included the first references to the divine nature of the Logos, were adopted and preserved by the early church but consequently were ignored by generations of Rabbinic Jews.

Maimonides was also concerned with expunging any notion of anthropomorphic qualities from Jewish imaginings of the Godhead. But his critics argued that this might leave the average Jew with no access to a personal God. However, Maimonides was not concerned with the average practitioner; he considered himself and his intended audience to be members of an educated rabbinic elite.

In his efforts at expunging Judaism of anthropomorphic references in order to achieve a pure image-less monotheism, he adopted the apophatic path, espoused in mystical Christianity by Pseudo-Dionysus the Areopagite in the fifth century. According to the philosopher Michael Sells, apophatic writing includes three elements:

> Classical Western *apophasis* shares three key features: (1) the metaphor of overflowing or "emanation" which is often in creative tension with the language of intentional demiurgical creation; (2) dis-ontological discursive effort to avoid reifying the transcendent as an entity or being or thing; (3) a distinctive dialectic of transcendence and immanence in which the utterly transcendent is revealed as utterly immanent. (1994, 6)

The *via negativa* claimed that no characteristic of any type could be attributed to a Godhead who was unimaginably Other (McGinn 2007). As Pseudo-Dionysus wrote concerning the mystical path:

> Again ascending yet higher, we maintain that he is neither soul nor intellect, nor has he imagination, opinion, speech, nor understanding, nor can he be expressed or conceived, since he is neither number nor order, nor greatness, nor smallness, nor equality or inequality, nor similarity, nor dissimilarity, neither is he immovable, nor moving, nor at rest, neither has he power nor is power, nor is he light, etc. (quoted in McGinn 2007, 289)

As will be discussed, this apophatic approach can also be applied to descriptions of the unconscious, a topic recently addressed by the Jungian analyst David Henderson (2014).

SPIRITUALITY AND REFORM

Attempts at religious reform initially tend to encourage radical and antinomian stances in favor of spirituality. But once these movements enter a phase of consolidation, newly won freedoms are invariably countered by the imposition of regulations designed to stabilize the new order to provide orthodoxy. Christianity was an effort to counter the legalisms of Judaism through a spiritual impetus. Fifteen hundred years later, the Protestant reform movement attempted to rid Christianity of its institutionalized canon laws by stressing the individual's spiritual relationship to God. Each of these movements saw little value in the law, the body, or the physical world, and, in this regard, both recapitulated the ancient Platonic tradition.

The Hasidic movement of the nineteenth century was aimed at reforming Rabbinic Judaism by devaluing the importance of Talmudic study and fostering spirituality for the masses through prayer and ritual practice. It interiorized the tenets of the medieval Kabbalah into a psychological system. But unlike the Christian reform movements, it remained faithful to the observance of the Law and the importance of sacralizing the physical world. Hasidism remained within the legal boundaries of Rabbinic Judaism and did not stray from them.

But with time it also grew progressively more conservative, and today it would hardly be recognizable as a reform movement, with the possible exception of Chabad Hasidim, which under the auspices of the late Lubavitcher Rebbe Menachem Mendel Schneerson embarked on a vast missionary project aimed at educating and reviving interest in traditional observance among non-observant secularized Jews.

In parallel to the Hasidic movement, the Lithuanian Mussar movement, founded by R. Israel Salanter in the mid-nineteenth century, promulgated a critical introspective approach focused on improving ethical behavior (Etkes 1982). Mussar claimed that textual studies, although of critical importance, should be linked to studies and practices designed to improve one's character traits. Mussar became a staple of the Yeshiva education in Lithuania.

Both Hasidim and the Mussar movement represented quantum leaps into the world of psychological interiority and scrupulous self-scrutiny and they are rightly considered prototypes of psychoanalysis, preceding it by almost a century.

As Yohanan Silman observes:

> The transition from psychology to discussion of the unconscious realms of the psyche took place in Rabbi Israel (Salanter) during the course of an organic and continuous intellectual development. The very possibility of the existence of "habits" implies the existence of a level of the psyche in which individual acts and desires are submerged and combine into "habits." This level is necessarily an unconscious one, as consciousness does not preserve its contents over a long period of time, while the very existence of "habits" requires the continuity of the impressions of isolated acts. (Silman quoted in Etkes 1993, 305)

As Etkes notes, there were a number of nineteenth-century thinkers who preceded Freud in discovering the unconscious life of the mind, including Immanuel Kant, from whom Salanter drew the idea of the dark and bright powers of the mind (Etkes 1993, 304). It appears that by the nineteenth century ideas were in bidirectional flux between the secular and religious worlds.

Freud's psychoanalysis was also a reform movement. It aimed at secularizing society, liberating it both from religious ideas and the sexual repression of the Victorian age. Despite its initial radical stance, it quickly grew conservative and efforts at modifying its tenets were met with staunch resistance by Freud during his lifetime.

The Jungian world has also had its experience with efforts at reform. Jung's psychology was essentially a counter-reformation that sought to reintroduce spirituality back into Freud's secular and materialistic approach to the psyche. As Jung states in *Psychotherapy or Clergy*:

> The fact that many clergy men seek support from Freud's sexual theory or Adler's theory of power is astonishing as both are hostile to spiritual values being as I have said, psychology without psyche. They are rational modes of treatment which actually hinder the realization of meaningful experience. . . . This means that the great majority if patients are actually alienated from a spiritual standpoint. (233–34)

The modern "developmental school" of Jungians, which has sought to reintroduce Freudian ideas into Jungian analysis has been criticized by classical Jungians for abandoning Jung's spiritual symbolic approach. For them, any return to Freud might be conceived as Judaizing, as the Church Fathers termed it, a return to the old Law that fails to acknowledge the supersession of Jung's ideas.

CHAPTER 7

Mysticism: Word and Image

What is mysticism? For many the word brings to mind something strange and uncanny, even bizarre. Others see mysticism as the hidden core at the heart of all religions.

—Bernard McGinn

In many respects, Freud's relationship to mysticism parallels the wariness of Rabbinic Judaism on this topic; for like the rabbis, although he recognized its attraction, he chose to distance himself and psychoanalysis from it. Jung was kindly disposed to mysticism and referred to it liberally in his writings.

The earliest written descriptions of mystical practices of Judaism date to rabbinic times but are based in the ancient Israelite religion. The Torah contains numerous references to mystical practices with respect to the sanctuary. In 2 Kings, the prophet Elijah is described as sitting with his head between his legs, which, according to Rav Hai Gaon, appears to have been a posture adopted for achieving trance (De Conick 2006a). Other techniques for enhancing visions were fasting and crying, and several apocryphal texts (e.g., 4 Ezra) make reference to this. The visions reported by those in mourning may reflect the tendency for tears to evoke the imagination, an explanation that has been suggested for the post-crucifixion sightings of Jesus by those in mourning following his sudden unexpected death (Ehrman 2014).

The three great mysteries of Judaism include the prohibited sexual relationships (*aroyot*) described in Leviticus 18:1–30, the creation ex nihilo of Genesis 1, referred to as *maaseh bereshit*, and the nature of the Godhead or *maaseh merkavah* (story of the chariot) in Ezekiel 1.[1] The major types of medieval Jewish mystical practice were *merkavah* mysticism, based on Ezekiel's vision of the divine chariot, and *hekhalot* mysticism, based on the vision in Isaiah 6 of God sitting on a throne within His palace surrounded by myriads of angels (Elior 1999). Although the *hekhalot* literature of late antiquity includes both types of mysticism, it offers no description of meditative techniques. Scholars continue to debate whether these texts were meant simply to be read or instead represent performative exegeses, in which the mystical adept is informed by texts as to what to expect while in different levels of trance, thereby fostering his meditative experience via suggestion (De Conick 2006).

Mystics in the first century were acquainted with such meditations. In 2 Corinthians 12:2, Paul refers to a *hekhalot* experience, declaring, "I know a man in Christ who fourteen years ago—whether in the body I do not know, or out of the body I do not know, God knows—such a man was caught up to the third heaven." It is generally assumed that he is referring either to himself or to Jesus, although there is little basis for either of these conclusions.

Mystical experiences generally take one of two forms. They are either kataphatic (i.e., characterized by excitatory visual experiences possibly accompanied by auditory components or synesthesia), or apophatic (i.e., quietistic in an effort to achieve mental states devoid of content) (Katz 2000). Ezekiel's vision of the *merkavah* and Isaiah's *hekhalot* vision are examples of kataphatic experience. Whereas the Hebrew Bible includes no definite example of quietistic meditation, it is suggested by Elijah's experience of a "still small voice" in 1 Kings 19:11–13:

> And he said, "Go forth, and stand upon the mount before the Lord." And, behold, the Lord passed by, and a great and

1. The latter is based on the theophany described by Ezekiel of the divine chariot.

> strong wind rent the mountains, and brake in pieces the rocks before the Lord; but the Lord was not in the wind: and after the wind an earthquake; but the Lord was not in the earthquake. And after the earthquake a fire; but the Lord was not in the fire: and after the fire a still small voice. And it was so, when Elijah heard it, that he wrapped his face in his mantle, and went out, and stood in the entering in of the cave. And, behold, there came a voice unto him, and said, "What doest thou here, Elijah?"

As the historian of Jewish mysticism Eliot Wolfson has suggested, Jewish mystical experience is often described as auditory (1995). This may reflect the Decalogue's prohibition against making divine images. In general, the Hebrew Bible exhibits an unusual propensity to prioritize narrative over imagery. Consider the description of Noah's Ark in Genesis 5:13–17:

> So make yourself an ark of cypress wood; make rooms in it and coat it with pitch inside and out. This is how you are to build it: The ark is to be three hundred cubits long, fifty cubits wide and thirty cubits high. Make a roof for it, leaving below the roof an opening one cubit high all around. Put a door in the side of the ark and make lower, middle and upper decks.

Surely, it would have sufficed from the perspective of a convincing narrative to describe "a large boat made of wood," perhaps with mention of its distinguishing features. Certainly, that is how most of us today would imagine the Ark, and it is likely how the Hellenized mind would have represented it in antiquity, as well. Instead, the Hebrew Bible provides the equivalent of an architectural plan. This emphasis on narrative detail speaks to a fundamental difference between the psychology of Judaism with its aniconic God, and that of Christianity whose incarnate God is frequently depicted in paintings and statuary.

RATIONALITY AND MYSTICISM IN PSYCHOANALYSIS

Freud's approach to the mind aims at the conversion of images into verbal narratives. This cognitive-linguistic approach is reminiscent of Jewish modes of textual interpretation. Freud conceived of the translation of symbols into words, i.e. the transformation of primary process to secondary process thinking, both as therapeutic and as an evolutionary advance from a primitive mode of imaginal mental representation to one of cognitive differentiation. For Freud, secondary thinking was the path of discernment and for making what had been previously been unconscious, conscious. The recovery of repressed affect and psychic structuring through cognition, and the transfiguration of sexual drives through sublimation, are the cardinal aims of Freud's psychoanalysis. On the other hand, Jung, following in the footsteps of the early church, primarily emphasized the ego's relationship to imagery, symbols, and myth as the therapeutic transformative elements of analysis.

The word is the primary medium of Freud's analysis, as Freud, like Jacques Lacan, conceived of the psyche as being structured by language (Homer 2004). Jung, on the other hand, imagined the unconscious as primarily structured through image-symbols. Jung's experiences, detailed in his recently published *The Red Book*, demonstrate his personal primary encounters with the symbols and images of his unconscious (2009). It is evident that the emphases of Rabbinic Judaism and Christianity continued to flow into how Freud and Jung imagined the psyche and aims of analysis, respectively.

There has been interest recently on the part of Freudian and Jungian analysts concerning what may be therapeutic in each other's approach. Unfortunately, dialogue has been hampered by the distinct sets of jargon adopted by each. Jungian parlance is concerned primarily with symbols that cannot be explicated in terms that Freudians can easily comprehend without a substantial unpacking of symbols. For example, when a Jungian refers to the *anima*, this includes a host of allusions that must be elucidated. But doing so impedes affective experience and is contrary to the symbolic approach. Whereas transduction of symbols is helpful for the purpose of communication and cognitive meaning, it impedes the evocation of affect, which is apparently hard-wired in the brain in regions that are proximate to areas that represent imagery. In turn, from the perspective of the Jungian audience, the moment-to-moment specifics of transference recognition and interpretation, which are based primarily on the ability to express declarative memories, seem arid and unappealing. This leaves each group at a loss when trying to comprehend and adopt the techniques of the other.

THE EARLY EUROPEAN KABBALAH

Although its theology is theoretically aniconic, Judaism is by no means devoid of imagery. By medieval times, and likely in large measure influenced by Christianity, one encounters a reemergence of mystical symbolism in Jewish practice (Green 2003). Kabbalistic thought emerged primarily out of two regions in Europe: the Languedoc (i.e., Provence, Gerona, and Castile) and the Ashkenaz, or what is now eastern France and western Germany (Green 2003). The Languedoc was the home of the Cathars, a Gnostic sect that practiced a spiritualized form of Christianity based on Neoplatonic myth. The Cathars were targeted as heretics by the Albigensian Crusade and its members slaughtered in the early thirteenth century.[2] It is very likely that this region provided fertile intellectual soil for the intermingling of ideas between Christian Gnosticism and Rabbinic Judaism, in order to yield a syncretistic Kabbalah.

The first non-biblical Jewish text to address an esoteric topic was *Sefer Yetzirah* (Book of Formation). Its provenance is uncertain, and although tradition credits it to Abraham, it was compiled sometime in the first centuries CE, making it one of the older extant texts of Rabbinic Judaism. Tersely written—it is roughly two thousand words

2. It has been suggested that Catharism was carried back from the Holy Land by Crusaders who encountered the Gnostic form of practice among the Bogomils and Paulicians in Eastern Europe. The Albigensian Crusade against the Cathars initiated by Innocent III was lengthy and merciless, succeeding in either exterminating the sect or driving it underground. See Jonathan Riley Smith, *The Crusades* (New Haven: Yale University Press, 2005).

long—it states that God created the world via the combination and permutation of the twenty-two letters of the Hebrew alphabet and the ten cardinal numbers.

In *The Hebrew Letters*, R. Yitzchak Ginsburgh describes how the Hebrew letters were conceived as elements in creation:

> Each of the twenty-two letters of the Hebrew Alphabet possesses distinct creative powers which in the teaching of Chassidut (Hasidism) are termed energy (*koach*), life (*chayut*), and light (*or*). Physical matter, as we now understand it from modern science, is no more than concentrated energy. In organic matter, the mysterious phenomenon called life becomes manifest. In the mind and soul of higher life forms, Divine Consciousness, here referred to as light, becomes revealed. In the creative process, the Hebrew letters appear at each of these three levels. (1995, 3)

Sefer Yetzirah was widely read and cited by both the rabbis and the kabbalists. A Talmudic story in *Sanhedrin* 65b states, "On the eve of every Shabbat, Judah HaNasi's pupils, R. Hanina and R. Hoshaiah, who devoted themselves to cosmogony, used to create a delicious calf by means of the *Sefer Yetzirah*, to eat on the Sabbath." It was also said that Abraham used this method to create the calf prepared for the three angels who foretold Sarah's pregnancy in the biblical account in Genesis 18:7.

Sefer Yetzirah expands on the text of Genesis 1:1, in which God creates the universe through ten utterances (e.g., "Let there be light, and there was light"). The idea of words and numbers (i.e., the elements of thought, speech, and rationality) giving rise to material forms can be discerned in Freud's theory of how images must be translated back into words in the course of analyzing dreams, in the service of creating psychological structure.

Sefer Yetzirah includes the first known reference to the term *sefirot*, which would become an all-important set of symbols for the Kabbalah. The text refers to *sippur* (to tell), *sefira* (to count), and *sapir* (sapphire), the latter referring to the base of God's throne described in Exodus 24:10 and later adopted in Ezekiel's vision of the *merkavah*,[3] as cognate terms to the *sefirot*.

Sefer ha Bahir (Book of Illumination) is widely accepted as the first kabbalistic text (Kaplan 2013). At first glance, it appears to be a standard example of rabbinic *midrash*, but on closer inspection its aim is obviously distinct, as instead of serving as the exegesis of a text, it continually raises obscure and paradoxical questions concerning the nature of the Godhead. As Arthur Green has suggested (2003), the text challenges its reader's knowledge concerning the mystical basis of Judaism. Historically, it is an important bridge in the development of the concept of the *sefirot*.

THE ZOHAR

The concept of the ten *sefirot* developed in the kabbalistic texts and was expanded upon, initially along Neoplatonic lines. Early in the earliest kabbalistic texts, the *sefirot* took the forms of guardian angels, as they often do in Gnostic myth; however, Judaism transformed them into symbolic representations of the attributes of the Godhead (*middot*).

The great advance in the history of the Kabbalah was the discovery of the *Zohar*, a text traditionally credited to the followers of the second-century tanna R. Shimeon bar Yochai (Rashbi). The *Zohar* appeared in Castile at the end of the thirteenth century, and was brought to light by R. Moses de Leon, who claimed that he had copied it from a previously lost ancient manuscript.

The book's provenance remains a matter of debate among scholars (Green 2003). It is written in a grammatically unusual Aramaic, the language of the early rabbis of both the Palestinian and Babylonian Talmuds, and contains a limited, and obscure, vocabulary. The text includes anachronisms and inconsistencies, with large portions appearing almost verbatim in other texts authored by de Leon. Based on lexicographical criteria, Gershom Scholem, the great twentieth-

3. I am indebted to R. Nehemiah Polen of the Hebrew College in Newton for noting that another obscure reference of the trilateral root is to a "wilderness boundary," which may in part explain how the terms has been used to connote "structure."

century scholar of Jewish mysticism concluded that de Leon authored the *Zohar* by himself, a theory supported by de Leon's wife's confession that she had discovered her husband writing it from his own imagination rather than copying it from an existing ancient manuscript (Scholem 1963). However, recently scholars have offered compelling arguments that while the *Zohar* may have been penned by de Leon, it was conceptually an effort inspired by a group of kabbalists, who modeled their lives on their imaginings of R. Shimeon Bar Yochai and his disciples (Liebes 1993). Whoever the author(s) was, he was undoubtedly an accomplished mystic.

The *Zohar* is replete with extensive symbolic elucidation of the *sefirot*, which served to standardize their subsequent meanings. An idea that is developed within the *Zohar* is that of the *sitra achra*, or "other side," a term that refers to those dark evil forces that function in opposition to the benevolent forces of divine light. In the *Zohar*, the *sitra achra* is attributed to the primordial uninhibited activities of the *sefira Gevurah* (i.e., restriction or law), and its elements do not interact directly with the Godhead but nor are they independent of it. The dualism of the *Zohar* is less radical than that encountered in Augustinian Christianity's notion of evil as the *privatio boni*, or absence of the all-good deity. Despite being restricted from the primary structure of the Godhead, the elements of the *sitra achra* are energized by it sufficiently to wrest away the lowest *sefira*—imagined as the feminine *Malchut* or *Shekhina*—and to hold her in captivity.[4] While in captivity, she is abused and longs to be reunited with her male counterpart, *Tiferet*, who resides in the higher supernal realm. She is released on the Sabbath for the purposes of conjugal right with *Tiferet*.

The age of the *Zohar* coincides with the emergence of the troubadours and romantic love in Provence and Castile. The attitudes expressed by the kabbalists concerning *Malchut* reflect their polarized fantasies about the feminine. On one hand, like the troubadours, they tended to hold the feminine in high esteem, and as pure and virginal.

4. The *Legend of Zelda* was a popular video game in the 1980s that included elements that are strongly reminiscent of the narratives in the *Zohar* in which *Malchut* must be rescued from the *sitra achra*.

On the other, she was imagined as a harlot and subjected to continued abuse by the *sitra achra*, representing their misogynistic fantasies (Green 2003).

The *Zohar* exhibits the rudimentary features of a novel, long before the appearance of *Don Quixote* (1605). Its text includes a series of amusing tales of misadventure, together with references to the paths leading to enlightenment. The *Zohar* consistently upbraids it characters for any hint of elitism or airs of superiority, but it is primarily concerned with establishing the unity of the Godhead and reaffirming the relationship of the average Jew with God.

Its protagonist, R. Shimeon bar Yochai, is described as quasi-divine. He is the archetype of the spiritual master, what would later become the Hasidic *tzaddik*. His insights are uncanny, his wisdom profound, and his charisma unparalleled. As Green notes, he is what the anthropologist of religion Mircea Eliade referred to as the *axis mundi*, as he can transmit the prayers of his disciples towards heaven where they can be received and responded to, a task previously held by angels (Green 1977).

The *Zohar* portrays the dynamics between the *sefirot* in frankly erotic terms that intimate an ecstatic spirituality. It borrows from Genesis 1:27, in which God creates man and woman together as one creature, akin to the Platonic myth. However, within the *Zohar* one does not observe the split between spiritual and carnal love that characterizes Christianity. Instead, body and mind are valued equally and in this regard, the text aims at achieving what neither Freud nor Jung are able to achieve with their respective psychological approaches. The kabbalists meld physical sexuality and spirituality without devaluing either (Mopsik 2005).

The *Zohar* also imagines the divine in terms that are personal and immediate rather than as the formless abstraction of the deity that Maimonides argues for in his *Guide*. Imagination takes priority over intellection for the kabbalists, much as it does for Jung. The theosophy of the *Zohar* insists that man's prayers and efforts are critical, as they serve to restore *Malchut*, the receptive feminine element of the Godhead to her rightful place in the unity of the Godhead. The *Zohar* with overt erotic allusions to insemination encourages man to initiate a flow of masculine divine energy from the world above into the receptive feminine *Malchut*, thereby fructifying the physical world.

In this fashion, a dialogical intercourse is created in which man and God cooperate in a dynamic of near symmetric mutuality. This, as will be seen, is comparable to Jung's notion of how consciousness and the unconscious function together to achieve a dynamically shifting psychological balance. The *tzaddik* is also comparable to the analyst who assists the patient in translocating elements from the unconscious into consciousness for the purpose of constructing meaning.

KABBALAH AND PARADOX

Despite the multiplicity of the *sefirot*, there is an implied unity to the Godhead of the kabbalists. But what chiefly supported their claim to being an orthodox element within Judaism was that, unlike trinitarian Christianity or Gnosticism, the kabbalists never abandoned the Law; rather they argued for exacting observance. Despite its numerous anthropomorphisms, the *Zohar* provides repeated disclaimers that its metaphors must not be reified. Like Maimonides, the kabbalists acknowledge that they serve an imageless Godhead. Indeed, the entire sefirotic system is ultimately dismissed as a purely imaginal construct.

Such paradox is characteristic of mystical theology. Although the *Zohar* does come uncomfortably close to Christianity in its multipartite depiction of the Godhead, its abiding faith in the Law sets it apart from polytheism. However, as both Christianity and Jewish mysticism borrowed from the Neoplatonic myth of emanation, the *Zohar*'s imagery must be seen as a "return of the repressed," (i.e., as an influx of multiplicity and imagery) within rabbinic monotheism. Copies of the *Zohar* were disseminated throughout southern Europe and into Poland, where they became a topic of intense scrutiny by scholars (Green 2003). In the sixteenth century, an elite group of Jewish rabbis versed in the *Zohar* and other kabbalistic writings gathered in the Galilean city of Safed. R. Yosef Karo, whose compendiums of Jewish law, the *Shulchan Aruch* and the *Bet Yosef*, would eventually become the definitive codification of the Law for modern Orthodox Jewry, attracted a group of talented students to him in Safed (Werblowsky 1977). However, the dominant personality to emerge from Safed was R. Isaac Luria of Ashkenaz, the Holy Ari, whose conceptual modifications of the Kabbalah had an important impact on Judaism and arguably on psychoanalytical thought, as well.

Little is known about Luria's life, but there is little doubt that he was highly charismatic with an uncanny insight into psychology and the cure of the soul (Fine 2003). For the brief time that he was in Safed before dying of plague, his life was modeled on that of R. Shimeon (Rashbi) in the *Zohar*. Luria's powers for foretelling the future, recognizing the history of reincarnated souls, and identifying the tombs of the early sages (*tannaim*) in the Galilee parallel those of the legendary Rashbi.[5]

The cardinal contribution made by Luria to the Kabbalah was the cosmogonic notion of the *shevirat ha kelim* or the "breaking of the vessels" and their repair (*tikkun ha olam*). Luria arrived at this by expanding on the kabbalistic idea of *tzimtzum*, a term that roughly means contraction. A problem that, until then, had not been satisfactorily addressed by the kabbalists was how the Godhead or *En Sof*, "without beginning or end," could create the cosmos without undergoing any change, since by definition the Godhead was considered immutable. To answer this question, Luria suggested that the *En Sof* desired to create the world by undergoing a contraction of his essence, leaving a partially light-filled space, into which a ray of divine light was projected. The source of this divine light was imagined to represent the archetypal man, Adam Kadmon or the Anthropos. It was accepted without criticism that this took place without any change in the divine essence, yet another paradox accepted by the mystic mind.

The light emanating from Adam Kadmon was meant to be received by the ten *sefirot*, now imagined as vessels (*kelim*) for the purpose of containing and structuring creation. The first three *sefirot*, *Keter* (crown), *Chochmah* (wisdom), and *Binah* (discernment), were

5. If one travels today in the Galilee, one encounters multiple gravesites of famous rabbis who lived in the first centuries CE. Most of these graves were identified by Luria based on his supranormal powers rather than archeological findings.

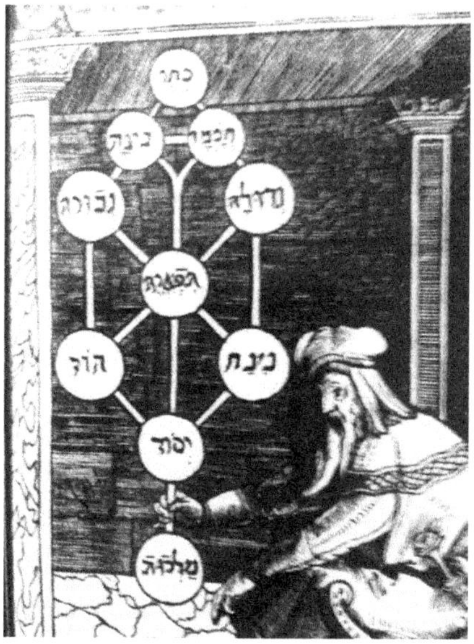

Figure 6. The standard sefirotic kabbalistic diagram includes the ten *sefirot* arranged in triangular form.

able to contain the emanated divine light of *En Sof*, but the energy could not be contained by the lower seven, *Chesed* (love), *Gevurah* (strictness), *Tiferet* (compassion), *Netzach* (victory), *Hod* (glory), *Yesod* (foundation), and *Malchut* (kingdom) (Figure 6), which shattered into shards. The shattered sefirotic vessels were spontaneously reconfigured and reinforced themselves as *partzufim* (faces).[6]

Sparks of light (*nitzizot*) entrapped within the shattered vessels descended into the lowest world of *asiyah* (making), where they coalesced into matter. Those shards that were devoid of divine light became the metaphysical source of evil. But the divine light contained within other shards of matter naturally seeks to return to its source in *En Sof*. According to Luria, through faithful observance of the Law, with intention (*kavvanot*), fostered by imaginal reunifications (*yechudim*) of letters and words, man is able to elevate the sparks in matter to their divine source, thereby restoring (*tikkun ha olam*) the

6. The Lurianic myth comes remarkably close to several ideas of modern physics. The shattering of the vessels is reminiscent of cosmological Big Bang theory. In addition, the idea of self-organization, such as occurs in the reconfiguration of the shattered *sefirot* to form the *partzufim*, is also reminiscent of modern theory of how complex systems tend to self-organize.

stability of the cosmos. The purpose of creation, according to Luria, is God's desire to engage man in a dialogue of mutual rectification. In one respect, this is simply a restatement of the ancient Israelite religion's goal of sacralizing the material world, but what is new is the notion that in doing so one also restores a broken divine realm. The kabbalist imagined a critical connection between his lower world and the metaphysical upper one, and that God and man were mutually reliant on each other for achieving wholeness, a notion that is recapitulated in Jung's model of the self correcting psyche.

But like the *Zohar*'s notion of the *sefirot*, the Lurianic myth of creation is simply another metaphor in Jewish tradition that is not to be taken literally. It is an image of primordial trauma, which reflects a basic fault within creation out of which evil also arises, and one that provides the model for modern theories of psychological trauma and dissociation.

THE EMERGENCE OF THE HASIDISM

Today, there are few practicing kabbalists largely because the technical practices of *kavvanot* and *yechudim* are difficult to master, as they require intense concentration and considerable mental gymnastics. In keeping with the general trends of esoteric Judaism, kabbalism was the domain of a rarified elite, and beyond the ken of most Jews. However, the Lurianic Kabbalah fostered spiritual experience and touched all Jews by contributing to the traditional liturgy.[7]

The *Zohar* and the Lurianic Kabbalah were a practical effort on the part of its practitioners to speed the arrival of the messiah (Gay 1976; Scholem 1995a). It cannot be sufficiently emphasized that life for the Jews in Christian Europe, as well as in Muslim Spain and Palestine, was fraught with economic difficulties, persecutions, and the threat of forced conversion. This led to a fervent communal yearning for

7. A number of changes in the prayer book were made by Luria and other kabbalists from Safed. These include the intentional unifications (*yechudim*) that are set out before prayers and songs like the Sabbath *Lecha Dodi*, which is held in reverence by practicing Jews. The prayer book of the *Arizal* would later be adopted by the Hasidim in preference to the Ashkenazic liturgy.

redemption and the coming of a messiah who would redeem the Jews from their plight. The Lurianic Kabbalah did inspire several would-be messiahs, the most famous being Sabbatai Tzvi.

Scholem authored the definitive biography of Sabbatai Tzvi, who is described as a prodigious scholar, a charismatic personality, and a severe manic-depressive (Scholem 1995a). With encouragement from his prophet Nathan the Wise, Tzvi declared himself to be the messiah in 1665. When he did, a furor of hope spread throughout the Jewish world, especially among *conversos*, those Jews forced to convert to Christianity against their will, who now imagined the possibility of returning to Judaism without the fear of being persecuted by the Inquisition. Large numbers of Jews throughout the world sold their businesses and left their homes in expectation of the long awaited redemption.

But when Zvi, who lived in the Ottoman Empire, was imprisoned by the caliph and ordered either to convert to Islam or be killed, the messiah chose the former and emerged with a new Arabic name wearing the Islamic turban. His conversion spelled a rapid end to his messianic claims for most Jews, although a small group of Sabbateans continued to believe that this act was part of the expected tribulations of the true messiah. As previously noted, Bakan promoted the idea that Freud may have been a crypto-Sabbatean, but there is little evidence to support this claim (Bakan 1958).

MYSTICISM OF THE HASIDIC REFORM

Throughout the Jewish world there was disappointment but continued belief that the coming of the messiah was imminent. It was suggested that he would appear in 1648, but instead that year yielded one of the most deadly pogroms recorded, with the massacre of thousands of Jews by Cossacks led by Bogdan Chmielnicki in Poland. This was compounded by the collapse of the autonomous Jewish governance of the Polish Pale and increasing social distance between the educated rabbinate and the uneducated Jewish poor, who were left in a state of economic and spiritual hopelessness with no one to champion them. The result was a profound melancholy amongst the Jews of Eastern Europe (Rapoport-Albert 1996).

In the last part of the seventeenth century, and in response to widespread disillusionment, a new defender of the Jews emerged in Eastern Europe. Israel ben Eliezer, an itinerant charismatic healer known popularly as the B'aal Shem Tov ("master of the good name") or by the acronym of Besht, is generally credited with being the founder of the Hasidic movement. Like the Ari, the Besht's biography is hagiographical, although there is recently discovered documentary evidence that he was a member of the Jewish community of Medzybich and had been awarded a stipend by the town for his activities as a healer (Etkes 2005).

The Besht offered a simplified approach to the service of God, one based on heartfelt prayer rather than Talmudic erudition. His mystical approach was not based on the complex *kavvanot* of the Lurianic kabbalists but on the idea of *devekut* (cleaving to God), in which one could induce trance and achieve an experience of oneness with God via the contemplation of words and letters. His followers described the Besht as a charismatic leader with supernatural powers, who like the Ari had a special connection to God.

Like Luria, the Besht wrote little, if anything, during his lifetime. His teachings were later authored by his disciples, most notably Joseph of Polonye and Dov Ber the Maggid of Mezyritch. The Maggid became the primary spiritual and political leader of the new Hasidic movement after the death of the Besht and attracted many disciples. Unlike the Besht, who was itinerant, the Maggid created the prototype of the Hasidic court, to which disciples and curious onlookers would travel large distances for an audience (Rapoport-Albert 1996).

The Maggid was actively engaged in promoting the tenets of Hasidism and countering the fervent anti-Hasidic sentiment of its opponents, the Mitnaggdim of the scholarly rabbinic class, led by the audacious Talmudic scholar, Elijah the Gaon of Vilna. The Maggid raised many talented disciples who disseminated Hasidism throughout Europe, founding their own Hasidic courts.

It is not possible here to examine the diverse philosophies and practices of Hasidim. For this reason, the present text will focus on

ליקוטי ספר של בינונים אמרים ה
פרק א תניא [בספ"ג דנדה] משביעים אותו
תהי צדיק ואל תהי רשע ואפי' כל
העולם כולו אומרים לך צדיק אתה היה בעיניך כרשע
וצריך להבין דהא תנן [אבות פ"ב] ואל תהי רשע בפני
עצמך וגם אם יהיה בעיניו כרשע ירע לבבו ויהיה עצב
ולא יוכל לעבוד ה' בשמחה ובטוב לבב ואם לא ירע לבבו
כלל מזה יכול לבוא לידי קלות ח"ו . אך הענין כי הנה
מצינו בגמרא ה' חלוקות. צדיק וטוב לו צדיק ורע לו רשע
וטוב לו רשע ורע לו ובינוני. ופירש בגמרא צדיק וטוב לו
צדיק גמור צדיק ורע לו צדיק שאינו גמור וברעיא
מהימנא פ' משפטים פי' צדיק ורע לו שהרע שבו כפוף
לטוב וכו' ובגמרא ספ"ט דברכות צדיקים יצ"ט שופטן כו'
רשעים יצה"ר שופטן בינונים זה וזה שופטן וכו' אמר רבה
כגון אנא בינוני א"ל אביי לא שביק מר חיי לכל בריה
וכו' ולהבין כל זה באר היטב וגם להבין מה שאמר איוב
[ב"ב פ"א] רבש"ע בראת צדיקי' בראת רשעי' כו' והא
צדיק ורשע לא קאמר . וגם להבין מהות מדרגת הבינוני
שבודאי אינו מחצה זכיות ומחצה עונות שא"כ איך טעה

Figure 7. The first page of R. Schneur Zalman's classic text of Chabad Hasidism *Likutei Amarim* or the *Tanya* (תניא) based on its first word.

that branch of Hasidism that both philosophically and historically most closely prefigured the ideas of depth psychology. Arguably, the most esteemed disciple of the Maggid was the Lithuanian Talmudic scholar R. Schneur Zalman of Lyadi. He founded a branch of Hasidism distinguished by its focus not only on fervent feeling for God but on a systematic and rational theosophy, which he explicated in his text *Likutei Amarim* (Collected Sayings), popularly referred to as the *Tanya*, which is the first word of the text (Figure 7).

The *Tanya* became the defining text of Chabad (*chochmah*, *binah*, and *daat*) Hasidism,[8] a name based on the acronym referring

8. The second Chabad rebbe, Dov Ber the son of Schneur Zalman, moved the court to Lubavitch in Russia where it was based for one hundred years. The Chabad or Chabad-Lubavitchers eventually moved their center to New York City where the last and seventh rebbe, Menachem Mendel Schneerson died in 1994. Under his

to the three highest *sefirot*.[9] Schneur Zalman adopted the Lurianic Kabbalah but transformed it from a theosophy into a sophisticated depth psychology. Lovingly referred to as the Alter Rebbe ("old Rebbe") or *the B'aal ha Tanya* ("master of the *Tanya*"), Schneur Zalman was writing for the average man or *beinoni*.[10] He promulgated an acosmic view of the universe in which God was paradoxically at once immanent (*maale olam*) and transcendent (*malle sovevim*), a theological position scholars have referred to as panentheism (Uffenheimer 1993).

The panentheistic idea of God as both the "center and circumference of the circle" is a shared mystical notion. According to the *Tanya*, the Lurianic *tzimtzum*, or contraction, of the Godhead, represented the reduction of intensity of divine light from man's perspective. It created the illusion of multiplicity while in fact God was present everywhere and in everything. This reality of no boundaries is a profound definition of monotheism. According to the *Tanya*:

> In like manner, God again projected and caused to issue forth and descend a radiation of the radiation from the effulgences of the letters; and likewise He again caused it to issue forth and to descend to the lowest level in the category of descents, until the completely inanimate, such as stones and dust were created. And their names even and afar are substitutions of substitutions, and transpositions of transpositions. . . . (179)

---

leadership, Chabad grew into a highly organized outreach movement for Jews all over the world. A subset of Chabad Chasidim consider the late rebbe to have been the messiah, following a familiar trope, and this has in part split the movement internally, although they show little evidence of external strain. See Samuel Heilman and Menachem Friedman, *The Rebbe*: *The Life and Afterlife of Menachem Mendel Schneerson* (Princeton: Princeton University Press, 2012).

9. In fact, most schemes have *Keter*, *Chachmah*, and *Binah* as the three highest *sefirot*, so the acronym Chabad represents the addition of another *sefira* that serves a purpose in their cognitive-oriented approach.
10. Lest one err in thinking that the *beinoni* was an average person, he was not. He was sinless, but unlike a *tzaddik* still struggled with internal desires. Even a single sin made one a *rasha* (bad person), although one could raise one's status. Schneur Zalman was convinced that through the exercise of will power anyone could attain the state of *beinoni* by just saying no to temptation.

It was possible via *tzimtzum* to create elements devoid of divine radiance, and these shells, or *kelippot*, correspond to the *sitra achra* of the *Zohar*, as forces of evil both in the world and in the mind of man.[11] According to R. Schneur Zalman, the *kelippot* of the Jewish soul were all *nogah* that contained sparks of divine light entrapped within dense shells, but could be elevated by proper religious observance.

The Chabad model includes two important psychological ideas. The first is that the divine soul, or what might be imagined as the healthy aspect of the psyche, does not develop ex nihilo based on proper nurture but is present from birth. This idea would have been dismissed by Freud, who saw the child as polymorphously perverse, but it is implied in the Jungian concept of the archetype of the divine or golden child. It can also be discerned in the writings of the object-relations theorist, Donald Winnicott as his notion of the true self, which he describes as follows:

> In typical cases the imprisoned true self is unable to function and by being protected its opportunity for living experience is limited. Life is lived by the compliant false self and the result clinically is a sense of unreality. . . . Life can only come from the true self. . . . (Winnicott 1989, 43)

The second idea is that, despite the accretion of shell-like defenses, the divine essence of the individual remains intact and potentially in reach, so that transformation of the personality is possible. Most Jungian psychoanalysts accept this and most Freudian analysts, while tending to eschew the language of spirituality, would agree that there must be hope for change whenever one accepts a new patient in analysis.

Some neo-Freudian psychoanalysts are beginning to reconsider the therapeutic importance of spirituality in the treatment of patients. As the non-Jungian psychoanalyst Karen Starr notes in *Repair of the Soul*:

---

11. In the *Tanya*, the Jewish soul contains *nogah*, which is a *kelippa* that contains divine sparks, whereas the non-Jew has a *kelippa* that is devoid of divine sparks. According to the Alter Rebbe, only the Jewish soul has the capacity for transformation, a point that has been questioned by non-Jews and Jews alike.

> Although the faith in transformation is more frequently a topic of discussion in religious circles than in psychoanalysis, I contend that faith is pivotal to psychic change . . . the faith that I am referring to is in the unfolding potential that exist in the world and in one's self. . . . (2008, 63–64)

Unfortunately, many Freudians have little awareness that this area is a staple of Jungian psychology and have not read his ideas on this topic in depth.

The healing path of the *Tanya*, at least in its broad strokes, is comparable to that of the psychoanalytical approach, as it includes analytical scrutiny, honesty, and efforts at modifying and refining behavior. One can discern within the *Tanya* the precursor of the psychoanalytical notion of working through the resistances of a false self construct, which may be compared to the shell of the *kelippa*, in order to arrive at the inner true self, as Winnicott termed it (1989).

Furthermore, Hasidism includes the idea that, at times, a regression into sinful behaviors may be required in order for the soul to attain a higher level of purity, an idea that is comparable to Freud's "regression in the service of the ego" (1916), and what Jung was apparently referring to in his notion of a *nekiya* or descent into the unconscious (1911).

CHAPTER 8

God and the Unconscious

All anthropomorphic projections were withdrawn from the object one after another, with a two-fold result: firstly man's mystical identity with nature was curtailed as never before, and secondly the projections falling back into the human soul caused terrific activation of the unconscious that in modern times man was compelled to postulate the existence of an unconscious psyche.

—Carl Jung

THE FREUDIAN UNCONSCIOUS

Freud did not discover the unconscious; the term was coined by Schilling in the eighteenth century, and its history has been traced by Ellenberger (1970). In the nineteenth century, mesmerism and hypnosis demonstrated that behaviors could be influenced by suggestion outside of conscious awareness. Indeed, many aspects of experience occur outside of consciousness, as man's ability to perceive the spectrum of the physical world is limited. He is blind to certain wavelengths of light, deaf to the extremes of sound, and insensate to the momentary physiology of the nervous system that regulates the heartbeat, digestion, and non-volitional automatic reflexes.

But what was difficult for man to accept was that his thoughts and actions also arose from beyond conscious control and might be, even in infancy, driven by sexual instincts, as Freud argued.[1] This was arguably

1. There is a famous experiment in which a subject is asked to report when he is about to move a limb, while the muscles and the brain are monitored for electrical activity. What has been demonstrated is that the muscles and brain are activated before the

Freud's most outstanding contribution, for, like the Copernican revolution, it shifted man's perspective to an awareness that the locus of an individual's control lay outside of consciousness.

Freud identified many examples of the activities of the unconscious mind. These included dreams, somnambulism, and automatic speech and writing. The unconscious influenced virtually all aspects of relational experience through what he termed transference (i.e., the unconscious mental projections of the patient onto others). Freud recognized that unconscious activities were always operating in the background and were normally only thinly guised by consciousness. The unconscious—often erroneously reified as a noun, despite being an active process—is phenomenologically speaking like God, in that it is both transcendent in its inability to be accessed directly, but also immanent in that its effects are always present, a notion paralleling the panentheistic theosophy of R. Schneur Zalman.

The most profound level of mystical experience, framed in religious jargon as the fusion of the soul with God, is the *unio mystica*. Jung argued that this experience was the result of a direct psychological encounter of the ego with the unconscious archetype of the self.[2] In *Tractate on Ecstasy*, R. Dov Ber, the second rebbe of Lubavitch Chasidism, argues that the quietistic experience that Hasidism terms *bitul*, the ultimate psychological abrogation of self, is devoid of ego-consciousness (Uffenheimer 1993).[3] Wilfred Bion, an early Kleinian

---

subject claims any awareness of a motivation to move. This experiment raises profound questions concerning mechanisms of free will.

2. Mystical experiences in Judaism are particularly hard to characterize. Scholem argued that Judaism proscribed experiences of full union with the divine (i.e., the *unio mystica*). However, Moshe Idel has argued against this notion and Dov Ber of Lubavitch's detailed treatise includes reference to a complete loss of any conscious awareness at the height of the mystical experience, even that of ecstasy.
3. The great scholar of Hasidism, Louis Jacobs, suggests that one must be careful in attributing the idea of *unio mystica* to the early *tzaddikim*, as it may be difficult to distinguish psychological connotation from the theosophical ones of the kabbalists. Louis Jacobs, *Their Heads in Heaven* (London: Valentine Mitchell, 2005). In the case of the *Maggid* of Mezyritch, R. Solomon of Lutzk recorded his experiences of *unio mystica*. However, variants of the *Maggid's* teachings, in this case the phrase "Make thee two trumpets (*hatzotzerot*) of silver" of Numbers 10:2 was reported by

psychoanalyst influenced by his childhood observations of Indian mystics, referred to the ineffable root of consciousness as "O" (Bion 1963), or what the kabbalists termed *ayin* ("nothing") (Eigen 2013). In any case, mystical experiences are difficult to define or to recount with clarity (Katz 1978).[4] Such experiences, like the unconscious, can be intimated in apophatic terms (i.e., through the *via negativa*) or through a kataphatic approach.

Freud referred to the unconscious as dimensionless and as devoid of knowledge of time and space (1940). Psychoanalysis also fosters the notion that it is a matrix located beneath consciousness. Man necessarily experiences God as the ultimate unconscious, and as transcendent, and located somewhere above. Here again, one encounters the Platonic and Aristotelian biases, with the real world either above or below, depending on one's perspective and values, as Raphael's painting of the *School of Athens* famously depicts (Herman 2014).

Metaphorically and dimensionally speaking, the Freudian unconscious is imagined as "smaller" than Jung's version of it, as the latter includes a collective unconscious whose boundaries are impossible to define. It is reasonably safe to conclude that Freud, as a biologist of the mind (Sulloway 1979), limited his notion of the unconscious to the body container, much as Aristotle and Maimonides did for the soul, whereas Jung, in his spiritualized approach, speculated that the unconscious, like the Platonic soul and the *yechidah* component of the soul in Judaism, might in fact be acting outside of the individual as part of a metaphysical *anima mundi* ("world soul"). As Jung states:

> The rescue of the human soul and the salvation of the cosmos in other words, they go hand in hand. . . . From the

---

R. Israel of Kosnitz, another disciple of the *Maggid*, as referring to the *coniunctio* between *k'lal Yisroel* and the *sefira Malchut*, and not with *En Sof*.

4. There is a small cottage research industry that is investigating the neurobiology of mystical experience, although few consistent results have been generated. Eugene D'Aquilo and Andrew Newberg in the *Mystical Mind* (Minneapolis: Fortress, 1999) suggested that mystical experience is conditioned as a progressive de-afferentiation of consciousness, so that sensory input is progressively and actively inhibited, resulting in states of consciousness that lack content.

> alchemical perspective the human individual may be a necessary focus but cannot be a sufficient one; the rescue of the cosmos is equally important. Neither can take place without the other. Soul and world are inseparable: anima mundi. (*CW* 12, para. 244)

Uncertainty concerning the boundaries of the unconscious parallels the religious vision of the Godhead in Ezekiel 3:12 "Then the Spirit lifted me up, and I heard a great rumbling sound behind me, Blessed is the glory of the Lord from His place!" Where "His place" within Jewish tradition is unknown even to the angels who, according to the sages, serve God intimately, but like all created creatures are unable to see Him.

Maimonides suggested in *The Guide* that the prophetic visions of the Hebrew Bible come either in the form of dreams or as what Jung termed active imagination or waking visions. In *Through a Speculum That Shines*, the scholar Eliot Wolfson argues that such mystical experiences are, in following Scholem, conditioned and contextualized by the previous experience of the mystical adept (Wolfson 1995). However, Wolfson further contends that there is no way to parse the actual mystical experience from subsequent descriptions, as imagination and its accompanying affects are coincident, so that the latter is not simply an interpretation of a quietistic experience, but an integral part of the experience itself.

Maimonides argues for a singular exception to the prophetic experience for the prophet Moses, who is hagiographically said to have been able to experience God directly through pure intellect, or "through a speculum that shines" (Wolfson 1999). But this statement is not supported by the biblical text, for in Exodus 33:17–123, we are told of Moses' request "to see God's face" directly:

> Then Moses said, "Now show me your glory." And YHWH said, "I will cause all my goodness to pass in front of you, and I will proclaim my name, the YHWH, in your presence. I will have mercy on whom I will have mercy, and I will have

> compassion on whom I will have compassion. But," he said, "you *cannot see my face*, [italics added] for no one may see me and live." Then the YHWH said, "There is a place near me where you may stand on a rock. When my glory passes by, I will put you in a cleft in the rock and cover you with my hand until I have passed by. Then I will remove my hand and *you will see my back* [italics added]; but my face must not be seen."

This argues that no direct visual experience of God is possible, even for Moses.

In psychological terms, the text of Exodus 33 further suggests a critical relationship of consciousness to the unconscious. Temporally, unconsciousness is an a priori of consciousness. On the micro-temporal scale, even behaviors thought to be initiated in consciousness (e.g., the voluntary movement of a muscle) have been shown to be preceded by measurable electrical activity in the body part that is being willed to be moved, before a report of an awareness of the desire to move it (Kradin 2008). This finding raises questions concerning the independence of free will.

The meaning of God's name in the Hebrew Bible, the tetragrammaton of YHWH, may shed some light on this dilemma. Today, the name is never pronounced, but the high priest and the Israelites uttered it aloud once yearly on the Day of Atonement when the Second Temple was still standing. The name is first revealed to Moses in the desert during the miracle of the burning bush in Exodus 3:13–15 (Figure 8):

> Moses said to God, "Suppose I go to the Israelites and say to them, 'The God of your fathers has sent me to you,' and they ask me, 'What is his name?' Then what shall I tell them?" God said to Moses, "*'ehyeh asher 'ehyeh.* This is what you are to say to the Israelites: *'ehyeh asher 'ehyeh* has sent me to you." God also said to Moses, "Say to the Israelites, YHWH (יהוה) the God of your fathers—the God of Abraham, the God of Isaac and the God of Jacob—has sent me to you." This is my

Figure 8. Moses the Lawgiver as portrayed by Charlton Heston in the Cecil B. DeMille blockbuster *The Ten Commandments*.

> name forever, the name by which I am to be remembered from generation to generation.

The proper translation of *'eheyeh asher 'eheyeh* is "I will be what I will be," as it reflects the first person imperfect or future tense of the verb to be or *hoveh* (הוה). Some commentators have interpreted this as a dismissive response, as the idea of denying access to a divine name occurs in several places in the Hebrew Bible, due to the ancient belief that knowledge of the name could be used for theurgic purposes. Alternatively, the divine response may have been meant to discourage the possibility of applying any word-image to the Godhead.

In the context of the present discussion, it indicates a specific temporal relationship of the unconscious to consciousness, which is that it precedes consciousness and therefore is always experientially part of the individual's past. All any being can know has literally already been preceded: as Exodus 33:20 suggests in God's response to Moses request to see his face: ". . . you will see my *back*; but my face cannot be seen."

Mystical experience is contextual and conditioned by previous experience and belief. Christian mystics report visions of Jesus or the Virgin Mary, whereas Jewish mystics virtually never report such images. Based on this and other phenomena, there is reason to conclude that the structuring of the unconscious, and the images that emerge from it, differ between Jews and Christians due to their religious milieus. Based on this, one might honestly question whether the tenets of either Freud or Jung's psychoanalytical approaches are universal (Wolfson, 1999). Although this may be less true today, as the secular world moves farther away from the symbologies of specific religious traditions, it was clearly when Freud and Jung were developing their theoretical stances.

Metapsychological differences might be viewed by some today as politically incorrect, but, in this regard it is important to recognize that political correctness has its origins in Christianity (Taylor 2007). As Jung noted, "the age of rational Enlightenment has eradicated nothing. Even our method of rational Enlightenment is Christian" (Jung 1934, 165). Modern political correctness shares with Pauline Christianity a distaste for particularism. As Howard Schwarz states in *Society Against Itself: Political Correctness and Organizational Deconstruction*, "The individual has disappeared. The subjects of the narratives that give sense to life are groups" (2010, 26) Although diversity is theoretically applauded within modern politically correct society, this is only the case when differences fit into the larger society's conception of what is correct.

Tolerance by politically correct society for traditional Judaism remains limited, as the latter prescribes separation from the dominant group with respect to food, dress, etc. Consider those within politically correct society who argue against Jewish ritual circumcision of male infants as cruel and unnecessary, or Jewish ritual slaughter of animals in a similar vein. Such views pose a subtle, yet no less problematic version, of what Nirenberg refers to as Christian "anti-Judaism,"[5] and they can

5. I am editing this chapter while in Jerusalem in July 2014, during Israel's war with Gaza, which was initiated by unprovoked missile attacks on the State of Israel, by the terrorist organization Hamas, which has repeatedly stated a policy of aiming to annihilate Jews and Israel. This unprovoked attack on civilians engendered a

obfuscate the ability to discern the religious roots of psychoanalytical thought by inappropriately limiting inquiry.

FREUD AND THE DRIVES

Freud imagined the unconscious as a compartment set apart from consciousness by an imaginal barrier of ego defenses. Within the psychic economy, the Freudian unconscious served two functions. It was, first, the source of the instinctual drives and, second, a repository for repressed ideas and affects. Influenced by Darwin, Freud viewed man as bestial at the core and motivated primarily by self-preservation and pleasure. The unconscious or id was envisioned as an impersonal cauldron of seething instincts, which like the Godhead was oblivious to time, space, and discernment.

Compare this notion of the unconscious with the description of *En Sof* (Godhead) in the *Tanya*: "For just as He was All Alone, Single, and Unique, before *it* was created, beside Him everything is as nothing, verily as null and void" (85). If one substitutes consciousness for the term "it," one is left with a description of the unconscious prior to the emergence of consciousness. Jewish commentaries envision creation in much the same way that psychoanalysis sees consciousness arising de novo from the unconscious.

Freud initially posited that the unconscious was motivated by the pleasure principle, i.e., by the impulse to fulfill hedonistic desires or wishes. Although this idea may sound antithetical to one's expectation of God, consider the scholar Roman Foxbrunner's synopsis of Chabad theology:

> R. Schneur Zalman insists that there is invariably and necessarily a transcendent reason hidden in the recesses of the divine Mind, which is also the first vessel for divine pleasure.

---

measured but lethal response by Israel. Several truces have been violated by Hamas since the beginning of the war. Yet much of the civilized world, fueled by disturbing images of war televised by the press, while accepting Israel's right to defend itself, has once again condemned it for brutality. How exactly this differs from the Augustinian dogma concerning the Jews (i.e., they can defend themselves but are not allowed to win) is unclear to me.

> This Pleasure, in turn, derives from the hidden essence of the Godhead and is its highest power. In simple terms, *God's motive for acting any given way is pleasure.* (1993, 42; italics added)

The divine mind, like the Freudian unconscious, is, according to the *Tanya* and the Lurianic kabbalists, pleasure-seeking and desirous of creation. Aharon ha Levi Horowitz of Stroselye, a major disciple of R. Schneur Zalman,[6] states in his commentary *Avodat ha Levi* that the human soul is the "crown of Creation" and contains all of the divine characteristics, with desire at the top of the list (Horowitz 1987, 6). Rabbinic Judaism and the nineteenth-century Mussar movement both equated the *yetzer ha ra* or "bad impulse" with man's carnal desire.

In Freud's model, the unconscious serves as a repository for repressed ideas and affects that potentially disturb consciousness. This mental chaff is subject to repression, and its restoration to consciousness is a primary goal of psychoanalytical treatment. As Freud stated, "Where *Id* was, *Ego* will be," (Freud 1916) conscious choice can counteract repetition compulsions. For Freud, the unconscious motivates behavior, but consciousness has a say, reminiscent of Akiva's statement in the *Ethics of the Fathers* (3:15) that, "All is foreseen, but choice is given."

In 1920, Freud modified his model of the unconscious to include aggression as a second drive. In *Beyond the Pleasure Principle*, Freud indicates that his own clinical observations, and the psychological effects that he attributed to the trauma of the World War I, had motivated him to conclude that repetitive self-defeating behaviors could not be explained solely by the pleasure principle.

Alongside the drive to procreate, Freud concluded that there must also be a psychological force favoring psychic annihilation. He posited

6. Aharon ha Levi was a companion of Schneur Zalman's son, Dov Ber. He split with Chabad in order to start his own branch of Hasidism, which he claimed was closer in philosophy to the Alter Rebbe's than what was taught by Dov Ber. However, the group did not prosper and is no longer extant. However, the largely forgotten writings of Aharon ha Levi reveal a theologically creative mind that in many respects closely resembles that of the Alter Rebbe. Many of the quotations are in R. Schatz-Uffenheimer's text *Hasidism as Mysticism* (Jerusalem: Hebrew University, 1993).

a grand competition between Life (Eros) and Death (Thanatos) instincts that resulted in ambivalence and both self-affirming and self-defeating behaviors:

> If we may assume as an experience admitting of no exception that everything living dies from causes within itself and returns to the inorganic, we can only say "The goal of all life is death and casting back; the inanimate was there before the animate." (Freud 1920, 161)

This theory encountered considerable resistance from Freud's followers.[7] But the idea was already prefigured in Deuteronomy 30:19:

> This day I call the heavens and the earth as witnesses against you that I have set before you life and death, blessings and curses. Now choose life, so that you and your children may live and that you may love the Lord your God, listen to his voice, and hold fast to him.

Jewish mysticism, like early Christian Gnosticism, describes an impulse within man's divine soul to return to its origins in the supernal void. Rachel Elior describes (1999) an ongoing tension in Hasidic theology between what emerges from nothingness (*ayin*) to assume the vestments of materiality (*yesh*), as well as the latter's reciprocal attraction to the return to the primordial void. Divine energies, as well as man's divine aspirations, rush to and fro (*ratzoh v'shuv*) between *ayin* and *yesh* (1999).[8]

7. The idea of Thanatos was roundly rejected in most psychoanalytical circles, but was adopted by the child analyst Melanie Klein, a Jewish psychoanalyst who was analyzed in Budapest by Ferenzci, and whose work has formed the basis for one of the major schools of object-relations theory in psychoanalysis. Although she took issues with Freud on a variety of matters, she always considered herself to be a Freudian psychoanalyst. See Phyllis Grosskurth's biography *Melanie Klein* (New York: Knopf, 1986).
8. A similar notion has been proffered by the physicist David Bohm, who hypothesized a dynamic flux between an unseen implicate and explicate order, in which

This paradoxical tension is described by R. Schneur Zalman, "For this is the purpose of the creations of the worlds, from *ayin* to *yesh*, so as to reverse the aspect of *yesh* to the aspect of *ayin*" (*Torah Or, Va-Yetze* 64). R. Aharon ha Levi expanded on this as follows:

> And this matter is written "and the living creatures (*chayot*) darted to and fro"—which means that the divine force ascends and descends. The aspect of ascent (*ratzoh*) is the desire of the heart to cleave to Him, blessed be He, and it is also from running (*merutza*), like someone running from where he is. . . . And also all of the souls of Israel in their source and root have this aspect of ascent in the will and desire to cleave unto Him, to the Infinite, blessed be He, as it is written, "and for your husband will be your desire." (Elior 1999, 44)

What Freud viewed as psychopathology due to conflict was understood by Jewish mystics as the soul's effort to restore itself to its divine source, an idea that Freud could not entertain as part of his "scientific" approach.

THE UNCONSCIOUS AND THE BEGINNING OF WISDOM

Freud's view of the psyche is essentially Aristotelian and materialistic. Although he abandoned his efforts at describing mental phenomena as neuronal activities (Freud 1895), his psychoanalysis needed to be firmly rooted in the material world. In this regard, the first ego, according to Freud, was a body ego, with complex mental structures assembled over time upon rudimentary somatosensory templates of experience (Freud 1923). Virtually all of the developmentally based theories of psychoanalysis are derived from this perspective. The Freudian psychoanalytical project is a bottom-up process, and one vectorially directed by the arrow of time.

One might erroneously conclude that Freud's ideas were rooted in scientific materialism rather than in hermeneutics. Freud's view of the

---

matter emerges from a background of energy only to disappear back into it at the quantum level (2002).

psyche was bound, like Judaism, to the material world. The Hebrew Bible often refers to metaphysical phenomena using physical metaphors. Consider Micah 7:18–19, which states:

> Who is a God like You, who *carries* iniquity, and *passes* by transgression, who has not maintained his wrath forever against the remnant of His people because he loves graciousness. He will return and have compassion on us; *He will wash away our sins, You will hurl all of our iniquities into the depths of the sea*. (italics added)

But in abandoning the *Project for a Scientific Psychology* (1895), Freud in fact had conceded that the language of psychoanalysis, like that of religion, was metaphor, and reflected the vicissitudes of the imagination rather than concrete materialism. Like the Israelites' reaction to YHWH at Sinai, Freud imagined the unconscious as a source of danger, and he adopted a series of martial metaphors, including defenses, resistance, etc., to describe how the ego defended itself against the unconscious. Consider the description of the events surrounding the revelation of the Torah to the Israelites at Sinai in Exodus 19:10–12:

> And the Lord said to Moses, "Go to the people and consecrate them today and tomorrow. Have them wash their clothes and be ready by the third day, because on that day the Lord will come down on Mount Sinai in the sight of all the people. *Put limits for the people around the mountain and tell them. Be careful that you do not approach the mountain or touch the foot of it*." (italics added)

It is evident that YHWH could not be trusted not to spontaneously break out with fatal force if approached directly:

> The Lord descended to the top of Mount Sinai and called Moses to the top of the mountain. So Moses went up and the Lord said to him, "Go down and warn the people so they do

> not force their way through to see the Lord and many of them perish. Even the priests, who approach the Lord, must consecrate themselves, or YHWH will break out against them." Moses said to the YHWH, "The people cannot come up Mount Sinai, because you yourself warned us, 'Put limits around the mountain and set it apart as holy.'" (Exodus 19:20–23)

The idea of limits and boundaries, as previously discussed, pervades both Judaism and Freudian psychoanalysis. Jews see the fear of the Lord as the beginning of wisdom and Freudian psychoanalysts view fear of the unconscious in the same light.

As the Law is the revelation of YHWH, it must be treated comparably with awe. The initial passage in the *Ethics of the Fathers* 1:1 summarizes the wisdom of the ancient Jewish sages as follows:

> Moses received the *Torah* from Sinai and gave it over to Joshua. Joshua gave it over to the Elders, the Elders to the Prophets, and the Prophets gave it over to the Men of the Great Assembly. They [the Men of the Great Assembly] would always say these three things: Be cautious in judgment. Establish many pupils. And make *a fence around the Torah*. (italics added)

Indeed, within Freud's psychoanalysis, like in Judaism, one observes the necessity to construct fences to contain the unconscious processes of the analyst and patient, so that they will not go dangerously awry. This strategy is reiterated repeatedly in Freud's thought, just it was by the rabbis, in order to contain the unconscious/God image at a distance such that it can be approached safely.

Freedom both for Freud and Judaism implies boundaries, frustrations, limits, and loss. Psychoanalysis aims at liberating the personality but in a determined "lawful" manner. Life is seen as a struggle from birth until death that should be accepted and enjoyed, to the extent possible. The idea of meetings five to six times weekly in classical psychoanalysis (these are almost unheard of today) was meant not only to foster the intensity of the process but to emphasize its mundane nature as well. Much like the observance of the Law for the Jewish practitioner, one attends psychoanalysis as part of one's daily routine, whether or not one is in the mood. In this regard, what is at first extraordinary becomes mundane. One attends analysis not simply to achieve new insight or emotional catharsis but also to learn to accept life's unavoidable banalities. As Freud states in *Studies on Hysteria*, "much will be gained if we succeed in transforming your hysterical misery into common unhappiness" (Breuer and Freud 1895, 305).

THE JUNGIAN UNCONSCIOUS: A GOD OF LOVE

The shedding of the Law by early Pauline Christianity yielded not only a theology that was distinct from that of Judaism, but also a distinct structuring of the unconscious by those subsequently immersed in the matrix of Christianity. Unlike Freud, Jung attributed a generally positive valence to the unconscious, viewing it as a source of creativity and renewal. This is the reason that he saw no need to posit the presence of ego defenses. He imagined the unconscious as bipartite, with personal and collective elements, the first closely corresponding to the Freudian unconscious, which Jung termed shadow, and the latter, to the collective unconscious, which he conceived of as a deeper wellspring of mental experience.

In redefining the unconscious, he borrowed from the Platonic Idea and the Kantian a priori by suggesting that the unconscious was structured by archetypes that determine the contours of human experience. At times, Jung imagined that these archetypes were not limited to the psyche but represented an extension of the natural laws of the cosmos that could manifest in one pole as matter (infrared) and in the other as spiritual energy (ultraviolet) (Jung 1980). In this regard, his concept parallels that of Einstein's quantum explanation of light as both a particle (photon) and a wave, but also the Jewish mystical idea that divine light could be transformed into matter in its emanations from *En Sof*. The Jungian psyche is essentially a spiritualized construct.

Obvious comparisons can be made between the Jungian archetypes and the kabbalistic *sefirot* that structure the Godhead. Whereas

Freud imagines the unconscious, much like the ambivalent force of the Jewish God, as chaos that must be contained, Jung posits an innate structure to the unconscious, much as God was structured as the incarnate Jesus in order to express a message of love before ascending back into the heavens. The Jewish God is an unimaginable ambivalent force; the Christian God is embodied and all good. The Freudian notion of the unconscious as a seething cauldron of chaos and repressed contents becomes for Jung an ordered and structured system, one interconnected, valenced, whose elements are in dynamic tension.

Jung imagined consciousness as the extremity of an unconscious whose chthonic depths, like *En Sof*, were unfathomable. Sparks of consciousness (read divine light) needed to travel an indeterminate distance from their source in the unconscious (read *En Sof*) in order to emerge as thought, just as the metaphysical divine light needed to descend before materializing within the world.

As in the Kabbalah, Jung imagined the creative potential of the ego as nourished by the unconscious archetypes (*sefirot*) that channel the flow of libidinal energies into consciousness, in a manner analogous to the flow (*shefa*) of divine light from *En Sof*. The Jungian model of the unconscious includes *syzygies*, as the male psyche is invested with an unconscious element of femininity termed the *anima* ("soul"), whereas women have a corresponding masculine element, the *animus*. These contrasexual elements, according to Jung, play an important role in linking consciousness to the deeper strata of the collective unconscious.[9] Like the kabbalists, Jung's idea of a *coniunctio* ("union") of the *zivvug* ("opposites") was a critical element in achieving wholeness, although for Jung this was an *eros* of psycho-spiritual activity and not Freud's carnal Eros.

9. In today's unisexual society, there are now volumes being written concerning the flaws in this mode of gendered thinking concerning the unconscious. See, for example, Lewis Aron and Karen Starr, *A Psychotherapy for the People* (New York: Routledge, 2013). However, whether the deepest level of unconscious process is transformed by changes in the ambient culture remains to be seen, although there is good reason to imagine that it may be, in the same ways that current imaginings of God likely differ from those in antiquity. Writing on such topics without falling into the pitfalls of anachronisms is virtually impossible.

Like James, Jung was unabashedly interested in the psychological underpinnings of religion, and he imagined the self as the source of the psychological image of the metaphysical Godhead. All of the descriptions of visions by mystics for Jung were such images of the self.[10] As Jung wrote in response to Martin Buber:

> God has indeed made an inconceivably sublime and mysteriously contradictory image of himself, without the help of man, and implanted it into man's unconscious as an archetype; not in order that theologians of all times and places should be at one another's throats, but in order that the unpresumptuous man should glimpse an image in the stillness of his soul, that is akin to him and is wrought of his own psyche. This image contains everything that he will imagine concerning his gods or concerning the ground of his psyche. (*CW* 18, para. 661)

In his autobiography, Jung describes having himself experienced a variety of such images and describes his life's work in psychology as his effort at explaining them (Jung and Jaffe 1989). Critically, Jung imagined these symbolic images as having a healing function when properly integrated with consciousness, although he warned that under uncontrolled circumstances they could devolve into the hallucinations of disabling psychosis. As in kabbalistic texts, where the *sefirot* are often depicted as a tree or as the body of a primordial man (Adam Kadmon) with a right and left side and a central axis forming the middle way between the opposite tensions of the lower seven *sefirot*, Jung interpreted the image of Adam Kadmon as symbols of the self that arose spontaneously in dreams. In some texts, the kabbalists depict the *sefirot* as a set of concentric circles,[11] which Jung also took to be an image of the self in the form of a mandala, and he noted the

10. Jung himself never capitalized the term self, which has become standard fare amongst post-Jungians and others.
11. According to a verbal communication from Arthur Green, when the various depictions of the *sefirot* originated has not been determined, and might be an interesting topic for future investigation in the area of the Kabbalah.

appearance of such circular symbols in the unconscious manifestations of psychotics, shortly preceding their recovery. On this basis he argued that they were innate healing structures offered up spontaneously by the unconscious in order to repair states of psychological disintegration.

In *Mysterium Coniunctionis*, Jung stressed what he perceived as the bivalent structuring of the unconscious as opposites,[12] and emphasized that the goal of psychotherapy was to bring these together imaginally in order to harmonize them (Jung 1955). This is reminiscent of the kabbalists who strove to achieve balance between the oppositely valenced *sefirot* (e.g., *Chesed* [love] and *Gevura/Din* [power/law]), the first prone to excessive love, the other to restriction. The conjunction, or more accurately the harmonizing, of these supposed opposites was expected to produce a third middle path, which directed the optimal flow of libidinal energies within the psyche.

Jung argued throughout his collected works that psychical ills were in large measure due to the one-sidedness of the ego's perspectives that resulted in psychological imbalance, much as the kabbalists viewed imbalances in the structure of the Godhead as undesirable. As Jung notes, "Good [read *Chesed*] does not become better by being exaggerated, but worse, and a small evil [read *Gevura*] becomes a big one through being disregarded and repressed" (*CW* 11, para. 286) (instruction bracketed in by present author). But he also argued that the attributes of man should not be projected onto the metaphysical Godhead:

> Good and evil are feeling-values of human provenance, and we cannot extend them beyond the human realm. What happens beyond this is our judgment: God is not to be caught with human attributes. Besides, where would the fear of God be if only good—i.e., what seems good to us—were to be expected of Him? (*CW* 11, para. 291)

12. The post-Freudian Jacques Lacan claimed that the unconscious was structured as a language.

Jung expressed an interest early in his career with Christian Gnosticism, and in mid-life he became deeply immersed in the study of medieval alchemical texts. The historical links between Jewish alchemists and the kabbalists have been explored by Scholem (Berlin et al. 2004), Idel (1990), Patai (1995), and others. The sixteenth-century kabbalist Chayim Vital, in his autobiographical statement to the introduction of *Etz Chayim*, describes having spent two years of his life practicing alchemy prior to abandoning it in order to study Kabbalah with Isaac Luria. Thus, it is likely that there were substantial areas of conceptual overlap between the Jewish alchemists and the Lurianic kabbalists (Vital 1988).

Jung was not fluent in Hebrew or Aramaic, the languages of the Hebrew Bible and the Talmud and *Zohar*, respectively, and it was only late in life that he became acquainted with the works of the Jewish mystics in German translation. By his own admission, however, he was struck by the parallels with his own psychological ideas (Drob 2000). Following a mild heart attack in 1944, he described the following kabbalistic vision in his autobiography *Memories, Dreams, Reflections*:

> Everything around me seemed enchanted. At this hour of the night the nurse brought me some food she had warmed. For a time it seemed that she was an old Jewish woman, much older than she actually was and that she was preparing ritual kosher dishes for me. When I looked at her she seemed to have a blue halo around her head. I was myself so it seemed in the *Pardes Rimmonim*, the Garden of Pomegranates and the wedding of *Tiferet* with *Malchut* was taking place. Or else, I was Rabbi Simon bar Yochai, whose wedding in the afterlife was being celebrated. It was the mystical marriage as it appears in the Kabbalistic tradition. I cannot tell you how wonderful it was. (Jung 1989, 294)

Jung was clearly inspired by the Zoharic myth, and it profoundly influenced his ideas in *Mysterium Coniunctionis*, which he personally viewed as his ultimate statement on the unconscious (Jung 1955).

The impulse to reify symbols in order to make them more accessible to the ego is encouraged in Jungian analysis. This parallels Christianity's incarnation of the Godhead, as Christ Jesus becomes an accessible image for devotion. As Jung notes, "It is impossible to demonstrate God's reality to oneself except by using images which have arisen spontaneously or are sanctified by tradition. . . ." (*CW* 11, para. 558). Note that Jung's approach to God is distinct from that of philosophers like Maimonides. Like the kabbalists, he adopts the kataphatic approach and is inclined to give substance to imagery in order to access affect, whereas the kabbalists applied symbolic imagery mostly to intimate the ever-changing relationships within the Godhead.

Jung's goal for psychoanalysis differs from Freud's. He does not focus on abrogating repetition compulsions, but instead he aims at achieving a conscious and felt experience of the archetypes, a process that he terms individuation.[13] The individuated person—it is important to note that Jung viewed Christ as the ultimate example of this, as he plainly states in his essay *Christ, A Symbol of the Self*—is consciously engaged throughout life with fate as determined by the expression of the archetypes (1951). Freedom for Jung, as in Christianity, is the result of successful individuation, which includes divesting oneself of the rules imposed by others, just as Luther in following Paul suggested that salvation was achieved only through faith (*sola fide*).

COMPLEMENTARITY

Like the Jewish mystics, Jung envisioned a bidirectional flow of information and complementary balance between consciousness and the unconscious, whereas Freud focused predominantly on the effects of the unconscious on consciousness. Freud saw no healing role for the unconscious, likely reflecting his negative view of God, while Jung postulated that the two systems of the psyche were engaged in a homeostatic dynamic, with the unconscious serving as a gyroscope that either complements or affirms the positions of the ego. In this

13. It is easy to imagine that through this goal Jung was also redeeming his father whose appreciation of the archetypes was evidently limited to reason and lacking in emotion.

regard, the unconscious serves as an innate corrective factor for what Jung referred to as the overly rational one-sidedness of consciousness. This has parallels with the Lurianic task of *tikkun ha olam*. Jung opined that modern man had become excessively reliant on consciousness and had consequently devalued the influences of the unconscious. It was this imbalance that was responsible for the emergence of the modern neuroses:

> Since the differentiated consciousness of civilized man has been granted an effective instrument for the practical realization of its contents through the dynamics of his will, there is all the more danger, the more he trains his will, of his getting lost in one-sidedness and deviating further and further from the laws and roots of his being. (*CW* 9, para. 276)

Jung claimed that the unconscious mirrors the perspective that the conscious mind adopts towards it, "We know that the mask of the unconscious is not rigid—it reflects the face we turn towards it. Hostility lends it a threatening aspect, friendliness softens its features" (*CW* 12, para. 79). Compare this to the statement by the sixteenth-century kabbalist R. Meir ibn Gabbai:

> What does "the Lord thy shadow mean"? Like the Lord, just as thy shadow laughs back when you laugh to it, and weeps if you weep to it, and if you show it an angry face or a pleasant face, so it returns, so is the Lord, the Holy One, blessed be He, thy shadow. Just as you are present with Him, so He is present with you. (quoted in Shoham 2013, 138)

At the end of his life, Freud fixed his attention on Moses, the prophet and lawgiver who led the ancient Israelites out of a state of spiritual unknowing in Egypt. From his letters to Fliess, it is apparent that Freud envisioned the insights of psychoanalysis as revelation, and as one that he had been chosen to receive and to transmit to the world, as previously noted by Yerushalmi (1991).

Like Moses, Freud had also made the lonely and dangerous journey, into himself, and passed his personal revelation on to others as psychoanalysis. Jung's descent into his unconscious was a comparable journey. But what each man necessarily discovered was their *own* unconscious, structured in part by their respective religious milieus.

CHAPTER 9

Revelation and Psychoanalysis

So watch yourselves carefully, since you did not see any form on the day that YHWH spoke to you at Sinai from the midst of the fire, so that you do not act corruptly and make a graven image for yourselves in the form of any figure, the likeness of male or female.

—Deuteronomy 4:15–16

REVELATION IN JUDAISM

The life of the mind may be imagined as a process of continuing revelation due to the emergence of contents from the unconscious into consciousness. This stream of consciousness, as William James referred to it, is an incessant flow of cognitions and affects, of which one is at best dimly aware.

In the psychology of Chabad Hasidism, thought is envisioned as the microcosm of how creation emerged ex nihilo from *En Sof*. According to the *Tanya*, the emergence of thought begins with an intuitive flash of wisdom (*chochmah*), whose source is within the unconscious (*En Sof*) (Zalman 2012). Through discernment (*binah*), this flash of intuition can be retained, isolated, and examined thoroughly by the mind. Jungian psychology considers discernment as prefigured within dreams by binary images or the number two, which discern what had been until then an amorphous unity. Once the idea has been carefully considered, it may be integrated into the mental repertoire as knowledge (*daat*), which then influences future thoughts and actions.[1]

These steps are reminiscent of the Freudian idea of working through in analysis, where early cognitive insights progressively deepen until they are no longer held apart from the repertoire of self. Once this task has been achieved, there is no longer a compulsion to repeat what had previously been dissociated from awareness. This process can take years in some cases, but it is critically important for the analyst to recognize the difference between the patient's having achieved cognitive insight (*binah*) and this deeper level of knowing (*daat*), as far too many analyses terminate with patients keenly aware of their neurotic issues but without having been divested of them.

As noted, the primary divine revelation in Rabbinic Judaism was the giving of the Torah at Sinai. Although generally translated as "Law," the word "Torah" is derived from the Hebrew root *hrh*, which means to instruct. In normative Rabbinic Judaism, God is imagined to interact with creation in two fundamental ways. God sustains the world through the effects of his ten utterances, so, as the *Tanya* suggests, if God were to cease to speak, all of Creation would immediately dissolve into nothingness. The other is the notion that the Torah, although given only once in historical time, remains available as God's source of continued revelation through study and inspired interpretation. Jewish scholars in all times have been encouraged to penetrate new intra- and

1. I have purposefully avoided specific examples from my psychoanalytical practice in this text because of my personal literary preferences. But the following anecdote is worth mentioning here. I once had a female patient who had a variety of issues, but one was the inability to do well in her course work. She would study at great length but when it came time to take the exam, she would invariably do poorly. I questioned whether she thought that she actually knew the material. It turned out that her professor was one of the rare Chabad Hasidim who was working in the secular world of academics. He was anxious to help her pass the course but also at a loss as to what to do next. She met with him on a frequent basis, and finally I suggested that she deliver the following message. She was not Jewish and knew nothing about Chabad philosophy. My message to her teacher was that she "has *binah* but not *daat*," which he understood immediately. We discussed this issue at some length in the treatment. The fact is the lack of *daat* is probably the greatest limiting factor in psychoanalysis.

inter-textual meanings via exegetical systems that promote insight into what is imagined as an inexhaustible divine will.

The Torah is considered the directly revealed wisdom of God. For Jews, the Torah is comparable to the Logos referred to in the Gospel of John 1:1. In Judaism it is said that, "God looked into the Torah and from it He created the world" (*Yalkut Shimoni*, *Mishlei* 942). The Torah was present before the world was created, and represented the wisdom of the Godhead. This concept was adopted by Christianity, but with Christ replacing the Law.

Jewish legal scholars and mystical adepts both engage in efforts at extracting the divine wisdom from the Torah. The exegete does so primarily through an intellectual probing of its text, with the belief that all divine knowledge is somehow embedded there. The Jewish mystic attempts to achieve insight into God by contemplating the deepest secrets of the Torah. Consider the following statements concerning the text of the Torah by the twelfth-century scholar and kabbalist Moshe ben Nachman (Nachmanides) in his commentary on Genesis (Ramban 2009):

> The reason for the Torah being written in this form (namely, the third person) is that it preceded the creation of the world, and needless to say, it preceded the birth of Moses our teacher. It has been transmitted to us by the tradition that it (the Torah) was written with letters of black fire upon a background of white fire. Thus, Moses was like a scribe who copies from an ancient book, and therefore he wrote anonymously. . . . (8)
>
> We have yet another mystic tradition that the whole Torah is comprised of Names of the Holy One, blessed be He, and that the letters of the words separate themselves into Divine Names when divided in a different manner, as you may imagine by way of example that the verse of Bereshit divides itself into these other words: *berosh yitbateh Elo-kim*. (13–14)
>
> It would appear that the Torah "written with letters of black fire upon a background of white fire" was in this form we have mentioned, namely, that the writing was contiguous,

> without break of words, which made it possible for it to be read by way of divine Names and also by way of our normal reading which makes explicit the Torah and the commandment. It was given to Moses our teacher using the division of words which expresses the commandment, and orally it was transmitted to him in the rendition which consists of the Divine Names. (14–15)

The centrality of the Torah is highlighted by its public reading, which is the apogee of the liturgical service. Yet despite its unique role as divine revelation, the Torah is a text that consists of words and narratives, some straightforward, others vague and obscure. For traditional Jews, studying the Torah in its original Hebrew is essential for proper interpretation. The experience of Torah study is primarily a cognitive-linguistic exercise. Generally, its text is read out loud and then memorized. It is chanted with a consensually agreed upon musical notation that also serves as its proper punctuation.[2] While the Torah can be an evocative text, large portions of it are legalistic and repetitive. In the *Zohar*, Simeon bar Yochai comments that when the Torah is evaluated as a text per se, others might be judged as more interesting or enjoyable. But once accepted as divine revelation, it becomes idealized and holy, and no text can possibly be of greater relevance. Consequently the Torah must be repeatedly interrogated for its deeper meanings. Jewish mystics have mined the text for millennia in pursuit of new meanings, but they have never ignored its superficial meaning, as this determines the proper observance of its precepts.

Certainly, one can comment on the Torah in translation, but the actual letters and trilateral roots of the Hebrew language supply a level

2. The Torah is written on a parchment scroll without punctuation or vowels. Its standardized format was determined by the Masoretes and the oldest known Masoretic text was the Aleppo Codex. It is read ideally without error, and two individuals (*gabbaim*) carefully scrutinize the reading and correct any mistakes that have been made. If a single letter of a written Torah is in error, the entire scroll is invalidated.

of depth to interpretation that is lost in translation. Indeed, a major source of controversy between Judaism and Christianity was rooted in the fact that the latter based its interpretations on the text of the Septuagint, a third-century-BCE translation of the Hebrew text into Greek. This translation, like all others, involves interpretation. An outstanding example surrounds the translation of the Hebrew term *almah* into the Greek word for virgin, *parthenos*.

The Hebrew word *almah* in Isaiah 7:14, means young woman. An *almah* can be a virgin (*parthenos*), however, the word does not necessarily connote virginity. In fact, *almah* occurs seven times in the Hebrew Scriptures and none of these examples demand the translation of "virgin." The theologically critical notion of the virgin birth of Jesus as suggested in the Gospel of Matthew results from a mistranslation within the Septuagint, the biblical text adopted by the early Christian exegetes.

CHRISTIAN REVELATION

The primary revelation for Christianity is not the Torah, but the incarnation and resurrection of Jesus Christ, which supersedes the Law. Therefor the Hebrew Bible—there was no other Bible at the time—was no longer considered a binding covenant, but was instead read allegorically and typologically for its imagined predictions of the arrival of Christ.

What is critically important for the Christian psyche is Christ as the embodied image of God, a heavenly *anthropos* who could be seen, touched, and worshipped.[3] Christianity transformed the ineffable Godhead into the reified image of the Son of God, who, according to orthodox Christian theology, was the manifest hypostasis of a trinitarian Godhead.

3. Controversies concerning the role of imagery are not limited to Judaism or Islam but have surfaced at various times in Christianity, most notably with the question of iconography in the Eastern Orthodox Church. Iconoclasts argued that worship of icons was heresy and undermined the tenets of monotheism. Those who supported the use of icons argued that it was proper to revere them rather than to worship them; this group eventually prevailed.

Whether his earliest followers conceived of Jesus as part of the Godhead proper, or of one substance (*homousia*) with the Father and Holy Spirit, as the dogma of the Trinity suggests, is doubtful. However, there is reason to believe that the eponym Son of Man, which occurs in the book of Daniel written circa 165 BCE, referred not simply to a human being, as the eminent religious scholar Geza Vermes argued (Vermes 1981), but to a divine figure, although one not necessarily equivalent to God as the Nicene Creed, adopted by the church in 313 CE suggests (Ehrman 2014).

As the death and resurrection of Christ is the central revelation of Christianity, the apogee of the Christian liturgical service is the mass, in which the Eucharistic meal of Jesus' blood and flesh are transubstantiated and ingested by the congregant, who is expected to experience the bread and wine as body and flesh of the divine sacrifice. Christianity shares this element with Mithraism, an ancient Mediterranean mystery religions that was current in the first-century Roman Empire. (Patterson 1921). The Mithraic communion liturgy included the words, "He who will not eat of my body and drink of my blood, so that he will be made one with me and I with him, will not know salvation" (Vermaseren 1959, 101). This notion shares no features with any of the Second Temple sects of Judaism, which traditionally abhorred the ingestion of blood as the result of repeated biblical proscriptions in that regard.[4]

Abraham Ha Rav Kook (Figure 9), the chief rabbi of Palestine during the mandate years, suggested that Judaism was a system constantly in flux with both a spiritual component and a religious one, the latter referring to the practice of ritual Law (Yaron 1991). Adopting a Hegelian approach, Kook imagined that the current emphasis on rabbinic legalism was necessary in order to maintain the coherence of Judaism while in exile. However, Kook argued that with the establishment of the Jewish State of Israel, it was time for Judaism to reclaim its original level of spirituality, emphasizing that it is the balance between the material and spiritual elements that distinguishes Judaism from

4. Mithraism was the obvious source of many features in Christianity including the birth date attributed to Jesus. Mithra was also born on December 25th, corresponding with the winter solstice.

Figure 9. Avraham Ha Rav Kook, the chief rabbi of Israel during the Palestinian mandate. Kook was a scholar, poet, and a visionary.

Christianity, and from Eastern soteriologies that seek to abandon the physical world. Kook viewed the events of recent history as moving in a direction to restore the importance of a spiritualized Judaism against what he viewed as the bankrupt ideas of atheistic secularism, which he attributed ultimately to Christianity's shedding of the Law.

Virtually all monotheistic religions seek to explain how the One becomes many. The kabbalists in their reference to the emanations of the *sefirot* describe a multipartite Godhead; however, in view of their orthopraxy, and their professed confession of the unity of God, they were never considered heretics as the early Christians were. Heresy is rarely acted against in Judaism—Christianity and the Karaite sect were exceptions—as the rabbinic commentaries generally tend to make room for conflicting ideas. Christianity having arisen from an apocalyptic sect has traditionally been less tolerant. Scores of heresies were identified by the church and dealt with severely.

The aim of Judaism is to develop an abiding faith in God based on a life immersed in the observance of the Law. The rituals of daily life in Judaism are viewed as an ongoing meditation on the Law, one achieved via coordinated right intentions and the right actions.[5]

5. The language adopted in this phrase was purposefully chosen to mimic the traditions of Hinduism and Buddhism where they most clearly are stated. The many

Action requires a material world, so that adopting a one-sided focus on spirituality is anathema for Judaism, as the corporeal realm must be sanctified, and neither devalued nor denied. This focus on the physical world extended to what was expected of a Jewish messiah, as explained by Maimonides in his *Mishneh Torah*.

Judaism, like most great religions, presents a complete soteriology. It addresses how to conduct oneself at all times, how to be healed both emotionally and physically, ideas concerning the redemption of this world, and references to an afterlife. However, emphasis on the afterlife was downplayed by Rabbinic Judaism, likely in reaction to the importance placed on it by Christianity. Indeed, many non-traditional Jews are unaware that Judaism includes beliefs in resurrection and reincarnation.[6] In its emphasis on physicality and the present world, Judaism is unique amongst the world's monotheistic religions.

Christianity's struggle with the body and materiality, on the other hand, dates to its inception. Whereas there is no clear understanding of what actually constitutes the Kingdom of God preached by Jesus, there are several indications in the New Testament and in the apocryphal writings available to first-century readers that the early church preached a radical split between spirit and matter. The corporeal world was seen—much as it was for the Platonists whose ideas influenced the direction of the early church—as a distraction and obstacle to the eternal life of the soul, and one that could, in part, be shed in this life by ascetic practices. Consider Jesus' statement in Matthew 19:24 that, "It is easier for a camel to pass through the eye of a needle, than for a rich man to enter into the Kingdom of Heaven," or Paul's in 1 Corinthians 7:8–9 that, "I say therefore to the unmarried and widows, it is good for them if they abide even as I. But if they cannot contain, let them marry: for it is better to marry than to

parallels between Judaism and the great religions of India is a large separate topic that cannot be addressed here.

6. The liturgy of Reform Judaism has expurgated references to resurrection of the dead and Conservative prayer books have also tended to downplay such references as well as those that petition for the restoration of the Temple sacrificial cult.

burn." Such negative ideas about the material world and sexuality are foreign to Judaism, which abhors neither wealth nor carnal relations.

But the Law can weigh heavily on some of its practitioners, as Paul confesses in Romans 7:14–25:

> I am carnal, sold under sin . . . I can will what is right, but I cannot perform it. For I fail to practice the good deeds I desire to do, but the evil deeds that I do not desire to do are what I am [ever] doing . . . [I am] a prisoner to the law of sin that dwells in my bodily organs . . . I [with mind and heart] serve the Law of God, but with the flesh the law of sin.

Paul's devaluation of the Law as an unnecessary element of divine revelation, in favor of the divine incarnation of the Logos-as-Christ, represented a profound antinomic turning away from the other Second Temple sects of Judaism.

The fact is that Jewish observance of the Law does not expect or require perfection. Paul appears to have brought his own rigid perfectionistic ideas to the observance of Judaism. He apparently could not abide the pressures of his own harsh super-ego, and as a consequence longed to be free of the Law. A similar mindset is seen in the sixteenth-century writings of Martin Luther, who also chose to dispose of the law as it manifested in the Roman Catholic idea of works, replacing it with the salvific notion of faith alone in what became the Protestant Reformation. Luther's psychobiography by the psychoanalyst Erik Erikson highlights the intensely obsessional nature of "young man Luther," and his pathological level of self-castigation (Erickson 1963). For both Paul and Luther, discarding the Law was a personal attempt to achieve freedom from guilt. This attitude persists within modern secular society, which currently values personal freedom over either works or belief.

Harsh super-ego stances tend to split experience into valenced positions. In this regard, apocalyptic Christianity viewed good and evil as autonomous domains represented by God and Satan, respectively. It ignored the teachings of Isaiah 45:7, in which YHWH exclaims that,

"I make light and darkness, I create peace and what is bad," as the credo of monotheism. Christianity undermines strict monotheism by virtue of its acceptance of a trinitarian Godhead. Certainly, most Christian theologians would argue against this, maintaining that the trinitarian notion merely reflects the facets of an indivisible Godhead. They might also rightly point to similar trends in the Jewish Kabbalah. However, the Jewish mystics refer to the various perceived characteristics of God and not to co-equal aspects of the Godhead, as is the case in Christianity. Furthermore, the multipartite model of the Godhead is in fact dismissed by the kabbalists as a metaphor that must not be reified; this is not the case for Christianity. An embodied Godhead cannot be identified anywhere in Judaism, and the reification of Christ as pure God and pure man is foreign to it.

THE ROLE OF RELIGION IN THE STRUCTURING OF THE UNCONSCIOUS

Based on this, one can easily imagine that the unconscious of a traditional Christian might be structured distinctly from that of a traditional Jew. The compartmentalization of good and evil is strongly established in the Christian unconscious, a fact that even Jung bemoaned as problematic, for as such it is unduly prone to projection, which contributes to the materialization of evil at both the interpersonal and socio-political levels, and to the inability to integrate negative affects into consciousness (Jung and Stein 1996). Jung was very aware of how what he termed the shadow, those elements of experience that are judged as negative by the ego, which if not recognized tend to wreak havoc in projection.

It is to say that the propensity to allegorically spiritualize texts and to mythologize is also more deeply rooted in the Christian than in the Jewish psyche. Judaism has its myths, but it has traditionally rejected myths that include theogonies, such as the virgin birth, as the historian of ancient Judaism Yechezkel Kaufmann points out (Kaufmann 1972). Whereas Freud saw the value of myth in psychology, it was Jung who posited a primary role for mythopoiesis in the psyche.

The priority of the image is inherent in the notion of an incarnated God, who can be consciously imagined, represented in religious art, and worshipped. Jung's psychological approach prioritizes the image over narratives; it is essentially a continuation of the Christian tradition. As the former Pope Benedict XVI, Joseph Cardinal Ratzinger, concedes, different modes of exegesis necessarily yield to different notions of God, an idea that is extended here to include different notions of the unconscious mind, and therefore also to psychoanalysis as a mode of investigation and treatment.

THE PERSISTENCE OF RELIGIOUS DIFFERENCE IN A SECULAR WORLD

Increasingly, Jews and Christians are living in proximity to one another in the West, and without the traditional limitations that were made on contact between the two religions. As part of the post-Holocaust tradition, Christianity has shown an increased awareness, and acceptance, of the Judaism of the historical Jesus.

But for two millennia these religions defined themselves in opposition to one another, until the fault lines between the two religions became unbridgeable (Boyarin 2006). Although Judaism has never been devoid of spiritual impulses, or Christianity of its interest in the material world—especially after it became clear that the Second Coming was not imminent—the issue of materialism versus spirituality was a dividing line between the two religions. The Church Fathers insisted on viewing Judaism as invalid due to its unwillingness to accept the supersession of the Law; the rabbis rejected Christianity as an essentially pagan tradition that had corrupted the intentions of the Law.

Jung attempted to explain the differences between his approach to psychoanalysis and those of Freud and Adler by proposing that distinct personal typologies were responsible (Jung 1921). He claimed that Freud's emphasis on sexuality and Adler's on power dynamics differed from his own focus on the spiritual aspects of the psyche, and attributed this to the different ego functions dominating their personalities. But when viewed from this perspective, Jung's position is essentially the same as that traditionally adopted by the church in its derision of Judaism. Freud and Adler, both secular Viennese Jews, tended to focus primarily on the material world rather than the spiritual one, the latter being of paramount importance to Christianity and Jung.

It is noteworthy that the abandonment of traditional religious beliefs may have little bearing on their continued influence. The secular mind is essentially entrenched in religious values. It is currently difficult to know whether or how the modern secular unconscious is being restructured.[7]

7. In 2015, the once highly devout Catholic nation of the Republic of Ireland voted to accept gay marriage in the face of strong opposition by the Catholic Church. A month later the United Sates Supreme Court made it illegal to deny the legality of gay marriage, arguing that it was an inalienable right. Obviously, much has changed since the days of Freud and Jung. But rapid changes are not necessary stable or enduring. Only time will tell.

CHAPTER 10

Eros and Sexuality

Civilization is a process in the service of Eros, whose purpose is to combine single human individuals, and after that families, then races, peoples and nations, into one great unity, the unity of mankind. Why this has to happen, we do not know; the work of Eros is precisely this.

—Sigmund Freud

Freud stressed the primary importance of the sexual drive within the unconscious. For him, it stood to reason that the psychic apparatus would necessarily be dedicated to representations of sexuality. Freud limited his use of the term libido to the sexual drive, although he also included its possible canalizations with respect to the individual and society at-large. Following the dictum that ontology recapitulates phylogeny, he developed a complex theory of how sexuality progressively matures through psychological phases in which the libidinal drive is cathected to various body parts, until it achieves mature genital sexuality. He argued, contrary to Jung, that the essence of neurosis was the stunting of sexual maturation by traumatic developmental inhibition or overly repressive societal attitudes. Inhibited sexuality, according to Freud, interferes with sexual performance and pleasure, limits healthy interpersonal relationships due to phobic avoidance, and results in psychological immaturity.

Freud addressed the notion of creativity in his theory of libido. He saw the mature limit-setting of sexuality by consciousness, what he termed sublimation, as the primary requirement for creativity and the most advanced form of ego defense. The highest psychological attainment, according to Freud, was to work, love, and assume responsibility, without suffering crippling intrapsychic conflicts. In *Civilization and Its Discontents*, he outlined the opposing tensions between the demands of sexual libido and those of a rigorously ordered society, and suggested that when the demand for order is excessive, human sexuality necessarily suffers (Freud 1930).

Taylor attributes this insistence on order to an obsession with structuring society following the European Reformation (Taylor 2007). In medieval times, the celebration of carnivals and common public displays of bodily functions, birth, death, and sexuality helped society maintain a limited but necessary degree of disorder. But after the Reformation, messy public displays were either banned or forced behind closed doors, and increasingly perceived as shameful. By the Victorian era, sexual prohibitions were widespread, as were psychoneuroses, a phenomenon that Freud was hoping to reform with psychoanalysis.

Freud defined sublimation as the process of deflecting sexual instincts into acts of higher social valuation, being "an especially conspicuous feature of cultural development; it is what makes it possible for higher psychical activities, scientific, artistic or ideological, to play such an important part in civilized life" (Freud 1930, 79–80). But how libido is sublimated is never clearly explicated by Freud. He suggests that sexuality is transfigured by the ego in the service of creativity and socialization. Yet according to the psychoanalyst Volney Gay, transfiguration is a concept properly limited to religious thought, e.g., the transfiguration of Jesus in the synoptic Gospels. According to Gay (Gay 1992):

> . . . psychoanalysis per se cannot provide a complete explanation of sublimated behaviors. They lie beyond its ken. Psychoanalysis is the *scientific* study of the transformation of instinctual drives, not of their transfiguration. To be transformed is to be changed from one form into another according

> to natural laws. To be transfigured is to be *exalted, glorified, and raised from one state to a higher one.* (110; italics in original)

The psychologist Mordecai Rotenberg opined that Rabbinic Judaism had already discovered the idea of sublimation, as part of its musings on the *yetzer*. The term *yetzer* is cognate to *yetzirah* ("creation") (Rotenberg 2004). According to Rotenberg, "The non-repressive *yetzer-yetzirah* sequence strives allegedly to inculcate a reading-writing system, which teaches how to channel part of the physical *yetzer* energy into the spiritual *yetzirah*" (2004, 42). In other words, the rabbis had already postulated that libidinal impulses could be spiritually transfigured as creation. If one accepts this argument, Freud's sublimation of the sexual drive is simply a reformulation of this rabbinic idea.

JUNG AND EROS

Jung generalized the concept of libido to include the entirety of psychic energy, rather than only the sexual drive, and his final break with Freud in large measure concerned their respective definitions of libido. Jung contested Freud's claim that the psyche was driven exclusively by the biological desire to procreate. Although Jung was also drawn to Darwin (Lawson 2008), he did not limit evolution to biology; instead he included a role in evolution for man's spiritual development as well.

Like William James, Jung adopted a pragmatic approach to religion, viewing it as a factor in man's search for meaning. For Jung, it was myth, rather than procreation, that motivated the psyche, as through mythopoiesis the unconscious was able to create narratives for the teleological purpose of moving man through the life cycle. For Jung, procreation was one aspect of the life cycle, but man was no longer merely a slave to sexual instinct.

Jung adopted the Platonic/Christian concept of *eros* as relatedness, rather than sexual desire. *Eros* had multiple aims that could be directed either intrasubjectively or interpersonally. For example, the relationship between the ego and the self was also erotic to the extent that it fostered their relatedness. Sexuality was, like libido, a critical subset of *eros*, but not the one that Jung chose to focus on in his theory. His perspective is perhaps best illustrated by his unusual treatment of analytical transference, in which he ignores its obvious sexual overtones, to focus instead on its spiritual implications (Jung 1946).

Jung's approach to *eros* is comparable to how both Jewish and later Christian mystics spiritually transfigured the Song of Songs, in which verses describing carnal sexuality were allegorized, in order to arrive at their true spiritual meaning: the love between God and Israel/church. Jung also conceived of medieval alchemy as an example of *eros* in pre-modern times, in which materials were brought into relationship with one another as reified aspects of psychological dynamics, in the service of their transformation. He would, late in life, discover that this had been addressed directly and thoroughly by the Jewish kabbalists.

In the Kabbalah, the complementary flux between the supernal worlds and that of the kabbalist was dependent on the proper practice of the Law and on intentionality, *kavvanot*, in its performance. The required dialogical interaction between man and God placed man in a role no less important than the repair of the soul and the entire cosmos (Starr 2008). Man's ability to act intentionally with the aim of reconciling the divine opposites in the Godhead (e.g., the characteristics of love and strictness) was unparalleled in Christianity, as the kabbalists envisioned God also as dependent on man. The kabbalists' actions elicited an unimpeded flow of divine energy into the lower worlds, fostering the welfare of creation. They concomitantly evoked a parallel intrapsychic flow aimed at promulgating wholeness within man-as-microcosm.

The psychological features of the Kabbalah would become increasingly evident in Hasidism, but they were by no means unknown to the medieval kabbalists (Rotenberg 2003). Indeed, a recent text by the religious historian Lawrence Fine (2003) on the life of R. Isaac Luria emphasizes his role as a psychological healer and his ability to read the nature of another's soul including its previous incarnations via a process referred to as metoscopy.

Although Jung's psychological theories are framed in terms that closely resemble those of the Jewish mystics, Freud's approach arguably comes closer to putting them into practice. As noted, the cardinal commandments in Judaism are to both love and fear God. Freud was well aware of the importance of love as a healing factor in psychoanalysis, although he saw it primarily in sexual terms. He refers to it as the positive erotic transference, but he does not ignore its potential pitfalls, as love and fear must always be considered together:

> So long as it is positive it serves us admirably. It alters the whole analytic situation; it pushes to one side the patient's rational aim of becoming healthy and free from his ailments. Instead of it there emerges the aim of pleasing the analyst and of winning his applause and love. It becomes the true motive force of the patient's collaboration; his weak ego becomes strong; under its influence he achieves things that would ordinarily be beyond his power; he leaves off his symptoms and seems apparently to have recovered—merely for the sake of the analyst. (Freud 1936, 53)

Freud recognized the critical importance of allowing positive transference, with its erotic and idealizing overtones, to mature before deconstructing it in analysis. But, he concomitantly emphasized the therapeutic role of abstinence in the treatment, so that the desires of the patient might be afforded clear boundaries, recapitulating the kabbalistic concept of harmonizing *Chesed* (love) with *Gevurah* (restriction).

Freud expressed this in his paper "Observations on Transference Love" (1915) and reiterated it in his correspondence with Sandor Ferenzci as follows: "I have elsewhere made it understood that the analytical technique requires of the physician that he deny to the patient the satisfaction that she demands. The analysis must be carried out in abstinence. . . ." (Hoffer 1991, 466) Compare this kabbalistic notion of balancing love with restriction (or law) with the theology of Christianity as espoused by Joseph Cardinal Ratzinger (1969):

> Excess is God's trademark in Creation; as the Fathers put it, "God does not reckon his gifts by the measure." Excess is the real foundation and form of salvation history, which in the last

> analysis is nothing other than the truly breathtaking fact that God, in an incredible outpouring of Himself expends not only the universe but his own self in order to lead man, a speck of dust, to salvation. (262)

This is a different understanding of the Godhead from that of the kabbalists. The Christian God is associated with unmitigated love; there is no restriction within Him. It is a beautiful concept, but can it be effectively applied in psychoanalysis? Does unmitigated love cure? Certainly, some analysts, including Ferenzci (1994) and Carl Rogers (1989) have suggested that it does, and that one must aim at abrogating the super-ego in analysis. But the Freudian literature is replete with clinical examples of excessive analytical love turning out badly for both the analyst and patient, and I am not referring here only to love in an enacted physical way, but also the failure to provide structured boundaries for patients who require a balance between empathy and interpretation (Josephs 1996). Obviously this is an important difference of opinion, but one that appears to have its roots in the tenets and beliefs of Judaism and Christianity.

NUMBER AND ARCHETYPE

Most diagrams depict the kabbalistic *sefirot* group as three inverted triangles with the sefirotic opposites displayed on the right and left hand sides of the inverted base of the triangle, and the third *sefira* located below and in the middle, as the product of the balanced union of the two (e.g., *Chesed, Gevura, and Tiferet*). If *Chesed* is defined as love or grace, which is the standard definition, and *Gevurah* as restriction, law, or abstinence, as is also the case, then *Tiferet* in psychological terms is compassion or mercy, in that it represents the optimal balance of these two extremes.

Jung ascribed an important role in psychology to the number three and to triangles. He imagined numbers and shapes as archetypes—note the parallel with *Sefer Yetzirah*—and triangles as symbols capable of transmitting psychic energies in the vectorial direction of their apex, much as the kabbalists did. However, it was Freud who first recognized the importance of the triangulated situation in the family romance of the Oedipal myth. But unlike Jung, he chose not to investigate the role of numbers as such within the psyche.[1]

Jung suggested that the continued tension between opposites evoked a psychological transcendent function that served to direct the libidinal energies of the psyche beyond the conflict of opposites, i.e., to a new position in which they were reconciled, and conflict was transcended—reminiscent of the middle path of the kabbalistic model. But Jung does not discuss how the opposites are to be reconciled in the here and now, which is precisely the importance of the transference, in which love and abstinence are enacted in real time, according to Freud. Instead, Jung appears to imply that their reconciliation occurs spontaneously, as the consequence of a spiritually driven Hegelian dynamic of thesis, antithesis, and synthesis, which manages to divest the previously conflicted situation of intrapsychic importance:

> From the activity of the unconscious there now emerges a new content, constellated by thesis and antithesis in equal measure and standing in a compensatory relation to both. It thus forms the middle ground on which the opposites can be united. If, for instance, we conceive the opposition to be sensuality versus spirituality, then the mediatory content born out of the unconscious provides a welcome means of expression for the spiritual thesis, because of its rich spiritual associations, and also for the sensual antithesis, because of its sensuous imagery. The

1. Jung's understanding of numbers as archetypes may be supported by certain observations made by theoretical physicists in the last century. When mathematically modeling the behavior of two particles, physicists are able to come to a complete solution of the equations that describe their behavior. However, once a third particle is added the equations break down and cannot be solved with accuracy, suggesting that there is something intrinsically difficult about three in relationship, as is well known from psychological observation. However, even the Platonists and Pythagoreans recognized that mathematics could not be applied with perfect accuracy to the real world, especially as a result of dynamic change. So mathematics only approximates reality but does not actually reflect it.

> ego, however, torn between thesis and antithesis, finds in the middle ground its own counterpart, its sole and unique means of expression, and it eagerly seizes on this in order to be delivered from its division. (*CW* 6, para. 825)

Regardless of its mode of action, the transcendent function for Jung primarily directs the patient's psyche to a new spiritual level.

Jung envisioned the archetypes of the collective unconscious as the source of psychological healing. He refers to this in his description of the cause and treatment of depression (1916). According to Jung, depression resulted from a diminished flow of psychic energy from its source in the unconscious, due to diminished receptivity of the ego. He describes this in terms of fairy tales, in which the old king and his kingdom are floundering in a state of decay and must be revivified by the arrival of a new youthful hero. This is akin to the dryness that the kabbalists describe when *Malchut* is separated from *Tiferet*, and the perceived need to stimulate the feminine waters (*mayim nuvkim*) from below in order to evoke a comparable flow from the masculine Godhead above—a graphic reference to physical sexuality.

Jung refers to the ego's need to engage in activities that naturally stimulate the unconscious, including active imagination, excursions into nature, or other creative efforts, in order to overcome a deficit in intrapsychic *eros*. The kabbalists' activities were instead primarily aimed at re-uniting the tenth *sefira*, *Malchut* (*shekhinah*), referred to in the *Zohar* by a host of feminine—and occasional masculine—symbols, who was separated from her male counterpart *Tiferet*. Their congress fostered the renewed flow of creative energies and plenitude into the world.[2]

2. This inclusion of the feminine element within the structure of the Godhead is often ignored by those who refer to the monotheistic God as purely masculine. Indeed, it appears to reflect an ancient notion, and one that Jung reintroduced in his psychology, that wholeness requires the union of both masculine and feminine characteristics, which Jung refers to as reintegrating the *anima* in a man and the *animus* in a woman.

During the weekdays, the kabbalist focused on elevating his own mental state to the level of *Malchut*, but on the Sabbath the supernal coupling was also ritually reenacted by the kabbalist with his wife. Their sexual congress was imagined as an *imitatio* of *Malchut* and *Tiferet*, as well as a worldly act aimed at procreation. This emphasis on carnal sexuality is a critical idea within Judaism, which demands and values procreation, and has rejected the celibacy esteemed by the Roman Church. Certainly, ascetic inclinations have periodically emerged in Judaism (e.g., the Qumran community and the medieval Ashkenazic Hasids), but these invited criticism.

Like the rabbis, Freud emphasizes the importance of life in the material world, including a healthy physical sexuality. Jung, like Christianity, instead places his primary focus on the spiritual aspects of relatedness, or *agape*. There is virtually nothing in Jung's writings that expounds in detail on sexuality or the body.

Jung borrows from Jewish mysticism, but he neglects its focus on the physical world. Although he did espouse the importance of grounding individuals whose thinking or intuition were overdeveloped by encouraging them to attend to sensate details and feelings, his primary aim was to revitalize the psyche spiritually.

The conflict between sexuality and spirituality is by no means specific to a particular religion or form of psychoanalysis; rather it a straw man that is revisited by every generation. It is always possible to conceive of a relationship in both physical and spiritual terms. Being encouraged to choose one over the other creates an illusory and problematic material/spiritual divide, whereas an inclusive approach yields to both the demands of materialism and metaphysics. History repeatedly demonstrates that unbridled spirituality, as Paul discovered, tends to result in elitism and antinomianism that undermines the stability of the community. This was particularly unacceptable to Judaism, where the survival of the community has always been highly valued. Although individual life is also greatly esteemed, in times of duress a Jew may be called upon to give up his life in order to maintain the sanctity of God's name (*kiddush ha shem*) and to preserve the sacral integrity of the larger religious group. As former Chief Rabbi of Great Britain Rabbi Jonathan Sacks noted in his discussion of the Torah portion *Ki Tissa* in 2008:

> They (Jews) will suffer humiliation, persecution, even torture and death because of the name they bear and the faith they profess, but they will stay true to the covenant their ancestors made with You. They will go to their deaths saying *Ani maamin*, "I believe." This is a people awesome in its obstinacy—and though now it is their failing, there will be times far into the future when it will be their noblest strength.

CHAPTER 11

The Symbolic Realm

To be effective, a symbol must be by its very nature unassailable.

—Carl Jung

Jung and the kabbalists shared an appreciation for symbols in mental life. Unlike the Maimonidean approach of the *via negativa*, the *Zohar* provides a set of symbols with seemingly inexhaustible and changing referents that intimate, but do not reify, the divine attributes. Via this kataphatic approach, the kabbalists provided a means for the individual to imagine and participate in a parallel dynamic between intrapsychic and cosmic events, without allowing the mind to rest comfortably on a specific image. This approach effectively transforms nouns into verbs.[1] As Arthur Green suggests, whereas Maimonides in the spirit of the philosophers sought to divest the mind of any preconceived anthropomorphic notions of God, the kabbalists chose instead to flood the mind with divine images in order to achieve a comparable result (2003).

Both modes of Jewish mystical experience are encountered in Hasidism and the Lurianic Kabbalah. The *Tanya* transforms the Lurianic concept of divine constriction (*tzimtzum*) and emanation into a theosophy of paradox that resembles Maimonidean thought by highlighting the importance of intellection. The willed contraction of the Godhead

1. In a totally different time and place, the jazz musician John Coltrane attempted to deconstruct static chordal structures by playing each note of the chord sufficiently rapidly that it was deconstructed and transformed into a flux of notes.

is the source of creation in the Lurianic Kabbalah, for only after a potential space had formed in the Godhead could something new emerge. However, *tzimtzum* in Chabad theosophy is defined as a virtual emptying, a progressive dimming of divine light as witnessed from man's perspective, but from its source in the Godhead (*En Sof*) no change had occurred.[2] R. Schneur Zalman offers the example of light from the fiery globe of the sun that is experienced by man with greatly diminished intensity, whereas from the perspective of the sun there has been no change in its strength. Jewish philosophies insist that no change can occur in the Godhead, taking Malachi 3:6 as a proof text: "I, the Lord do not change."

This panentheistic acosmic theory views *tzimtzum* and all material reality to be paradoxical; the material world is at once both real and virtual. It is noteworthy that Chabad fosters a quietistic mode of mediation that strives towards the emptying of the self (*bitul*) in order to make room for an appreciation of the immanent fullness of God. However, these quietistic imageless states are not devoid of affect. Instead, like the descriptions of nirvana in Eastern psychologies, they are experienced as blissful, implying an outpouring of positive affect that accompanies the meditative achievement of the "fullness and nothingness" of *ayin* (Uffenheimer 1993).[3]

For some practical kabbalists, symbols served as reified nodes that could be contemplated in order to deepen trance in their imaginal approach to the divine (Idel 1990). Jung early in his career had suggested that affect was physiologically embedded within images and that the path towards its cathartic release was to imaginally attempt to reify the image. He believed that modern man's modern prioritizing of cognition had weakened his ability to experience imagery directly, which in turn interfered with the metabolism of affect.

---

2. Interestingly, this question of relative perspective may have been an influence on another twentieth-century Jewish genius, as it shares elements with Einstein's special theory of relativity.
3. The idea of emptiness is also encountered in Christianity as *kenosis* and in Buddhism as *sunyatta*.

Consequently, Jung encouraged working with images as part of dreamwork as well as in active imagination (Jung 1967). But his aim diverges from the Jewish mystical notion of *devekut*, in which the practitioner is encouraged to focus on images, not in order to release repressed affect, but to experience the bliss of divine immanence. Nevertheless, these approaches are not altogether distinct.

In contrast to Jung's notion of the symbol, which resembles that of the early Church Fathers and the Greek philosophers, the Freudian symbol is limited, as it is generally interpreted as a representation of a sexual wish. Israeli historian of Kabbalah Yehuda Liebes has argued that the symbols of the *Zohar* are projections of the kabbalist's repressed sexual desires (1993), and Bakan (1958) and Drob (2000) have made comparable suggestions. There can be little doubt that sexuality was a topic of considerable interest for the author(s) of the *Zohar*. In addition, Freud, Jung, the kabbalists, the alchemists, and the Christian Gnostics all displayed an interest in symbols of bisexuality and hermaphroditism (Mopsik 2005), representing the original state of man as reflected in Platonic myth and in Genesis 1:27.

However, reducing the religious impulses of the kabbalists to repressed sexual desire misses the point, as Jung suggested in his criticism of Freud's theory. Choosing between sexual and spiritual interpretations is not only unnecessary, but it can be psychologically a disservice to do so. Winnicott, for example, argued for not defining the transitional object for the infant, but instead allowing paradox to develop into intrapsychic tension without forcing artificial choices between seemingly irreconcilable positions (1959). This psychological advance must be carefully distinguished from neurotic ambivalence, in which rapidly alternating choices occur or doubt concerning choice may become paralyzing.

In Chabad psychology, the individual is encouraged to know his mind from within his inner being as embodied knowledge (*daat*), and not simply via ephemeral cognitions. The individual is asked to act out of conviction from an authentic core, and to avoid manic choices between anxiety-provoking possibilities. As the neurobiologist Anthony Damasio has argued, normal decision requires affective valence, and in its absence confident choices cannot be made, a problem that affects neurotic individuals whose affect is restricted (1994).

In the remainder of this text, the specific techniques, relationships, and disorders that characterize psychoanalysis will be examined together with the religious tenets that influenced them, beginning with the historical origins of psychoanalysis in dream interpretation.

CHAPTER 12

Dreams and Midrash

The dream is a little hidden door in the innermost and most secret recesses of the soul, opening into that cosmic night which was psyche long before there was ego consciousness, and which will remain psyche no matter how far our ego consciousness extends.

—Carl Jung

FREUD'S INTERPRETATION OF DREAMS

Freud claimed to have penetrated the secrets of the unconscious mind via the interpretation of dreams. He viewed the dream as the *via regia* of the unconscious, and as a communication that, once decoded, allowed the analyst to assess the state of the patient's unconscious (1900). His approach to dreams was a natural extension of his perspectives on the nature of the unconscious, which he regarded with mistrust. Paul Ricoeur (1970) referred to this as Freud's hermeneutic of suspicion.

Bakan suggested that Freud was disguising crypto-Sabbatean mystical sources in his writings on psychoanalysis (1958). But it is more likely that Freud viewed his own unconscious as a potential source of danger, whose productions needed to be disguised from consciousness.[1]

1. This attitude is commonly encountered in individuals with rigid ego defenses, including personalities along the spectrum of obsessional and paranoid ideation, which may have included Freud. In such individuals, the contents of the unconscious are particularly prone to projection, and one may observe an extroverted stance, in order to avoid the perceived dangers of interiority.

From Freud's viewpoint, discovering the proper interpretation of dreams required someone capable of confronting and decoding their unpleasant implications, and he claimed to be that man. In the years prior to 1899, he undertook an analysis of his own dreams. Freud was never analyzed by another, although he did use his colleague Wilhelm Fliess as sounding board for his ideas. Freud had—or at least imagined that he had—the rare gift of highly developed ego objectivity that is required for examining one's own unconscious (Borch-Jacobsen and Shamdasani 2012). As Freud viewed it, his self-analysis was a unique historical event. It followed that individuals who wished to become psychoanalysts would either have to be trained by Freud, or by someone in a training lineage that led back to him. Only those analysts would be prepared to recognize properly the manifestations of the unconscious, thereby creating a chain of authoritative transmission, comparable to that described for the Oral Law in the *Ethics of the Fathers*.

Freud posited that the reported dream was expressed as a manifest narrative that, like the text of the Torah, was imbued with deeper secrets. In the dream's case for Freud, this was invariably a sexual wish, which he termed the latent dream. The Freudian approach to the dream is therefore a paranoid one, not in a pejorative sense, but by virtue of the term's actual meaning of "knowing around"—what is at the surface.

Freud reasoned that the latent dream, which expressed derivatives of the unconscious drives, was edited during sleep by an intrapsychic activity that he termed the dream censor (1900). Its purpose was to purge the latent dream's wish of ego-dystonic sexual meanings, by creating a veiled ego-syntonic narrative. Freud suggested that this was achieved via a set of linguistic stratagems that condensed and transformed the contents of the manifest dream. The dream interpreter's task was to reverse this process in order to arrive at the dream's actual meaning.

In practice, this involved asking the patient to free associate to the contents of the dream, while the analyst scanned these associations for evidence of the latent dream wish. Of course, based on Freud's perspective concerning the unconscious drives, this was presupposed to be a libidinal wish, so that the generic features of the interpretation were already known a priori. It was this bias that caused William James and others to question the validity of Freud's approach.

Dream interpretation was not new; it had been practiced from time immemorial. The importance of dreams in antiquity is discussed in the Talmud in *Berachot* 55b, in which Rav Chisda remarks: "A dream that has not been interpreted is like a letter that has not been read." Indeed, dreams play an important role within the Hebrew Bible. They structure the Joseph cycle in Genesis, as they foreshadow the dramatic events that will unfold, and the foreboding dream of Nebuchadnezzar, in which he seeks an interpretation of the writing on the wall, is a key narrative element in the book of Daniel.

In all of the dreams depicted within the Hebrew Bible, the interpreter takes no credit for his skill but instead advises others that it reflects an insight into God's will (i.e., the gift of prophecy). The pre-cognitive implication of dreams is noted in *Berachot* 57b where it states, "Dreams are 1/60th of prophecy." From a psychoanalytic perspective, it might be said that the biblical dream interpreter's intuition concerning the unconscious was somehow inspired.

A small sampling of Talmudic interpretations of dreams from *Berachot* 57 is cited below:

> If one dreams of a funeral oration mercy will be vouchsafed to him from heaven and he will be redeemed.
> If one dreams that he has intercourse with his mother, he may expect to obtain understanding, since it says, "Yea, thou wilt call understanding 'mother.'"
> If one dreams he has intercourse with a betrothed maiden, he may expect to obtain knowledge of Torah, since it says, "Moses commanded us a law, an inheritance of the congregation of Jacob."
> If one dreams he has intercourse with a married woman, he can be confident that he is destined for the future world, provided, that is, that he does not know her and did not think of her in the evening.

These interpretations are simplistic, particularly with respect to their reliance on fixed meanings taken out of context of the dreamer's experience. However, they suggest the ancient awareness of the dream as a metaphoric statement, and provide evidence that sexual images, including those of incest fantasy, were well-known in antiquity. The last example above refers to the "day residue," which Freud suggests in *The Interpretation of Dreams* can be incorporated into the manifest dream (1900). However, the rabbis recognized that the symbolic nature of dreams precluded any single correct interpretation. Whereas Freud imagined that he had discovered the secret to decoding a dream's meaning, he apparently was unaware of or chose to ignore the following statement in *Berachot* 55b:

> A dream is realized according to its interpretation: "There were twenty-four dream interpreters in Jerusalem. Once I dreamed a dream and went to all of them. What one said the next did not—and all came true, to uphold what is said: All dreams follow the mouth."

Freud's dream interpretation includes the analytical deconstruction of the manifest dream, Jung's the synthetic amplification of symbols. Freud's approach favors language, as it seeks to transform images into narratives. As previously noted by Bakan and others, Freud's method of dream interpretation shares features with rabbinic *midrash* (1958). *Midrash* represents the exegesis of a biblical text in order to arrive at a deeper meaning, just as the manifest dream is interpreted in order to identify the latent dream wish. Freud's notion of condensation and transposition of dream symbols resembles the operations described in *Sefer Yetzirah* as a mode of creativity. Similar methods were adopted within ecstatic Kabbalah, notably by R. Abraham Abulafia, and were later included in the mystical speculations of the Hasidism (Idel 1990).

It also parallels rabbinic *midrash*, in its propensity to read into the dream narrative (i.e., to superimpose interpretations that are not necessarily suggested by the dream's images directly, fostered by the technique of free association). According to the historian of Judaism David Weiss Halivni, in *Peshat* and *Derash* the "reading in" of meanings was an early element in the construction of the Oral Law (1998). In fact, the Oral Law that according to tradition was transmitted to Moses at Sinai, is not specifically referred to in rabbinic literature until the second century. It appears to have been the legacy of R. Akiva, who personally introduced many new laws that had no clear basis in the written Torah. In some instances, the plain meaning of the Law was revised in order to abrogate its original intention. Such was the case of the *Prozbul*, reputedly introduced by the first-century sage Hillel in order to suspend the Torah's statutes of forgiveness of debts in the last years of the seven-year cycle (*shmittah*), so that there would be no hesitancy on the part of lenders to extend credit, as this might lead to economic collapse in the community.

The technique of reading in was aimed at establishing rabbinic authority. Once rabbinic power was consolidated, the approach was abandoned and conservatism in interpretation rather than innovation became of paramount importance. Like the early rabbis, Freud did not feel compelled to adhere strictly to the images of the dream, as part of his purpose was to establish his sexual theory of psychoanalysis.

JUNG'S DREAM INTERPRETATION

Jung's criticism of Freud's approach to dream interpretation was that it focused excessively on a reductive analysis of a sexual wish and failed to recognize the extent of the dream's creativity (Jung 1945). But as communications from the unconscious, dreams exhibit both a shared and stereotypical quality and highly idiosyncratic features. Comparable to the exegesis of the revealed Torah, the potential meaning of dreams is virtually inexhaustible. Consider the statement of R. Isaac Luria:

> There are 600,0000 aspects and meanings in the Torah. According to each one of the ways of explaining the Torah, the root of the soul has been fashioned in Israel. In the Messianic age, every single man in Israel will read the Torah in accordance with his own root. (Scholem 1995b, 205)

Jung called for an image-bound approach to the dream (Jung 1945). He imagined dreams as a mode of psychological creativity, in which the unconscious selects, for obscure reasons, highly specific images in the service of creating a new symbolic narrative. Rather than being a meaningless concoction of images by a brain attempting to rid itself of toxic metabolites during sleep, as the late Nobel laureate Sir Francis Crick suggested (Crick and Mitchison 1983), dreams for Jung were microcosmic examples of nightly creation, meant to be witnessed by the dream-ego and shared with others for the purposes of communication and the co-construction of meaning. Like all acts of creation, dreams, for Jung, were the result of the novel transposition of previously learned ideas and images assembled via archetypal processes.

Dream interpretation plays an inordinately important role in Jungian analysis. Having de-emphasized the importance of transference dynamics, the practice of classical Jungian analysis is highly dependent on working with dream imagery.[2] Much like the *Zohar*,[3] which is awash in a sea of symbols each with multiple possible referents, Jung viewed the dream as a set of symbols with mythic and metaphysical implications. Jung referred to living symbols as having inexhaustible referents that always point beyond themselves, an idea meant to capture their spiritual potential. The repeated interpretation of a symbol via the same referents limits its meaning; this was Jung's criticism of the overuse of phallic and vaginal references in dreams, although Jung also tends to over apply certain meanings, (e.g., water for unconscious, house for psyche, etc.).

---

2. It must be recognized that Jungian, like Freudian, analysis has evolved over the last one hundred years. However, many of the innovations in the different theoretical schools of Jungian analysis have borrowed from the techniques of post-Freudian treatments (e.g., Self psychology, Kleinian analysis, etc.). Jung left no systematic writings on the topic of technique and may have been opposed to the idea. In the Jungian community, one observes large differences in the therapeutic styles and emphases of analysts.
3. Modern scholars like Yehuda Liebes have questioned whether Gikatilla, the author of *Shaarei Or*, may have in fact been one of a group of Castilian kabbalists who contributed to which offers an exhaustive number of referents for each of the sefirot the authorship of the *Zohar*. See Yehuda Liebes, *Studies in the Zohar* (Albany: SUNY Press: Albany, 1993).

Jung also objected to the method of free association, in which patients are encouraged to speak of whatever comes to mind without editing—no simple task—with respect to the dream images. Jung argued that that when allowed to free associate, patients time and again tended to discover their own complexes, thereby limiting the potential implications of their unconscious imaginings.

Another important idea in Jungian dream interpretation is related to the dream's inherent novelty, as it is expected to convey new information to consciousness that the ego previously had not been able to recognize or integrate. This includes repetitive dreams, which Hillman suggested may reflect the insistence of the image in reaction to the inability of the ego to integrate its implications (2014).

Jung insisted on amplifying the symbols of the dream based on their specific details; for example, a metal table in a dream is not the same as a wooden table, and such differences, no matter how subtle, said Jung, must be considered, and efforts made at interpreting them. To this end, he encouraged the technique of circumambulation (Jung 1967) of the dream image, amplifying associations, but always returning to it, as opposed to Freud's technique of free association. In analysis, this amplification of symbols may be achieved in dialogue with the patient, or at times by the analyst alone, who can subsequently choose an optimal time to introduce some new symbolic meaning with possible relevance to the dreamer.

For Jung, like Freud, the dream was the *via regia* to the unconscious, but from the former's perspective the ego and the unconscious act together as a homeostatic system, with the dream either complementing or compensating the ego's conscious position. This idea parallels that of Luria's notion of *tikkun*, as previously described. The unconscious and consciousness serve comparable positions to God and man in this dynamic of mutuality. The goal of dreaming, and its interpretation, according to Jung, was primarily to foster balance within the psyche, rather than to identify a repressed sexual wish.

The experience of working with Jung's mode of dream interpretation is difficult to explicate simply with clarity. The multiplicity of symbolic referents tends to create a network of new associations and essentially becomes a creation of the analyst and analysand. In some cases, the symbols may be related to mythological referents that Jung believed were guiding the individuation process, and this idea can produce an experience that feels potentially deeper, although at times less personal.[4]

Jung's approach of circumambulation of the image is nearly identical to that of the *Zohar*, where a symbolic image based on a biblical phrase is repeatedly revisited and expanded, sometimes for many pages within the text. The kabbalists approached the mystical structure of the Godhead by immersing themselves in a seemingly inexhaustible set of images concerning the relationships of the *sefirot*. As Pseudo-Dionysus the Areopagite noted with respect to kataphasis:

> There are too those other sacred pictures used to represent God, so that what is hidden may be brought out into the open and multiplied, what is unique and undivided, may be divided up, and multiple shapes and forms be given to what has neither shape nor form. All this is to enable the one capable of seeing the beauty hidden within these images to find that they are truly mysterious, appropriate to God and filled with a great theological light. (Henderson 2014, 17)

Unlike linguistic deconstruction that utilizes cognitive processes to construct rational meaning, the amplification of symbols fosters novel connections to the image and its associated affect, thereby intimating its deeper secret meaning. Liebes referred to this as the creative impulse of the authors of the *Zohar* (1993), whereas Jung referred to it as creativity in the service of the self.

Another parallel with the *Zohar* is Jung's statement that the images of the dream are not hidden per se but are, in fact, transparent

4. Although the Jungian focus on myth for some carries a certain numinosity and appears to link the individual to antiquity, it may be said that it reflects what has been alternatively termed the seven basic plots, which determine the number of human narratives that can be examined. This does not deny the mythopoietic potential of the unconscious but curiously does tend to de-mythologize it.

(Jung 1967) What Freud saw as a disguised manifest dream, Jung considered the natural expression of the symbolic unconscious. According to Jung, "Dreams do not deceive, they do not distort or disguise" (*CW* 7, para. 189). Like parables, the interpretation of imagery is accessible to those who have the capacity to think symbolically. But as symbols are ambiguous, they can reveal or conceal, depending on the audience. To those accustomed to thinking symbolically, the stories told via symbols are indeed transparent.

A famous parable in the *Zohar*, *Sava de Mishpatim* 2:99a, illustrates this point. It describes a young man who is attempting to court a maiden concealed behind a window within a tower. The maiden symbolizes the Torah; she exposes herself increasingly to the sight of her befuddled suitor, who symbolizes the scholar working at interpreting scripture. Slowly, and in an eroticized manner, the maiden reveals her secrets to her suitor. But in the end, it is apparent that all of her secrets had been obvious from the outset.

The rabbis took the term *pardes* (from the parable in *Chagigah* 14) as an acronym for *p'shat*, *remez*, *d'rash*, and *sod*, translated here as literal, allegorical, allusive, and esoteric meanings, respectively, of a passage. The parable of *Sava de Mishpatim* 2:99a in the *Zohar* suggests that paradoxically the deepest secrets of the text are in fact always present in the manifest version of the text (i.e., its *p'shat*, paralleling Jung's notion of the transparency of unconscious imagery, includes its deepest meaning for those who have "eyes to see and ears to hear" [Mark 8:18]). The symbolic approach does not require linguistic decoding; rather it calls for a different way of thinking. Interestingly, both Freud and Jung wrote about these two different types of thinking (directed and symbolic), and it is frankly uncertain whether their ideas were independently arrived at or inadvertently borrowed (Jung 1911 and Freud 1900).

Symbolic thought allows virtually any text to be re-interpreted metaphorically, as early Christianity did in its allegorization of the Hebrew Bible. It is evident that Jung, and likely the Jewish kabbalists, were influenced by Christian tradition in their use of symbols, whereas Freud's approach remains closer to classical rabbinic *midrash*.

CHAPTER 13

Transference: Personal or Not?

Experience has taught me to keep away from methods as much as from diagnoses.

—Carl Jung

The idea of transference, as previously noted, has roots in the ancient Israelite religion. The penitent Israelite would place his hands on the animal to be sacrificed, thereby symbolically transferring his sins to it before offering it up to the priest to be sacrificed (Chilton 2002). Similarly, on the Day of Atonement, the high priest would transfer the sins of Israel onto one of an identical pair of goats (i.e., the scapegoat). This animal was then led away into the desert and offered up to the demonic spirit Azazel, while the other goat was offered to YHWH as atonement (Klawans 2004).

Transference, as Jung freely admitted to Freud at their first meeting (Jung and Jaffe 1989), is the alpha and omega of psychoanalytical treatment.[1] Freud's critical observation was that as transference, images, objects, relational schemas, etc.—in part dependent on the various post-Freudian developments of the idea—are projected onto the analyst. In the absence of an identifiable transference, Freud

1. This reference also alludes to the New Testament where in Revelation 22:13 Christ says that "I am the Alpha and the Omega, the First and the Last, the Beginning and the End."

insisted that psychoanalysis was unable to cure, as from his perspective only interpretations made from within the transference were mutative. It is, according to Freud, impossible to work on repairing the patient's distorted and non-adapted perceptions while working at a distance, because as he states in his 1912 "Dynamics of the Transference," it is impossible "to destroy anyone in effigy" (Freud 1912, 108).

Transference is the single most important idea linking all of the modern derivatives of classical Freudian psychoanalysis. It is a method used to interrogate the present in order to interpret the past, as it assumes that the patient brings his specific personal memories to each session, where they eventually will manifest as old interpersonal schemas and affects. These are directed at the analyst, who although not a tabula rasa, as Freud initially claimed, is only vaguely known to the patient. This vacuum of knowledge is filled by the projections of the patient, and, in turn, responded to by the counter-projections of the analyst (Kradin 2007). As a result of the analytical training and sensitivity of the psychoanalyst to the vicissitudes of transference, he or she is positioned to question the historical sources of the dynamic that is transpiring in real time. The optimal interpretation of transference should be timed to the preparedness of the patient's mind, and directed at both the here and now and the roots or "genetic" aspects of the projections.

Like many concepts in psychoanalysis, transference matured within Freud's own lifetime and afterwards. Initially, analysts focused on the erotic yearnings expressed directly or in guised forms by female patients for male analysts. The positive erotic transference was judged as unavoidable but it had to be recognized, interpreted, and responded to with abstinence. However, a wide range of affects and cognitive schemas invariably emerge in a long-term psychoanalytical treatment, and the analyst must become skilled in listening with the third ear for their thinly guised expressions.

In practice, it is the relative lack of emphasis placed on the details of the transference dynamics that most clearly distinguishes Freudian from Jungian analysis. After parting with Freud in 1912, Jung progressively tended to rely less on the interpretation of transference as a therapeutic technique, and he ultimately questioned whether the Freudian preoccupation with it might be detrimental to therapeutic progress (Kradin 2014). This no doubt reflected his personal difficulties with managing the erotic transference in analysis, as well as his increased interest in transpersonal aspects of the psyche.

Jung recognized transference as sufficiently important to examine what he perceived to be its archetypal features (Jung 1946). But his exposition of archetypal transference is devoid of personal or sexual references, and he explains in the introduction to his monograph on "The Psychology of the Transference" (Jung 1946) that he assumes the reader to be acquainted with Freud's approach to it. To illustrate his thesis, Jung interprets a series of woodcut images from a medieval alchemical text, the *Rosarium Philosophorum*. Whether these images in fact illustrate transference is virtually impossible to ascertain. It is unlikely that the alchemist or artisan who created these woodcuts consciously had anything like what Freud or Jung had in mind. But Jung imagined this as the all-important feature of the alchemical texts, which he concluded were unconsciously talking about the unconscious (Jung 1980).

Jung is a master of the symbolic approach; and he is facile in identifying what he is seeking. He takes the images of the *Rosarium* out of their original context and allegorizes them in the service of a predetermined goal, which was precisely what he criticized Freud for doing in interpreting dreams. It is impressive proof of Jung's creativity that he was able to approach ancient alchemical texts and find novel meanings in them, but his approach is essentially the same as that of the Church Fathers, who read the Hebrew Bible out of context in order to find references to Christ. It is naive to accept Jung's claim that this constitutes evidence that the alchemy endeavor was a proto-psychological one, but his hypothesis may carry some validity.

TRANSFERENCE IN PRACTICE

Recognizing and interpreting transference requires the ability to listen for subtle metaphoric expressions, as well as the capacity to think symbolically. As Freud recognized, these are more the talents of a poet than a physician, especially as symbolic thinking is no longer a primary feature of medical training. This skill must be learned from one who has received specific training in the identification and interpretation of transference. As the vicissitudes of the transference cannot be learned from reading books or attending talks, few Jungian analysts are adept at working with the transference, having never received specific supervision on the topic.

Having gleaned from my own Freudian psychoanalysis and supervision the vital importance of transference, I have attempted to teach this topic to Jungian analytical trainees, some of whom have had no formal background in clinical psychology. But the topic invariably engenders negative reactions by some of the trainees, who criticize it as reductive and overly focused on sexuality.

What has repeatedly impressed me in this exercise has been the trainees' expressed desire to dismiss the importance of negative affects and sexual feelings in the treatment, and instead to re-interpret them in spiritualized forms, or in other words, to see the erotic transference, which is almost certainly at least in large measure based on felt sexual desire between the analytical couple, as the unconscious longing of two souls to engage with the transcendent divine. One candidate commented that her Christian beliefs did not support Freud's reductive and critical notions, reinforcing my impression that the Jung/Freud divide was based in large measure on religious difference. For at least some Jungians, Freud represents Judaism in the flesh, and Jung, Christianity in the spirit.

In this regard, they are merely restating the ancient bias of Christianity. As Robert Michael states in *Holy Hatred* (2006), where he reviews the opinions of the fifth-century Church Father Jerome:

> Jews are attached to the Old Law, which means the "flesh" and "sinful passions," but Christians are dead to this "old written code" and slaves only to the "new life of the Spirit." Jews walk "according to the flesh," Christians walk "according to the Spirit." (26)

CHAPTER 14

Trauma, Psychopathology, and Jewish Mysticism

Analysis had led back to these infantile sexual traumas, and yet they were not true.

—**Sigmund Freud**

PSYCHE AND MEMORY

At the *fin de siècle*, hysterical patients appeared in Freud's consulting room with physical symptoms and signs that could not be explained by modern scientific knowledge of anatomy and physiology. Today this entity is referred to as a psychosomatic conversion disorder (Kradin 2012).

Hysteria was known to the ancient Greeks, but its symptoms and theorized causes have changed with time. During medieval times and through the witch craze of the sixteenth and seventeenth centuries, hysteria was considered evidence of demonic possession.[1] By the end of the nineteenth century, it was widely held to be a degenerative disease of the nervous system. Jews were considered particularly prone to developing hysteria, especially those from Eastern Europe, which was late in its reception of the Enlightenment (Gilman 1993).

1. Hysteria was accepted by the male medical establishment as a disease of women. When Freud attempted to present a case of a man with hysteria to the Viennese Medical Society in the late 1890s, he was harshly criticized by his colleagues. See a recent review by Lewis Aron and Karen Starr, *A Psychotherapy for the People* (2013).

In the late nineteenth century, the French neurologist Jean-Marie Charcot concluded based on his experiments with hypnosis that patients with hysteria were suffering from a mental disorder (Kradin 2012). Freud spent several months observing Charcot's practice and was sufficiently impressed to continue his pursuit of this topic. His first publication on hysteria was based on the treatment of a young Jewish woman, pseudonymously referred to as Anna O., by his older colleague, the respected Jewish Viennese internist Josef Breuer.[2] Breuer had observed, with his patient's guidance, that the symptoms of hysteria tended either to dissipate or disappear entirely once memories encoded under adverse emotional conditions were retrieved.[3]

The talking cure, or as Anna O. referred to it, chimney sweeping, was conceptualized by Breuer and Freud as the treatment of a psychological disorder attributable to the trauma of incest (Breuer and Freud 1893).[4] Freud suggested that memories, feelings, and fantasies disavowed

2. As Gilman notes, there was an established custom of recording the histories of the mentally ill and then analyzing them. Freud did this in his famous case of Schreber the paranoiac and Jung also based his first major text, *Symbols of Transformation*, on a case that he had not personally observed.
3. The story of Anna O., in reality Bertha Pappenheim, a woman who, apparently largely cured of her disabling symptoms, went on to play a role in the founding of social work services, is complex and in many respects disturbing. Freud never treated the woman. Breuer, an accomplished physician and physiologist, apparently got substantially involved with her care. It is said that he abandoned her treatment when she developed symptoms of what was termed pseudocyesis (i.e., imagined pregnancy), claiming that Breuer was the father. Freud, highly talented, ambitious, and recently having observed Charcot's work with hysterical patients, joined with Breuer in writing up the case. Breuer, however, himself apparently traumatized by the experience, dissociated himself from the future of psychoanalysis. Thus, one is left with the curious dilemma of deciding who in reality was the first psychoanalyst, Freud, Breuer, or Anna O. History has subsequently decided for us. See Henri Ellenberger, *The Discovery of the Unconscious* (New York: Basic Books, 1981).
4. The question of retrieved memories of incest or, more broadly, sexual abuse has never been successfully resolved. Freud withdrew his original theory in part because of its scandalous implications, but also because he apparently became convinced that at least in some cases such memories were in fact fantasies. Nevertheless, it has been argued, most vocally by Jeffrey Mosson *In Assault on Truth* (New York: Farrar, Strauss, Giroux, 2012), that Freud purposefully denied the truths of sexual abuse in his patients in order not to jeopardize the future of psychoanalysis. Whatever the historical truth, it raises the more pressing issue in this thesis as to the fine line between reality and imagination.

by consciousness were split off and repressed into the unconscious. These repressed reminiscences, as the authors referred to them, produced symptoms through unconscious pathways of psychophysical excitation. Treatment required that the repressed memories of infantile sexual trauma be retrieved, first, by dismantling the patient's defenses, and then by raising split-off ideas and affects to their original source in consciousness.

Since its inception, the idea that psychological trauma is the cause of psychopathology has dominated the theory of psychoanalysis, but this begs the question of what exactly is meant by "psychological trauma." The fact is that prior to the Enlightenment, the concept of traumatic psychopathology did not exist. Of course there were always people who were considered insane or eccentric; but most of them were thought to be possessed or bearing the wages of sin. The modern notion of traumatic nurturing was not considered a cause of adult psychopathology.

There has undoubtedly always been psychological trauma, but one must guard against anachronizing one's conceptions of it. For example, one of the premier works of pagan antiquity, Homer's *Iliad*, is replete with graphic descriptions of battle trauma, yet one cannot identify a clear description of post-traumatic stress disorder (PTSD) within it. In fact, clinical examples of war neuroses were rarely documented prior to the World War I.

Freud was sensitive to this issue. As he wrote in *Civilization and Its Discontents*:

> No matter how much we shrink with horror from certain situations—of a galley salve in antiquity, of a peasant during the Thirty Years' War, of a victim of the Holy Inquisition—*of a Jew awaiting a pogrom*—it is nevertheless impossible for us to feel our way into such people—to divine the changes which original obtuseness of mind, a gradual stupefying process, the cessation of expectations, and cruder or more refined methods of narcotization have produced upon their receptivity to sensation of pleasure and unpleasure. (1930, 89; italics in original)

As Gilman notes, Freud's reference to the Jewish pogroms stands in contrast to other examples from antiquity, as pogroms were contemporary for Freud. Nevertheless, he appears to register them as in the past, not in the present. Harold Bloom has suggested that "Freudian memory and Freudian forgetting are a very Jewish memory and a very Jewish forgetting" (Gilman 1993, 3), a topic examined in depth by Yerushalmi in both *Zachor* (1982) and *Freud's Moses* (1991).

This idea merits further explication with respect to Freud's psychoanalysis. Judaism has historically exhibited a tendency to integrate new traumatic events into its history. For example, the destruction of both the First and Second temples is commemorated each year as a fast day on the ninth of Av (*Tisha B'Av*). Other traumatic events in Jewish history (e.g., the pogroms of the crusades) have also been incorporated into the fast day of Av, and many Jewish historians think that the twentieth-century Holocaust will also be in the future (Yerushalmi 1991).

This reflects the propensity of the rabbis to imagine history as circular rather than linear. Historical accuracy, as we currently know it, has until recently not been a priority in Judaism's recountings of its own past. Instead, new events tend to be re-imagined and integrated into older ones. This is identical to Freud's notion of *Nachträglichkeit*, translated here as "retroaction," which in Freud's theory connotes the attribution of traumatic meaning to earlier events.

On the contrary, both Christianity and Jungian psychology, borrowing from Hellenistic philosophy, tend to see history unfolding with purposeful intention (*telos*) into the future. This can be discerned in the typographical reading of the Hebrew Bible by the Church Fathers, in Hegel's notion of history unfolding into the future under the influence of the Holy Spirit (Hegel 1976), and in Jung's idea of individuation, in which the patient literally becomes what he or she was meant to be.[5]

Freudian psychology interprets events in the present as expressions of the individual's developmental past. History, and therefore

5. An example that is often given is of an acorn, which somehow knows that it is destined to become an oak tree. This is its *telos* or implied purpose.

memory, are essential in the understanding of present behavior, the latter being viewed as rooted in memoric re-transcriptions of pre-existing templates of experience. On the other hand, Jung's mode of analysis calls for relatively little knowledge of an individuals' earlier life. Rather, he seeks to examine how life is unfolding towards some future outcome through the serial analysis of dreams. The template for the configuration of the individual's psyche is primarily seen as the mythopoietic activity of the unconscious rather than developmental history. In this regard, Jung's view parallels the attitude of Christianity towards Judaism. It sees Judaism (read Freud) solely as an antiquated mode of belief that has been rendered irrelevant by the new covenant (read Jung). It rejects its laws (read psychoanalysis) as unnecessary for the conduct of a Christian life.

TRAUMA AND THE SHATTERED PSYCHE

Until recently, psychological trauma was defined as an "out of the ordinary experience" (Howell 2008). It was limited to unusually brutal events that the psyche—most often the immature psyche—was incapable of containing. The result was the imagined splitting of psychic contents along some unexplained fault line that safeguarded affects that could not be metabolized. Although specific genetic and experiential vulnerabilities to the results of trauma have been suggested, none have been confirmed.

The extraordinary event definition of trauma does not jibe with modern research into this area. According to the psychologist Elizabeth Howell, in a recent national survey of two thousand randomly selected youths ten to sixteen years of age, one half of boys and one third of girls reported having been subjected to violent victimization (2008). Almost forty percent of girls in the US in another study reported sexual abuse as children before age eighteen, with a reported incest rate approaching sixteen percent. Modern psychology has adopted the notion of trauma as the primary cause of psychopathology, but if these studies are correct serious trauma is very ordinary (Howell 2008).

Scientifically speaking, the term trauma in psychology has no clear basis, any more than psychological stress does (Kradin 2012).

Although increasing numbers of studies suggest that neurobiological pathways can be disrupted by trauma, psychology as a social science is far from establishing a mechanistic definition. In addition, the field itself is vulnerable to the phenomenon of suggestion (Borch-Jacobsen and Shamdasani 2012). For example, is it coincidence that at the same time physicists were describing the dissociation of radioactive particles and the splitting of the atom that Freud and Janet were discovering psychological dissociation? Perhaps, but there appears to have been a prevalent zeitgeist.

The fact is that there is currently no basis for attributing psychological trauma to any specific pathway of nervous system dysfunction, although considerable attempts have been made in that regard (Van der Kolk 2014). As the so-called science of psychoanalysis is in fact primarily one of hermeneutics, the reigning metaphor for the development of psychopathology has become that of psychic wholeness disrupted by serial micro- and macro-traumas. Alternatively, one may conclude that psychological chaos characterizes the infantile psyche, as Melanie Klein argued, and must subsequently be contained and structured through interpersonal nurture (1958).

As already discussed, the language of Freudian psychoanalysis is a language of trauma replete with martial metaphors: there is *conflict*, one struggles with *resistance*, the neurotic mind settles on *compromise* positions. Psychological *defenses* encapsulate dissociated elements of experience in order to maintain them outside of consciousness.

The idea of dissociation emerged in response to observations made during the course of experiments with hypnosis and dissociative hypnoid states. This undoubtedly played a critical role in how psychopathology was imagined and was reinforced by the widespread real traumas of modern warfare. But, interestingly, the most severe form of dissociative disorder, that of multiple personality disorder (or diffuse identity disorder) has been demonstrated to be largely, if not exclusively, an iatrogenic disorder, so that new personalities, or alter egos, actually tend to proliferate in response to suggestions made by the therapist (Lilienfeld et al. 1999).

As previously noted, Freud's psychoanalysis was criticized for being prone to the effects of suggestion. Following Charcot's retirement in the late 1890s, a scandal broke out concerning his widely publicized hypnotic experiments with hysterical female patients at the Hospital Salpetriere in Paris. At least some of Charcot's hysterics, many of them homeless streetwalkers, had confessed to acting out whatever they expected Charcot wanted from them in order to remain clothed and fed while in the hospital. Upon his retirement, Charcot's colleagues rejected his methods as unscientific.

In response to this affair, Freud ceased to practice as a hypnotist. He adopted a seated position out of the sight of his patient, and claimed to be nothing more than a tabula rasa or "clean slate" for the projections of his patients. In this way, Freud hoped to purge suggestion from psychoanalysis. But this was disingenuous. In fact, the analyst, like the kabbalist, is always an active participant in the therapeutic process. Psychoanalysis, like other social sciences, is always subject to suggestion (Borch-Jacobsen and Shamdasani 2012).

The earliest detailed psychological descriptions of traumatic psychological dissociation were not made by Freud but by his older French contemporary, the psychiatrist Pierre Janet (1926). Janet described what he believed was a propensity of the psyche to fragment in hysterical patients. Phenomenologically, according to Janet, this produced autonomous sub-personalities capable of actively re-enacting remembered relational disturbances. Dissociation was, for Janet, a psychological response that led to structures that Jung subsequently termed complexes.[6] Whereas the idea of dissociation is similar to Freud's concept of repression, it differs in an important aspect. According to Freud, elements that are unacceptable to consciousness are actively repressed, and this implies that they, at one time, had

6. Jung was a student of Janet; Freud was a student of Charcot and later of Hippolytus Bernheim. The latter replaced Charcot in Freud's mind because Charcot was a classic anti-Semite, whereas Bernheim was a Jew. However, all of these masters were skilled hypnotists, and their ideas are in fact based on the effects of suggestion. See Sonu Shamdasani *Jung: A Biography in Books* (New York: Norton, 2012).

been part of consciousness, if only fleetingly, and then lost. Currently, the bulk of modern scientific evidence tends to support Janet's viewpoint.

Dissociation, as Janet imagined it, and as it is currently widely conceived, is a spontaneous psychological reaction to overwhelming affect. In the presence of a sufficiently disturbing environmental event, the psyche is imagined to fragment. Dissociation has been described—or perhaps more accurately imagined—by observers in infants as occurring in the context of so-called disordered attachments to caregivers.[7] These micro-traumas may go unobserved except by trained observers. Nevertheless, it is inconceivable that such micro-traumas are not, in fact, normal. And if all have been traumatized, what is the proper place for a concept of trauma in the psychiatry?

TRAUMA AND KABBALAH

The motif of traumatic psychological dissociation was prefigured uncannily by the sixteenth-century Lurianic myth of the shattering of the vessels. The shattered vessels, some still containing sparks of divine light, descended through four imaginal worlds until they reached the earth. The Lurianic myth focuses on cosmology, but Hasidism reframed the Lurianic theosophy in psychological terms by interiorizing it. In Chabad philosophy, not only the cosmos was disrupted by the breaking of the vessels, but the wholeness of the soul as well, and *tikkun* becomes a process of inner psychological work. R. Dov Ber of Lubavitch claimed that it was only with the admission of psychological brokenness (*tsubrokenkeyt*) that the process of psychological repair can begin in earnest (Jacobs 2006).

In Judaism, a sinner whose psyche is broken and who seeks ardently to repair it through the process of *t'shuvah* (return or repentance) is

7. It is hard to know what to make of the science of infant observation. It should be obvious that the inability of the infant to report its own experience leaves substantial room for projections by the observers. It is one thing to make observations and yet another to try to correlate them with the mental states of a non-verbal infant.

held in higher esteem than a *tzaddik* who has never sinned, and only with rare exception is a broken man judged to be beyond redemption.[8]

The Lurianic myth is an apt image of traumatic dissociation. According to Luria, creation was never meant to achieve perfection; instead, God had flawed the process purposefully from its beginning, so that man could participate in its repair. Luria places the basic fault back to its origin in the divine will. Sin reflects man's failure to participate with God in a relational dynamic of repair. This is in many respects the core dynamic of modern psychoanalysis, in which both analyst and patient tend to disrupt and then repair the relationship.

DISSOCIATION AND TRAUMA

Jewish mystics reported dissociative states. R. Yosef Karo was famously visited by a maggid who chided him concerning lapses in his studies (Werblowsky 1977). R. Isaac Luria (Vital 1988), the Besht (Etkes 2005), and others described out of body experiences as heavenly ascents, apparently while in trance.

Victims of severe psychophysical trauma also frequently report having aspects of consciousness split off, and observe what is taking place from outside and above their own bodies (Van der Kolk 2014). Interestingly, individuals with borderline personality disorder, a severe and fairly common form of psychopathology commonly associated with sexual and other forms of abuse, report an extraordinarily high frequency of spiritual and mystical experiences (Gunderson and Links 2008).

But as William James warned, one must be careful not to reduce religious experience to psychopathology, especially when these experiences are meaningful to the individual and not disruptive to others. Controlled dissociative experiences do not necessarily have the same

8. One such exception is Acher who is encountered in the Talmudic tale of the *Pardes*. It is said that he "uproots the shoots," which is interpreted by the rabbis as shedding his ties to the Law and possibly becoming either an early Christian or some other form of Jewish Gnostic. He was the teacher of Rabbi Meir who figures prominently in the Talmud. See Peter Schafer, *The Origins of Jewish Mysticism* (Princeton: Princeton University Press, 2009).

implications as severe psychopathology. Rather, they suggest that it is possible while in a trance to imagine mental images as arising from outside of the self.

As might be imagined, the effective psychoanalytical treatment of dissociation is prolonged and painstaking, like the task of *tikkun olam*. Indeed, the rabbis had long been aware of the fact that character flaws were highly resistant to change. As Rav Yisroel Salanter, the famed Mussar (ethics) teacher, reportedly remarked, "It is easier to learn the entire Talmud than to change one character trait" (Etkes 1982, 242). Modern psychoanalysts would do well to heed these words of Mussar when faced with the reality of promoting personality change in their patients.

CHAPTER 15

Obsessionality and Historical Traumas

Life, as we find it, is too hard for us; it brings us too many pains, disappointments, and impossible tasks. In order to bear it we cannot dispense with palliative measures.

—Sigmund Freud

In his parting address to the Viennese Psychoanalytic Society, Freud referred to the traumatic history of the Jewish people. Whether or not one accepts what Jewish historian Salo Baron referred to as the lachrymose tradition in Judaism (Carroll 2001), there can be little doubt that socio-political and physical traumas have shaped Jewish history.

Like the history of religion, the historical factors that formed the context for psychoanalysis must be considered. To ignore the specific challenges facing Freud would be to extract him from his proper matrix. Freud lived (1856–1938) through some of the worst anti-Semitism witnessed on the European continent since the crusades and perhaps nowhere in Europe was it worse than in Freud's early Vienna (Gilman 1993). It would be foolhardy to imagine that this had no bearing on Freud's ideas.

In his introduction to Daniel Matt's *Zohar*, Arthur Green argues that it is impossible to separate the Kabbalah and its Lurianic modification from what was happening to the Jews of the Iberian Peninsula from the thirteenth to the sixteenth century (2003). During that period, they were publically humiliated, forced either to undergo conversion or be exiled, and in some instances killed. The *shekhina*-in-exile that preoccupies so many of the stories of the *Zohar* should rightfully be imagined as a projection of the traumatized soul of the Iberian Jew. Exile is a serious ordeal that is too often underestimated. Socrates chose to drink hemlock rather leave Athens (Herman 2014) and Dante, exiled from his beloved Florence, offered a vision of hell in his *Inferno* that included individuals who had been instrumental in his banishment.

In order to appreciate Freud's position, a brief review of Jewish history is required. Judeophobia was well known in the ancient world (Schafer 1998). The ancient Israelites were already, as Balaam says in Numbers 23:9, "a people who live apart and do not consider themselves one of the nations." This was a consequence of their self-identification as a kingdom of priests with prescribed rules of ritual purity. The destruction of the First Temple in 586 BCE was a major challenge to Israelite theodicy and the idea that YHWH specifically protected them. However, rather than view themselves as an abandoned people, they developed a new notion of history in which events, no matter how catastrophic, were construed as part a divine plan for their continued existence. Prophecy officially ceased following the abrogation of the Davidic monarchy, and this signaled another loss, this time a spiritual one, for Judaism.

The rebuilding of the Second Temple, according to the books of Ezra and Nehemiah and 2 Chronicles, was accompanied by increased emphasis on Torah study and ritual purity. Pharisaism, which appears to have roots in the Babylonian Exile (Scholem 1963), was a reform movement that attempted to convey aspects of Temple-based ritual purity into the daily life of the householder, and in so doing added significantly to the required daily ritual practices of the Jews.[1] It is likely, as the historian E. P. Sanders suggests, that many of the argu-

1. Modern scholars of Christianity, including E. P. Sanders, have argued that many of the controversial confrontations between Jesus and the Pharisees may relate to Pharisaic regulations that were not widely accepted in the first century (e.g., the washing of hands before eating) (Sanders 1996).

ments between Jesus and the Pharisees in the New Testament were based on priestly ritual practices that had not yet been widely adopted by Jews, such as ritual hand washing before eating (1996).

Following the destruction of the Second Temple in 70 CE and the cessation of the sacrificial cult, the new rabbinic movement stressed the importance of Torah study, together with prayer and ethical behavior, as a replacement for the Temple rites (Neusner 1978). Jewish mysticism had a brief re-emergence during the first and second centuries as evidenced by the parable of the *Pardes* in *Chagigah* 14b and the mystical ascents of R. Nehuniah ben HaKanah described in the *hekhalot* literature (Schafer 2009). But following the defeat of Bar Kokhba in 135 CE, mysticism and messianism were seen as dangerous and were discouraged by the rabbinic authorities.

After the Oral Law was codified as the *Mishnah* in 200 CE and the Talmud around 500 CE, the study of the Law preoccupied the attention of Jewish scholars. This led to intellectual pursuits and a proliferation of rabbinically imposed rules, which often resulted in an uninspired and rote performance of rituals, further depleting the once-spiritual core of Jewish religious experience.[2]

With the Enlightenment, the hold of rabbinic Judaism on its congregants was challenged, first in Western Europe, and later in the East. Freud, as the product of this Jewish Enlightenment, was an educated secular Jew, who viewed the ritual practices of all religions, including Judaism, as superstitious and as examples of collective pathological obsessionality. As he states in *Future of an Illusion*:

> Religion would thus be the universal obsessional neurosis of humanity; like the obsessional neurosis of children, it arose out of the Oedipus complex, out of the relation to the father. If this view is right, it is to be supposed that a turning-away

2. In a recent biography of Elijah the Gaon of Vilna who was acknowledged as the greatest Torah scholar in historical times, it was noted that his focus on Torah study was rarely interrupted, and that when his sister came to visit him after many years of separation he summarily sent her away so as not to interrupt his studies. He became the major Mitnagged opponent to Hasidism, which he viewed as leading Jews away from the proper goal of Torah scholarship.

> from religion is bound to occur with the fatal inevitability of a process of growth, and that we find ourselves at this very juncture in the middle of that phase of development. (Freud 1959c, 27)

In his *Notes on a Case of Obsessional Neurosis*, Freud (1909) suggested that obsessionals show a deep concern for existential security, and that their repetitive rituals are efforts to magically ward off perceived dangers (Kradin 2014). He observed that, like some observant Jews, obsessional patients showed inordinate concerns with perfectionism, fears with respect to contamination, and an overdeveloped emphasis on cognition with a corresponding restriction of affect. They suffer from anhedonia and psychic and behavioral rigidity.

HASIDISM AND THE HEALING OF JUDAISM

There was a widespread perception of collective anhedonia among the Jews of Eastern Europe in the eighteenth century. As in the obsessional neurotic, concerns due to existential insecurity may have affected entire communities. The circumstances of the large number of Jews settled in the Polish Pale seriously declined during the seventeenth and eighteenth centuries. A series of traumatic events including the Chmielnicki massacres of Jews in 1648, invasions by Swedes and Russians, and the persistent rabid animosity of the Polish peasantry plagued the communities of the Pale (Rapoport et al. 2000). As Scholem notes, these events, superimposed on the earlier ignominious failed messianic movements of Sabbatai Zvi and Jakob Frank, contributed to the emergence of the new reform movement, Hasidism (Scholem 1969). The early Hasidic literature appears to see the rabbinic authorities' failure to meet the spiritual needs of their communities as the major cause of the general impoverishment of spirit that had gripped the Jews of Eastern Europe (Rosman 1996). This is curiously similar to the Gospels holding the Pharisees and scribes responsible for the ills of society while ignoring the obvious oppression of the Roman rulers. Perhaps the shared realization that nothing could be done about the external oppression tended to shift the burden of responsibility to the Jewish leadership in the eyes of those who were suffering.

Hasidism was conceived as the antidote to the joyless obsessionality that had depleted the religiosity of the Jews of Eastern Europe. Israel ben Eliezer the B'aal Shem Tov, or Besht, is credited as being the charismatic founder of Hasidism. He was an ardent supporter of the Jewish people, and willing to intervene both spiritually and materially in efforts at fostering their collective welfare (Etkes 2005). In a letter, the *Iggeret Ha Kodesh* (The Holy Letter) to his brother-in-law, the Besht makes reference to his own mystical ascents into the heavens. In one of these, he asks the messiah when he will be coming to alleviate the sufferings of the Jews. The messiah's answer is that he will come when all Jews are as spiritually accomplished as the Besht—which short of a miracle would not be anytime soon. But the Besht never ceased to encourage the Jews to work towards a brighter future.

As opposed to the kabbalist meditative approach of focusing on *kavvanot*, the Besht practiced the technique of *devekut*, or clinging to the divine. Scholem describes *devekut* as the singular aspect of Hasidism that distinguishes it from other forms of Jewish practice (Scholem 1969). The Hasidic scholar Roman Foxbrunner explicates the many ways that the term was applied by the early Hasidism (1993). Technically, *devekut* originally included the mystical technique of prolonging and clinging to the utterance of a letter or a word, in an effort at penetrating to the divine essence hidden within them, thereby elevating the sparks of the divine essence embedded within the letters back to their source. It was also a mode of textual study informed by both love and fear of God. But mostly, it was conceived as a simple effort at approaching God in prayer and during the performance of *mitzvot*.

The Hasid was encouraged to approach all of his daily activities mindful of divine immanence. This approach is reminiscent of the technique of mindfulness, which has been modified from Theravada Buddhism and widely applied in modern psychotherapy. In it, the patient is counseled to focus his mind on the immediacy of the moment. Mindfulness has been demonstrated to be an effective treatment for a variety of psychological and psychosomatic ills, including borderline personality disorder and depression (Siegel 2009). But mindfulness is also part of the Hasidic approach, as Buber points out:

> A Master asked his disciples, "What is the most important thing in the world?" One answers, "The Sabbath"; another "prayer"; a third, "Yom Kippur." "No," the Master explains, "The most important thing is what you are doing at the moment." (Buber quoted in Dresner 2002, 54)

The Besht discouraged ascetic practices and unhappiness. The Hasid was encouraged to live joyfully in the world, even in the face of adversity. Sensitive to the limitations that the average Jew faced with respect to receiving an elite education, he introduced a perspectival shift that made God potentially accessible to everyone. The Besht reasoned that if God's presence is everywhere and in everything, then how could any man possibly be excluded from His presence?

The Besht also saw the need for an accomplished mystic who could serve as a spiritual link between the supernal realm and the community. If the average Jew could not attain his own high level of spiritual achievement, he could always attach himself with faith to a spiritual champion, one much like Simeon bar Yochai had been for his followers in the *Zohar*. This spiritually gifted individual was referred to as the Hasidic *tzaddik* or rebbe, who as Green notes represents the embodied *axis mundi* for his followers:

> In the writings of the kabbalistic and Hasidic masters, the holy man is often described in various terms highly reminiscent of the notion of sacred space. The *Tzaddik* may be Zion, Temple, Jacob's ladder, or Holy of Holies. While the transference of sacred space imagery to another realm might seem especially apt for the Jews, given their long history of exile, . . . such transference never meant the replacement of the

> geographical Jerusalem or Holy Land by the *Tzaddik*, but rather an additional locus of divine presence. . . . (1977, 327)

In many respects, the psychoanalyst is imbued with the features of the *tzaddik* for his patients. He is a spiritual adept whose knowledge is believed by the patient to exceed his own. In his interpretations, he raises the patient's unconsciousness to awareness, and serves as a life-line that the patient can cling to until he has achieved sufficient insight into himself.

CHAPTER 16

Master and Disciple

An ancient adept has said that if the "wrong man uses the right means, the right means works in the wrong way." . . . In reality, everything depends on the man and little or nothing on the method.

—**Carl Jung**

Like all ancient oral traditions, the transmission of Judaism relied heavily on the relationship between master and disciple, and this continues to be the case in the training of new rabbis and religious scholars. A comparable dynamic is seen in the relationship between Jesus and his apostles.

The master and disciple relationship was of particular importance in the transmission of esoteric traditions. The enlightened master was obliged to ascertain the ability of a disciple to receive concealed truths safely. The initiation of a disciple into an esoteric tradition is depicted in the aggadic passages of *Chagiga* 14b:

> The Rabbis taught in *Baraisa*: An incident occurred with Rabban Yochanan ben Zakkai, who was riding on a donkey, and going along the Road, while R. Elazar ben Arach was walking behind guiding the donkey forward. R. Elazar ben Arach said to Rabban Yochanan ben Zakkai, "My teacher, teach me one chapter of *maaseh merkavah*." Rabban Yochanan ben Zakkai replied to him, "I cannot do that! Have I not

> taught you regarding this: 'Nor may one expound upon *maaseh merkavah* in a class of one student, unless that student was a scholar who could arrive at an understanding of the issues on his own'?" R. Elazar ben Arach said to him, "My teacher, allow me then to recite before you one matter that you have already taught me." Rabban Yochanan ben Zakkai said to him, "Speak."
>
> Immediately Rabban Yochanan ben Zakkai descended from the donkey, wrapped himself in a garment, and sat upon a stone under and an olive tree. R. Elazar ben Arach said to him, "My teacher, why did you descend from the donkey?" Rabban Yochanan ben Zakkai said "Is it conceivable that you will expound upon *maaseh merkavah*, and the Divine presence shall be with us, and ministering angels shall accompany us. And I would be riding on a donkey?!"
>
> Immediately, R. Elazar ben Arach began his discourse on *maaseh merkavah* and expounded. And fire descended from heaven and surrounded all the trees in the field. All the trees began to utter song. What song did they utter? Praise Hashem from the earth: sea giants and all the water depths . . . fruitful trees and all cedars . . . Halleluyah. And angels spoke up from amidst the fire and said, "That is certainly *maaseh merkavah*." Rabban Yochanan ben Zakkai stood up, kissed R. Elazar ben Arach on his head and said, "Blessed is Hashem, God of Israel, who has given a son to our forefather Abraham, who knows how to comprehend, delve into, and expound upon *maaseh merkavah*. There are those who expound well but do not practice well, practice well but do not expound well; but you R. Elazar ben Arach are one who both expounds well and practices well. How fortunate are you, our forefather Abraham, that R. Elazar ben Arach emerged from your loins!"

This story demonstrates the restrictions on revealing concealed wisdom except to a qualified student. Ben Zakkai's dismounting from the donkey and wrapping himself in a fringed garment while sitting under a tree was not simply a spontaneous action, but a formal ritualistic statement concerning the examination process that the disciple must pass in order to achieve the status of master in his own right (Bakan 1991).

In this regard, the passage in *Chagigah* 14b continues to describe a mystical process that went amok. This is the famous story of the *Pardes*, which has already been mentioned, in which four scholars enter a mystical trance, but only one, the rabbinic hero of the second century, R. Akiva, returns from it unscathed. In this aggadic segment, R. Akiva warns his comrades concerning what to avoid, as he has apparently successfully undertaken this spiritual journey before and is therefore aware of its pitfalls:

> Our rabbis taught: Four men entered the Garden (*Pardes*), Ben Azzai, and Ben Zoma, Acher (Elisha ben Avaya) and R. Akiva. R. Akiva said to them: "When ye arrive at the stones of pure marble do not say 'water, water.' For it is said: 'He that speaketh falsely shall not be established before my eyes'" (Psalm 101:7). Ben Azzai cast a look and died. Of him scripture says: "Precious in the eyes of the Lord is the death of his saints" (Psalm 116:15). Ben Zoma looked and became demented. Of him, scripture says: "Hast thou found honey? Eat as much as is sufficient for you, lest thou be filled and vomit" (Psalm 25:16). Acher mutilated the shoots. R. Akiva went up unhurt and went down unhurt. (*Chagigah* 14b)

The tale warns against entering altered states without proper grounding, as one can potentially be carried away to the point of death, madness, or to a loss of faith, with the latter being the case for Elisha ben Avuyah, or Acher.[1] It is noteworthy that only Akiva is referred to as a rabbi, which may indicate that the other scholars had not yet

1. The story of Acher is fascinating. He was a great scholar and one of the teachers of R. Meir. It is said that when in trance he mistook the angel Metatron, who was seated on a throne, for a second ruler with YHWH. He apparently lost his faith in the Law and then openly transgressed it. This idea of a binitarian God image may

successfully achieved the role of master and therefore were unable to withstand the effects of divine revelation.

The roles of master and disciple play out prominently in psychoanalysis between the analyst and the analysand, as well as in the training of future analysts. Some have argued that long-term psychotherapy is more a spiritual exercise than a medical or psychological treatment (Malinen 2010). Many patients who enter analysis tend to view their analyst as a master early in the treatment. This is a desired response, as this idealization fosters the early positive transference, which is necessary if a therapeutic alliance is to be achieved. The remainder of the treatment includes the re-visioning of the master, when he or she invariably disappoints the patient. Such relational ruptures are viewed as opportunities for repair, which is considered to be mutative. In this regard, the analysis is analogous to *tikkun* (i.e., the repair of a damaged relational system).

But unlike the religious model, which is based on a pre-Enlightenment and Near Eastern master and disciple dynamic, the aim of a secularized analysis in the West is, in large measure, to promote the autonomy of the patient, and this goal, perhaps more than any other, defines the difference between secular psychoanalysis and the religious cure of the soul. The modern emphasis on personal autonomy and individuation is a by-product of what Taylor refers to as the buffering of the individual from the greater community (2007). Prior to the Enlightenment, individuals were contained and at times enmeshed within the matrix of family and community, a dynamic that persists for those who remain in traditional societies. From the perspective of a secular society preoccupied with individual autonomy, a patient must ideally learn from interpretations and internalize the approach and wisdom of the master/analyst, but with the aim of becoming autonomous.

Both Freud and Jung openly expressed concern for what they viewed as herd mentality and praised autonomy and individuation.

in fact reflect an early phase of Christian thought and the rabbi's polemical reaction to it (Schafer 2009).

However, as Schwartz notes (Schwartz 2010), the current climate of political correctness emphasizes the importance of shared community values, although it is not clear how these are determined. From this perspective, the individual's choices and autonomy are devalued, and it is too early to know what effect this may have on the practices of psychoanalysis.

Those psychoanalytical treatments in which the early master and disciple relationship is not modified are viewed as being impeded by a shared resistance of the analyst to criticism or the emergence of strong affects. But whether the goal of autonomy has fostered the mental health of individuals or, more broadly speaking, the quality of modern life is by no means clear, and there may be need for an unbiased reexamination of the goals of psychoanalysis in this regard.

With respect to analytical training, it should be noted that there are major differences between Freudian and Jungian institutes, which are in part dependent on regional differences, especially in the Jungian world. Whereas Freudian training includes technical supervision and evaluation, Jungian training in its classical mode more closely resembles a spiritual education. The candidate in Jungian analysis is judged not only on his or her knowledge and clinical expertise, but also on the progress of their individuation process.[2] As the term suggests, individuation emphasizes the primary importance of the individual and limits the role of relationships. What some may view as well individuated may to others resemble narcissism.

Jung argued that the analyst cannot take a patient further psychologically than he has been able to go himself:

> An analyst can help his patient just so far as he has gone and not a step further. In my practice, I have from the beginning

2. I have known analytical candidates who have spent upwards of twenty years in Jungian training because of sado-masochistic dynamics centered on the evaluation of their individuation. This has become less common, thankfully, but remains an issue. In some cases, the candidates have had little aptitude for symbolic thinking and limited intuition, both critically necessary for an effective analyst, and they should have been encouraged to stop training, but unfortunately for all involved, including the public who eventually must rely on them for help, this was not the case.

> to deal with patients who "got stuck" with their previous analyst, and this always happened at the point where the analyst could make no further progress with himself. (*CW* 16, para. 545)

But how far an analytical trainee has individuated is impossible for evaluators—who are usually *not* the trainee's personal analysts—to know. Like all master and disciple relationships, the question of evaluation is fraught with pitfalls related to the psychological biases of the couple. Yet this perspective persists in Jungian training as a remnant of a time when one's religious masters judged spiritual progress.

In the analytical pairings as conceived by self-psychological, relational, and attachment theorists, one sees parallels with that of the *tzaddik* and his disciple. Virtually all Hasidim report that in the presence of their *tzaddik* they have a sense of well being. However, there is a downside to an analytical approach that primarily values mirroring or holding environment, i.e., the love symbolized by the *sefira* of *Chesed* if it fails to counter it with limits, i.e., the *sefira* of *Gevurah*. Unfortunately, in the therapy of personality disorders, the expression of love without limits and correctives is rarely therapeutic. In my experience, unexpressed and undetected hostility are the reasons that most analyses fail to progress. It is critically important that analysts be in touch with their own anger, if they are to provide a productive therapeutic milieu. This may be a critical difference between analysts informed by Judaism versus Christianity. The latter as a religion of love has traditionally been strongly adverse to expressions of overt negative affect. When this is the case, both the patient and analyst may harbor unconscious anger expressed in ways that ultimately undermine the treatment.

CHAPTER 17

Losing Oneself: Narcissism and *Bitul*

Whoever loves becomes humble. Those who love have, so to speak, pawned a part of their narcissism.

—Sigmund Freud

What is the optimal position of the self? When is self-esteem healthy versus egotistic and non-relational? This is perhaps one of the greatest questions that must be addressed in psychoanalysis. Most religions tend to value humility as a virtue, and this is true of both Judaism and Christianity. However, decreasing the importance of self may prove problematic if a core sense of values has not first been established. It should be emphasized here that traditional religions assume the attainment of a healthy sense of self before arguing for its deconstruction.

Following the death of the Besht, the mantle of Hasidic leadership fell on the shoulders of his disciple, the scholar and accomplished mystic R. Dov Ber, the Maggid of Mezyritch. The Maggid adopted the teachings of his master but transformed them with his own distinct spiritual inflection (Uffenheimer 1993). As opposed to the Besht whose practices might best be termed theurgic, the Maggid was a contemplative mystic. Rivka Schatz Uffenheimer has examined this quietist element in Dov Ber's acosmic interpretation of Jewish theology (1993):

> The central axis of quietist thought is the pantheistic idea that all that remains following the erasure of self is God: God is present in man only in a passive way, which becomes able to act once the various garments or potential of the soul and the intellect cease to act. The only human act that may be identified with the divine will is that of total self-annihilation. Therefore one cannot speak of a voluntaristic outlook within the quietistic framework from man; God does not desire any particular thing from man—neither good nor evil, neither the performance of certain actions or the refraining from others. On God's part, there is only the pure will, which acts within us. It is clear that such an outlook is one of extreme quietism. (1993, 66)

In some respects, the practices of the Maggid represent a return to the influence of Maimonides, whose approach was primarily rooted on intellection. But Dov Ber's theology did not depend solely on a finely honed intellect; rather it was aimed primarily at self-nullification (*bitul*), (i.e., the eradication of greed and pride that separates man both from God and from his fellow man).

Dov Ber and his school called for a focus on contemplation and reduced the earlier emphasis on kabbalistic imagery. Hasidism retained much of the terminology of the Kabbalah, but imbued it with new meanings. Creation in sefirotic terms was now to be imagined both at the cosmic and psychological level. The Hasid was expected to rid himself of self-preoccupation (Rotenberg 2003). In this vein, the Maggid encouraged his followers to transform the I (*aniy*) into nothing (*ayin*) (Matt 1995), a radical perspectival shift based on the transposition of a single letter. As Dov Ber suggests:

> One must think of oneself as *ayin* and forget oneself totally. . . . If one thinks of oneself as something (*yesh*) . . . then God cannot clothe Himself in him, for God is infinite. No vessel can contain God unless he thinks of oneself as *ayin*. . . . (Matt 1995, 86)

The Hasidic transformation was interpreted by Buber as a new emphasis on existential values (1958). Hasidic tales were not focused on elite Talmudic or kabbalistic scholars; instead, they were concerned with the humility and selflessness of masters like R. Zusa of Hanipol. Now it was said that when one traveled to meet a *tzaddik*, it was not to be intellectually enriched, but to observe how a saintly man "ties his shoelaces," i.e., speaks, eats, and interacts with his fellow man on a daily basis. Grandiosity at any level was viewed as antithetical to the true goal of the Jew, just as Moses was referred to as the "most humble of men" in scripture.

FREUD ON NARCISSISM

In 1914, Freud published an important paper, "On Narcissism." The history of this paper is noteworthy, as it followed the rupture of his relationship with Jung, and was written in part to refute Jung's idea of introversion. Jung conceptually separated the attitudes of the ego as either outer directed (i.e., extroversion), or inner directed (i.e., introversion). He made no value judgment concerning these attitudes, preferring to conceive of them as primarily phenomenological differences in personality types, rather than features of psychopathology (Jung 2012). In this regard, Jung may have been expressing his approval concerning the merits of religious contemplation, which assumes an introverted stance by the practitioner.

But Freud argued that sustained introversion was not simply a personality type but a psychopathological stance. He conceived of it as the cathexis of libido to one's own self as opposed to others, and he pointed to the myth of Narcissus as an example of such extreme self-love. According to Freud, the grandiosity and contempt for others exhibited by narcissists made it impossible for them to sustain relationships with others.[1] He furthermore argued that these patients were not

1. The term narcissism is adopted from the famous Greek myth. Freud refers to it as a libidinal cathexis to oneself that cannot be transferred to others. Consequently, the narcissist is unable to love. Unable to develop any interest in another, he/she is incurable according to Freud by the development of transference that is a necessary feature in analysis.

amenable to psychoanalytic cure, due to their inability to develop productive transference responses to the analyst.

In the 1960s, Heinz Kohut, a Jewish Austrian-born psychoanalyst like Freud, developed a novel theory that countered Freud's pessimistic conclusion that patients with narcissism could not be analyzed. Kohut's personal history is noteworthy. He eschewed any references to his Judaism and went as far as to suggest, to those who did not know the truth, that he, as well as his mother and father, were Christians. In his biography, Charles Strozier, a historian and self-psychologist, states that both of Kohut's parents were Jewish and that his father had been at least to some degree observant (Strozier 2001). After emigrating to America, Kohut affiliated with the Unitarian Church, although there is no evidence that he ever formally converted to Christianity.

This is only one of several topics on which Kohut consciously chose to dissemble the truth. Having developed a novel theory concerning the self based on early developmental deficits (Kohut 1971), he published a now famous paper, "The Two Analyses of Mr. Z" (Kohut 1979). This was, in fact, an autobiography sketch guised as the case history of a patient. In it, he describes the struggles of a young narcissistic man, besieged by shame due to traumas suffered at the hands of his early caretakers, especially an intrusive and narcissistic mother who had been unable to mirror his early experience. He describes a profound failure in Mr. Z's ability to idealize his caretakers. These traumatic deficits, according to Kohut, resulted in fluctuations of self-esteem, narcissistic grandiosity, the inability to idealize others, and failures in empathy.

But rather than being incapable of developing transference responses, as Freud had suggested, Kohut (1979) argued that narcissists exhibited early self-object transferences that reflected deficits in early relational dynamics and that could be repaired through the analyst's identification as a self-object (i.e., a figure that could selflessly provide another with what is necessary for early mentalization).

According to Kohut, the optimal stance to be adopted by the analyst in the treatment of the narcissistic patient was to listen empathically, affirmatively mirror mental states via empathic attunement, and provide a milieu in which the patient could begin to idealize the analyst. Such self-object transferences support the fragile ego of the narcissist, providing it with sufficient strength to modulate shameful and envious affects that otherwise would necessarily be repressed or projected. But these early self-object transferences were not to be interpreted by the analyst until the ego was sufficiently strong to tolerate intrusions.

A Hasidic tale told by the itinerant Enlightenment scholar Solomon Maimon concerning his visit to the court of the Maggid of Mezyritch depicts an extraordinary example of what Kohut referred to as self-object mirroring:

> I arrived at Mezyritch and after having rested went to the house of the leader. . . . On the Sabbath I went to his solemn meal and there found a number of venerable men who had come from a variety of places. The rabbi greeted each of his guests and then we all sat down to eat . . . after the rabbi began to sing an exalting and uplifting melody. Subsequently, he held his hand on his brow for some time, and then called out the names and residences of his guests: Z. of the city of H., M. of the city of R. . . . and so on. The rabbi then asked each of us to recite some verse from the Holy Scriptures. As we finished the rabbi delivered a discourse in which he wove together all of the verses that we had recited for him. Since these were taken from different parts of scripture they were altogether disconnected, but with great skill he tied them together to make a single theme. Still more extraordinarily wondrous was that every one of the guests discovered in that part of the discourse, which related to his verse, special references to his private life and thoughts. At this of course we were greatly astonished. (Shochet 1990, 134)

Similar observations have also come from attachment theory, a post-Freudian branch of psychoanalysis, pioneered by John Bowlby (Bowlby 1969). This school argues from a biological perspective that the human infant, like other mammals, requires secure attachment figures. Based largely on infant observation, rather than on implied histories derived from adult narratives and transference observations, attachment theorists have compiled evidence that unstable attachments in the maternal infant pairing can yield anxious, chaotic and/or avoidant attachment styles, which predict the subsequent development of adult psychopathologies (Fonagy 2001). Current modes of psychoanalysis are virtually all preoccupied with the idea of providing a safe environment within which patients can express their ideas and feelings.

Freud's paper "On Narcissism" was an important theoretical breakthrough and it inspired an abundant literature on this topic. Indeed, the concept of narcissism has permeated Western civilization to the extent that some have suggested that we are currently living in a culture of narcissism (Lashley 1991). It has been my experience that many patients seeking Jungian analysis fall within the narcissistic spectrum of psychopathology. As might be expected, they prefer to view themselves as introverts. They resist efforts at examining their grandiosity, and choose to immerse themselves in dream imagery, fairy tales, and myth. Jungian analysts may collude with these notions, having never had their own narcissism subjected to a Freudian analysis. Of course, there are many exceptions to what I am suggesting, but it does represent, at least from this analyst's perspective, a feature of Jungian analysis.

MORALITY AND NARCISSISM

Freud's criticism of the narcissist includes a moral judgment. Indeed, the psychoanalyst Otto Kernberg has suggested that narcissism virtually always includes a sector of sociopathy (2000). Virtually all world religions convey a message concerning the importance of humility and concern for others. But in a secular world devoid of strong religious underpinnings, the standards of values and authenticity are difficult to define. Consider the opinion of Rabbi Lawrence Hoffman concerning secular values:

> As popularly practiced the new authenticity has no moral force to it. It is purely expressive, a kind of romantic individualism by which individuals claim the absolute right to express

> themselves in order to make themselves into the people they are meant to be. . . . But if the self is all we have and if the ultimate goal is self-expression, it is hard to see how anything could be a sin. . . . The result is a society of laissez faire, self-realization and therapeutic care. (2012, 29–30)

Certainly, the notion of innate natural morality has been repeatedly advanced. In his *Descent of Man*, Charles Darwin argued that moral behavior developed from an innate animal predisposition to empathize, and that morality was the result of natural evolution, rather than a product of externally imposed religious values (2004). In today's secular world individuals have increased freedoms concerning how and what they choose to value. Indeed, it may be suggested that one of the challenges facing psychoanalysis is whether the analyst and patient in fact share comparable values. When religious structures were stronger, it was possible to feel more comfortable in this regard. Currently, the goals of analysis must be clearly explicated, as in the absence of shared value systems it may be impossible to define what constitutes the grist for analysis and therapeutic progress.

The abrogation of ego is the path to the elimination of suffering in Buddhism. But it is not the final goal of the Jewish mystic. Rather, he aims at achieving a transient union with the divine and then returning to this world. In Judaism, there is a reigning idea that contact with the divine must be transient and cannot be sustained. The most one can hope for are glimpses of divinity as they appear and disappear moving to and fro. The mystic makes room for the divine to fill the space opened in the emptying of the self, the contraction of the ego, *tzimtzum*, or what the early church termed *kenosis*. But a final freeing of the soul does not occur until death.[2]

Western society is rooted in a conflicted syncretistic set of values derived in part from the ancient religions of the Near East and the Hellenistic world. In the West, we are as much heirs to the Greek idea

2. This is probably not very different than in Buddhism where enlightenment or *nirvana* may be achieved during life but final release only occurs at death with *paranirvana*.

of *arête* (i.e., excellence and virtue) as we are to the Judeo-Christian notion of humility. While the Greeks were aware of hubris (i.e., overweening pride that challenges the gods), pride was not frowned upon in the Hellenistic world, nor was there a moral system in place that would have viewed narcissism as pathology. However, like the Hasidic and Mussar traditions that saw pride as antithetical to spirituality, Freud recognized modesty as a virtue.[3] But with the decline of monotheistic religious systems, it may be argued that pagan values have begun to re-emerge.

In some branches of Hasidism, rigorous self-scrutiny with the goal of ridding oneself of prideful ideas and feelings became the primary task. R. Menachem Mendel of Kotzk was relentless in insisting on honesty as the ideal existential stance, and the Kotzker famously rejected any pretense in spiritual practice. As Abraham Joshua Heschel notes:

> The Kotzker conceived of living as an ongoing encounter, a fighting to the end, in which thought of surrender was inconceivable. He held moral cowards in contempt, disliked pusillanimous souls. The battle was fierce: it was an encounter with the ego and its treacherous delusions. (1995, 266)

In his analytical approach to the narcissism of patients, Freud was effectively following in the path of the Kotzker and the Lithuanian Mussar movement. His pursuit of truth with respect to analyzing the unconscious was relentless. As Freud remarked in a letter to Wilhelm Fliess, "Being entirely honest with oneself is a good exercise" (Freud and Fliess 1985, 172).

Can one assume that this mindset represents a calling of the Jewish psyche? The biblical prophets were unyielding in calling for just treatment of the poor, the widow, the orphan, and the slave, as well as for an end to hypocrisy. The Jewish rabbi Jesus of the Gospels also belongs in this category. This traditional truth seeking can still be observed in

3. Moses, the greatest of prophets and the only one to have spoken with God face to face, is repeatedly referred to in the rabbinic literature as the most humble of men, apparently linking his level of prophecy with a lack of egocentricity.

the *yeshivot*, where politeness often takes a back seat to an insistence on discerning the message of a Talmudic argument. The Talmudic style is recognized as potentially confrontational and challenging, but for those used to it, it is also experienced as well-intentioned. The prophet Isaiah's (49:6) call for Israel to serve as a kingdom of priests and as a "light unto the nations" has remained a prominent role for Jews. And despite Freud's secular atheism, these same moral values can be perceived in his humanistic theories and practices.

CHAPTER 18

Oedipus and Supersession

Jung finds that the Oedipus complex is not specific enough for the etiology of the neuroses and proceeds to attribute this quality to inertia, the most universal quality of matter, animate and inanimate!

—Sigmund Freud

An evolving concept in psychological theory is the importance of early relationships as critical factors in normal development. It was Jung, more than Freud, who emphasized the importance of the dyadic relationship in psychoanalysis. Unlike Freud's one-body model of psychoanalysis that stressed the intrasubjective dynamics of the patient's unconscious and ego, Jung's was a two-body model that recognized the need for the participation of the analyst and his or her concomitant transformation during the treatment, an idea that prefigured modern relational-based modes of psychoanalysis. Jung recognized the critical role of the mother as the source of how the unconscious was structured, as opposed to Freud's focus on the primacy of the father's imago in the child's mind. Jung was also persistently critical of the effect of the group on societal progress:

> The element of differentiation is the individual. All the highest achievements of virtue, as well as the blackest villainies are individual. The larger a community is, and the more the sum total of collective factors peculiar to every large community

> rests on conservative prejudices detrimental to individuality, the more will the individual be morally and spiritually crushed, and, as a result, the one source of moral and spiritual progress for society is choked up. (*CW* 7, para. 240)

In such statements, Jung is rehearsing the viewpoint adopted by the Protestant reformers of the Roman Church. Protestantism values, as Jung characterizes it, the spiritual and moral progress of the individual, not the group. For Luther and Calvin, each person must struggle to establish his own relationship with God. This is a very different notion than what is seen in Judaism, which places a high value on the well-being and preservation of the group so that virtually all events of religious gravity in the community require the participation of a quorum of at least ten men.[1]

As has been discussed, Freud pays particular attention to the relationship between fathers and sons in his psychoanalytical theory. He chose to elucidate the dynamics of the family romance through the myth of Oedipus, as presented in Sophocles' *Oedipus Rex*. As Freud states in *The Interpretation of Dreams*:

> If the *Oedipus Rex* is capable of moving a modern reader or playgoer no less powerfully than it moved the contemporary Greeks, the only possible explanation is that the effect of the Greek tragedy does not depend upon the conflict between fate and human will, but upon the peculiar nature of the material by which this conflict is revealed. There must be a voice within us which is prepared to acknowledge the compelling power of fate in the *Oedipus*. . . . His fate moves us only because it might have been our own, because the oracle laid upon us before our birth the very curse which rested upon him. It may be that we

1. A series of prayers that focus on holiness can only be recited in the presence of ten men or a *minyan*. In modern times, different sects of Judaism have moved away from this requirement, either to ignore it altogether, as Reform Judaism does, or to include women as part of the *minyan*. In addition, most prayer in Judaism is communal. There is a place for personal petitional devotion, but it has little formal status in the religion.

> were all destined to direct our first sexual impulses toward our mothers, and our first impulses of hatred and violence toward our fathers; our dreams convince us that we were. King Oedipus, who slew his father Laius and wedded his mother Jocasta, is nothing more or less than a wish fulfillment—the fulfillment of the wish of our childhood. But we, more fortunate than he, in so far as we have not become psychoneurotics, have since our childhood succeeded in withdrawing our sexual impulses from our mothers, and in forgetting our jealousy of our fathers. We recoil from the person for whom this primitive wish of our childhood has been fulfilled with all the force of the repression which these wishes have undergone in our minds since childhood. (1900, 223)

Oedipal dynamics also played an important part in Freud's theoretical writings on the origins of religion, including *Totem and Taboo* and *Moses and Monotheism*. Rizzuto explores this point in her analysis of the relationship of Freud to his father Jakob. Freud writes:

> Of all of the imagoes of childhood, which as a rule is no longer remembered, none is more important for a youth or a man than that of his father. A little boy is bound to love and admire his father, who seems to him the most powerful, wonderful, kind, and wisest creature in the world. God Himself is after all is only an exaltation of the picture of his father as represented in the mind of early childhood. (1913a, 243)

But Freud's early enchantment with his father eventually changed to disillusionment. In his letters to Fliess, he accuses his father of cowardice, jealousy, and of having committed incest with one of Freud's older brothers.

The Oedipal wish to displace the father and his values, according to Rizzuto (1998), may have been why Freud expressed such vehemence in his anti-religious stances, especially those directed against Jewish ritual practices (Freud 2010). Jakob Freud was evidently a man who remained tied to his belief in God and to a simple mode of Judaism; he was not an intellectually sophisticated man, and he evidently embarrassed his educated and gifted son.

There is an interesting parallel between Freud's rejection of the father and the history of the Hasidic movement. As Louis Jacobs suggests in *Honor Thy Father: A Study in Hasidic Psychology* (1965), an early controversy between the emerging Hasidic movement and their Mitnagged opponents concerned whether sons were allowed to disobey their fathers' wishes when the latter insisted that they abandon their allegiance to a Hasidic *tzaddik*.[2] In a polemic brought before the Russian authorities by the Mitnagged Avigdor ben Chayim, the rabbi of Pinsk, he complained that, "They [Hasidim] argue that a father only brings his child into the world to satisfy his lusts and there is consequently no obligation for a child to honor his father. The same applies to the mother except that some measure of respect is due to the mother by the child she suckled" (Jacobs 1965, 4).

Despite the religious and political motivations of this polemic, it does appear to have been based in fact. R. Schneur Zalman of Chabad argued that the Fifth Commandment did not include an obligation to obey the dictates of the father if he was interfering with the proper—the Hasidic—path of his son. As Jacobs notes, the Hasidic movement was in fact not only one of reform but also insurrection that often split sons from fathers and families, much in the same way Freud's ideas openly divided the psychiatric establishment and lay Victorian society. Both Hasidism and psychoanalysis called for new levels of freedom and autonomy for the individual. Indeed, the Hasidic literature is replete with parables concerning the relationship between fathers and sons, describing them, at times, in loving terms but at other times as conflicted. In many cases, these were allusions to man's relationship to God as well.

2. Discord within families on this account was often severe, and it is recorded that many fathers said *kaddish* for a son who joined the Hasidic movement. Indeed, R. Schneur Zalman's father apparently moved from Lithuania and never again mentioned his (in)famous son (Immanuel Etkes, *Schneur Zalman of Lyady* [Waltham: Brandeis, 2014]).

Freud claimed that the resolution of the Oedipal conflict for a son included his identification with the father (i.e., an unconscious adoption of the father's psychological positions). However, in some cases it may give rise to persistent hostility directed at the person and values of the father, as appears to have been the case for Freud. But the values of the father in such cases may later re-emerge, as Freud termed it, as the return of the repressed. Freud theorized about this in *Totem and Taboo* (1913a) and in *Moses and Monotheism* (1938). In fact, Yerushalmi has suggested that at the end of Freud's life, he had come closer to returning to his father's relationship to Judaism (1991).

Freud's idea of psychological identification may also have roots in Hasidic thought. R. Schneur Zalman, echoing the medical knowledge of his day, claimed that the male infant's soul was derived from semen arising in the brain of the father during the moment of conception. In this way, the soul of the child becomes identified with that of the father, as Freud suggested. As irrational as this may at first appear, it speaks to a pre-modern conception of how a male child was imagined to take on the attributes of the father.

Jung's relationship to his father was also oedipally strained. He appears to have initially taken Freud for a benevolent father figure, and to some extent, at least early on in their relationship, the feeling was reciprocated. But the differences between the two men undermined their ability to continue to collaborate. Freud appears to have displayed paranoid ideation concerning the aspirations of several of his more talented younger followers and he expressed concerns about their wishes to displace him and his sexual theory. Jung, in turn, was evidently an ambitious opportunist, and was deeply narcissistically wounded after being intellectually rebuffed by Freud. But there is another deeper parallel to the oedipal dynamic between the elder Freud and the youthful Jung, and this is one that has its basis in the history of religion.

THE PARTING OF THE WAYS: OEDIPUS AND SUPERSESSION

The path leading to the parting of the ways between Christianity and Judaism has been obscured by time, but modern scholars are currently reconstructing its historical elements. By the end of the first century, definite and open enmity had broken out between the early Jewish followers of Jesus and their fellow Jews. While the Second Temple still stood, it was possible to view Jewish Christians—who may not yet have considered Jesus divine—as simply another sect within the spectrum of Second Temple Judaisms (Ehrman 2014). But after the destruction of the Temple, Jewish Christians and the early rabbis began to struggle in earnest for legitimacy in the eyes of their fellow Jews and the ruling government of Rome. Rabbinic Jews controlled the synagogues, and they began to drive the heretical Jewish Christians out. Paul famously described himself originally as a zealous Pharisee who sought to persecute the early Jewish Christians, until undergoing his conversion to Christ on the road to Damascus.

The conflict had worsened considerably by the second century. The rabbinic movement became more aggressive in persecuting Jewish Christians (*notzrim*) and Gnostic sects (*minim*). A blessing was introduced into the standardized daily prayer that would have caused Jewish Christians to curse themselves, a serious implication in those times, and those who refused to recite it were hounded from the synagogues. The Talmud describes the need to remain strictly separate from Jewish Christians, to be careful not to find any pleasure in their conversation or books, and to avoid any of their healing practices even if it meant certain death, as the Talmudic historian Daniel Boyarin notes in his consideration of an aggadic passage in *Tosefta Chullin* (1999).

Matters may have reached a head during the Bar Kokhba rebellion of 132–135 CE. R. Akiva, the leader of Rabbinic Judaism, declared Simeon ben Kosiva (Bar Kokhba, "son of a star") to be the Jewish messiah, and supported him in what was widely recognized to be a doomed rebellion against Rome. In return, Bar Kokhba advanced the religious aims of the rabbis, including the persecution of heretical sects, most notably the Jewish Christians. The latter refused to fight under Bar Kokhba, as they had already declared Jesus of Nazareth their messiah.

In the first years of the rebellion, the insurrectionist Jews were able to wrest control of Jerusalem away from Rome and to govern it. Bar Kokhba may have taken this opportunity to persecute Jewish Christians and to execute them for their failure to support the insurrection. Shortly thereafter, Jewish Christianity all but disappeared.[3] After the end of the 132–135 CE rebellion, in which it is estimated that hundreds of thousands of Jews were killed and the rest banished from Judaea, newly converted gentiles with no religious or cultural ties to Judaism now constituted the majority of Christians. They aggressively made a point of reminding the Jews of their culpability in the death of Jesus, and insisted that Christianity had superseded Judaism by an obvious act of divine will, as evidenced by both the destruction of the Temple and the subsequent failed insurrection. This opinion was further encouraged when Constantine established Christianity as the Roman Empire's favored religion in the fourth century. The father-son relationship between Judaism (Laius) and Christianity (Oedipus) shifted, as it does in the myth, from the persecution of the young religion by its father to an attempt by the son to replace the father. Indeed, Freud makes reference to the role of patricide in the context of the struggle between Judaism and Christianity in his last work, *Moses and Monotheism*.

Jung proposes the supersession of Judaism by Christianity in his controversial text *Answer to Job*. There, he argues that the God image is constantly changing as a result of the continued evolution of the collective unconscious. He concludes that YHWH represented a primitive God in need of constant attention, with elements of an unstable

3. We currently have few if any documents that are clearly attributable to Jewish Christian sects. It is widely believed that the Ebionites, a transliteration of the term *evyonim*, which means, "the poor," were likely an early Jewish Christian sect. Paul speaks in his letters of gathering donations for the poor of Jerusalem, likely a reference to the Ebionites. The *Didache*, an early Christian document, may have its origins in Jewish Christianity, and several apocryphal texts appear to have originally been of Jewish provenance but were later edited to reflect Hellenistic Christianity. Helmut Koester, *Introduction to the New Testament* (Amsterdam: deGruyter, 2000).

borderline personality, and behaviors that were envious, angry, chaotic, and unpredictable. To Jung's mind, Christianity, the new God image of Christ who espoused unlimited love and compassion for man, represented a psychological advance in man's unconscious. Jung's argument is essentially a reframing of the ancient Christian idea of having superseded Judaism, which was viewed by most Christian academics and theologians in the late nineteenth and early twentieth centuries as primitive and irrelevant.

CHAPTER 19

Psychoanalysis and Altered States

The psyche creates the world every day. The only expression that I can use for this activity is fantasy.

—Carl Jung

The role of mystical altered states in psychoanalysis (Bromberg 2001) has rarely been examined. The reasons are manifold; however, they may parallel the early kabbalists' concerns of for safeguarding esoteric practices. The fact is that the training of a psychoanalyst has little in common with that of other professions. Substantial emphasis is placed on the master and disciple relationship and training analyses and detailed supervisions are designed to insure that trainees are ready to be initiated as masters in their own right.

Like the Hasid who comes to watch his *tzaddik* "tie his shoelaces," trainees do not so much learn didactically from their training analysts as observe how their analysts behave, and when and how they intervene to ask questions, make comments, or offer well-timed interpretations. Ideally, training should also include the direct observation of a patient treatment, but this is not available in most institutes.

The subjective mental states of the analyst, however, are totally unavailable for perusal. It should be noted that the practice of psychoanalysis has included altered mental states since its inception, being rooted in hypnosis. In his *Recommendations to Physicians Practicing*

Psychoanalysis (1912), Freud suggests to psychoanalysts that they adopt a state of "evenly-suspended attention," and "simply listen and not bother about keeping anything in mind," (1912, 112), an approach that constitutes a meditation. Wilfred Bion offered the advice that the analyst enter each session "without memory or desire" (1963). These are references to altered and paradoxical mental states, respectively, that can be likened to those of the mystics (Garb 2011).

Jung wrote about his personal experiences while in altered mental states. In *Memories, Dreams, Reflections*, he describes apparently dissociated states in which he would routinely converse with imaginary figures, comparable to Josef Karo and his maggid (Werblowsky 1977). Jung later termed this active imagination and encouraged analysts and patients to practice it and later to write down their experiences.

The psychoanalyst working out of altered mental states promotes communications in a manner that is distinct from the logically directed cognitions of everyday life, and in ways that have not yet been adequately explained. The Kleinian notion of projective identification, or what Jung refers to as participation mystique, represents an unusual mode of communication that is somehow able to influence the thoughts and affects of others. This may be attributable to very subtle bodily cues, but this is by no means certain. It is as possible that this phenomenon represents a primitive pre-verbal mode of communication of our forebears that has been retained in man. From the perspective of psychopathology, it is most often seen in obvious form in so-called borderline patients, where it appears to represent a primitive mode of mentalization, although it may be functioning in most people and most of the time but at levels that are not readily perceived.

Such altered states appear to foster psychological permeability to ideas and images, such as intuition and empathy, while Kohut defined it as vicarious introspection, or what might alternatively be termed attuned intuition. The recent psychoanalytical literature has focused on the so-called countertransference musings of the analyst while in states referred to as reverie (Ogden 1998). There is no other science that I am aware of that encourages comparable states of mind in its practice.

However, today the most common form of psychotherapy is a short-term cognitive-behavioral approach that does not include the elements discussed above. Dreams are rarely interpreted, symbolic images are largely ignored, and the primary goals of the treatment are rational and well-defined. This mode of psychotherapy, although demonstrably practical and valuable for some patients, continues the post-Enlightenment trend of expunging symbolic and imaginal approaches from the cure of the soul. Indeed, the aims of medical psychiatry have in large measure reverted back to those held at the end of the nineteenth century, with a primary focus on brain science, and with psychotherapy viewed as ancillary to psychopharmacology.

What is potentially lost in this approach? Perhaps it is the sense of meaning that was once supplied in a religious society that assisted the individual in his or her path through life. Brain science is gradually replacing those modes of symbolic thought that were once a valued part of psychoanalysis and more broadly human experience itself. However, man will almost certainly continue to seek meaning for his experience. The fact is that no one can benefit psychologically from being told that there is increased activity in their amygdala or that their serotonin levels are low. This is not to dismiss the importance of brain science in psychiatry or to adopt the position of a Luddite. But as Goethe responded polemically to Newton's optics, there is a great deal of difference between mathematically describing the behavior of light and the experience of seeing a summer's day in all of its color and beauty (1810). In this regard, it may be comfortably predicted that devalued elements of psychoanalytical thought will in the future be subject to a return of the repressed. If, as has been argued, psychoanalysis shares much in common with, and is in fact rooted in, religion, then their fates may also be linked. But only time will tell.

Conclusion

Judaism places an emphasis on God's Law; Christianity focuses primarily on God's love. This yields distinct images of God, and serves to differentially structure the unconscious minds of Jews and Christians. As Scholem. noted a direct psychological proof for this is the fact that the mystical experiences are contextually dependent on the religious background of the mystic (1969).

The psychoanalytical ideas and techniques promulgated by Freud show distinct parallels with the tenets of Judaism, whereas Jung's spiritualized approach more closely approximates the attitudes of the early church and the second-century Christian Gnostics. The Freudian psyche is rooted in the body and in sexuality. Freud's interpretive style and style of argument are reminiscent of Jewish *midrash*. In addition, Freud valued negation and abstinence in psychoanalysis as a method for fostering the psychic structure of his patients and protecting the analysis, just as the negative commandments of the Judaic Law are aimed at promoting ethical behaviors and ritual purity. Jung, on the other hand, placed little emphasis on the body or sexuality, and tended to allegorize the material world symbolically, like the early Church Fathers. Systematic rules for how to conduct an analysis received little attention from Jung.

The absence of a clear technique or statements with respect to how to create a framework for analysis can be viewed as a deficiency in Jung's approach. It can lead to therapeutic misadventures and psychological violations. By focusing almost exclusively on his own personality as the instrument of therapy, Jung showed little concern for his followers, who may not have been gifted with his therapeutic skills. His casual remark, "Thank God I am Jung and not a Jungian" (Stein 2005, 5) may have been an honest confession, but is of little assistance to those who are attempting to learn his psychoanalytical approach.

For this reason, it is common today for Jungian analysts to adopt some mode of neo-Freudian technique in order to structure their analyses. In my experience, it is often a self-psychological or relational mode of analysis, as classical Freudian thought and object-relations theory are viewed as overly reductive and strict. There are Jungian analysts who do not believe that Freud's notion of boundaries is critical for the success of psychoanalysis and many, who view it as detrimental. They criticize Jungians who adopt neo-Freudian approaches, much as the early Church Fathers criticized early Christians for Judaizing.

The differences in the therapeutic approaches of Freud and Jung are well recognized, but the influences of specific religious differences until now have not been formally compared. Questions of their religious difference have tended to focus primarily on claims of Jung's anti-Semitism and on Freud's struggles with the rabid anti-Semitism of his time. Jung attributed his theoretical differences with Freud to personal typology (Jung and Jaffe 1989). But in their private correspondence, both men acknowledged that religious difference was the unbridgeable barrier between them.

William James recognized the psychological benefits of religious belief (1988). Like the religious cure of the soul, he suggested that deeply transformative psychological healing requires faith. But faith has lost its footing in modern life and has largely been replaced by rational ideas. This loss has affected both religion and psychotherapy. But as Abraham Joshua Heschel argues:

> Faith in God cannot be forced upon man. The issue is not only lack of faith but also the vulgarization of faith and the abuse of freedom. Our effort must involve a total re-orientation about the nature of man and the world. And our hope lies in the certainty that all men are capable of sensing the wonder and mystery of existence, that all men have a capacity for reverence. Awe and reverence precede faith; they are at the root of faith. We must grow in awe in order to reach faith. We must be guided by awe to be worthy of faith. Awe is the beginning and gateway of faith, the first precept of all, and

> upon it the whole world is established. (Heschel and Hartman 1997, 251)

Jung noted in his time that Catholics rarely came for psychoanalysis because they attended confession and expressed faith in God (Jung 1933). Likewise, it is rare for those in the observant Jewish community to seek psychotherapy, unless they encounter psychological issues of substantial magnitude (Margolese 1998). As Jung noted, religion was, and continues to be, an effective mode of psychotherapy for many. However, for those who cannot find solace in the traditions of religion, secular psychotherapies must suffice.

Freud's classical psychoanalytical approach was criticized by Jung for lacking a spiritual component. It is true that repeated interpretations of sexual wishes and Oedipal dynamics can become rote and therapeutically stale, much as religion when practiced mechanically becomes arid and joyless (Kradin 2014). Obsessional styles must be avoided if analysis is not to become, as Freud recognized, empty ritual.

Jung's approach tends to counter this deficiency. Jung was almost certainly correct in envisioning the unconscious as an organ of creativity. His concept of the creative mythopoietic psyche engenders an imaginal increase in psychological capaciousness. His approach calls for a more positive attitude towards the unconscious than Freud's, and one that in some respects recapitulates that of the mystics. Jung's concept of the self is reminiscent of the religious divine soul, and his emphasis on its role as a motivating force within the process of individuation makes Jungian analysis an intrinsically spiritual exercise. It is encouraging that some modern non-Jungian psychoanalysts are re-evaluating the therapeutic importance of spirituality in their treatment of patients (Aron and Starr 2013), although there is a need to credit Jung's advances among psychoanalytical scholars, as claims that fail to recognize what has already been published border at times on plagiarism.

The field of psychoanalysis has progressed in many ways since Freud and Jung first developed their ideas. A modern psychoanalyst may take exception to much of what I have written here, as it does not rehearse all of the theoretical advances that have occurred. But my aim has not been to elaborate on the historical development of the field; rather it has been simply to highlight how the religious tenets of Judaism and Christianity influenced the ideas of Freud and Jung.

The validity of my arguments may be difficult to accept for those practitioners who are not versed in the histories and respective theologies of Judaism and Christianity, and for those who are not acquainted with Jung's ideas concerning the pre-modern roots of modern psychology. In defense, this text is an exercise in the history of unconscious ideas, which means that one can merely intimate proof for its arguments. It is impossible to prove that Freud was informed by notions of the ancient Israelite priest as healer, but there is circumstantial evidence to support this hypothesis, even if it never consciously entered Freud's mind.

The sensibilities of some may be offended by overt expressions of religious difference, but there is no doubt that such religious differences influenced Freud and Jung. After all, as Karl Abraham noted, one does not simply lose a two-thousand-year-old mode of thinking in a generation or two. And in this regard, it is important to realize that Freud was not as secular as he believed himself to be. Nor was he the universalistic humanist that some of his followers would prefer to imagine him as. The facts instead strongly suggest that he remained in many respects, psychologically speaking, a traditional Jew, and subject to the traditional prejudices that were rampant in early twentieth-century Europe. This is true even if he was a declared atheist who never practiced his religion, as his personal statements repeatedly confirm. Nor can Jung's Christianity, with its anti-Semitic sentiments, be dismissed, Although he may not have consciously considered himself to be anti semitic, this was not uncommon, as Goldenhagen points out (2013).

Today, and especially in America, it is easy to forget that the post-Enlightenment Europe of Freud and Jung was steeped in strong religious prejudices. The history of religious prejudice is deeply rooted in the orthodox beliefs of Christianity and Judaism and this will not likely change substantially, as long as these religions continue to adhere to them. The early church was persecuted by Rabbinic Jews in the first two centuries of the first millennium, a fact that is either unknown or ignored by most Jews. However, the subsequent anti-Semitic attitudes, official policies, and teachings of the Catholic Church and its subsequent Protestant reformers more than made up for any wrongs that ancient Christians might have suffered at the hands of the ancient Jews (Michael 2006). The religious antipathies of early twentieth-century Europe must not be denied, nor should they be revised anachronistically. Freud and Jung acknowledged their own prejudices and today's scholars must feel free and unencumbered if they are to examine how religious biases distorted the trajectories of psychoanalytical thought and tended to exclude aspects of potentially optimal psychological experience. Discussion of this topic must not be clouded by the atrocities of the Holocaust, modern ecumenical statements by the church, or by modern politically correct perspectives. Consider the following passage in Strozier's biography of Kohut:

> Kohut felt the goal for revitalizing psychoanalysis was to get the Jews and Protestants to work together. The Jewish medical dominance of psychoanalysis in contemporary America was unfortunate, but if the institutes were dominated by the Protestants alone it would probably move psychoanalysis toward nonscientific "healing through love" and other cures by identification. The result would be a rise in existential psychiatry and analysis, as it existed in Europe, which he clearly saw as unfortunate. (Strozier 2001,136–137)

Psychoanalysts, be they Jewish, Christian, or secular, who are genuinely interested in the topic of how psychoanalysis has, and is, evolving, must be able to recognize how religious differences shaped their field.

In conclusion, the points raised in this text have potentially important implications for psychoanalytical treatment. If my arguments are correct, one may indeed question whether Freudian analysis speaks more to patients with Jewish backgrounds and Jungian analysis to those with Christian ones. Patients tend to vote with their feet, and the religious demographics of who tends to seek out Freudian versus Jungian psychoanalysts may offer an important insight. Certainly, times have changed since the early twentieth century and cross pollination between schools of psychoanalytical thought has occurred. But it is naive to imagine that religious background no longer influences modern psychoanalytical ideas.

Having experienced Freudian and Jungian analysis first hand, both as a patient and as a practitioner, I have perceived differences that I interpreted, like Kohut, as strengths and deficiencies in both. In general, I found that my Jewish analysts, both neo-Freudian and neo-Jungian, were more apt to be challenging and more interested in developmental issues. I experienced my Christian analysts, again from both schools, as supportive but less comfortable addressing negative affects and intimate personal issues. Whether my observations can be generalized is uncertain, but my experience has been seconded by others, including Kohut, as noted above.

After pondering this topic, I suggest that the remedy for what ails psychoanalysis may be found precisely in those areas where Judaism and Christianity have diverged. Judaism and Christianity defined themselves both in positive ways and by mutual denigration. Dimly conscious impulses have almost certainly caused them to accentuate their areas of difference. It is undeniable that Judaism lost an important element of spirituality in reaction to the rise of Christianity. Rabbinic Judaism found it increasingly necessary to turn inward in order to survive the repressive effects of Christianity over two millennia. It is not surprising that Freud's approach tends to lack spirituality and seeks to maintain a materialistic stance.

In its abandonment of the Law, Christianity gained certain freedoms but also sacrificed rules that foster ethical concern. In its dualistic perspective, it tends to split the good and the bad in ways that potentially compromise mental health and the conduct of analysis. Is it a surprise that Jung's approach, informed by Christianity, is basically antinomian?

Judaism and Christianity eventually evolved as the shadows of each other via a continued process of positive and negative selection. A religion that attends to rules must necessarily be different from one that attends primarily to love; although both Judaism and Christianity share laws and love in common, their accents are distinct. In a recent biography of Menachem Mendel Schneerson, the last Lubavitcher rebbe, he is noted to have suggested that modern Judaism needed to reintroduce elements of mysticism if it was to attract secular Jews back to their religion. As the author Chaim Miller notes:

> For the contemporary Jew to remain passionate, for many lost souls to find their way back home and for the Jewish spirit to be revived, dry legalism and even exhilarating Talmudic dialectics are important but not enough. Jews need the transcendent holistic vision and spiritual vitality that only esoteric teaching . . . brings. (2014, 214)

A comparable argument can be made concerning psychoanalytical approaches. Analysis as practiced by Freud, can be dry and appear harsh to a Jungian analyst who is focused on loving his or her patient and exploring their spirituality.

I am not suggesting that Freudians abandon their focus on boundaries or that Jungians become less concerned with spirituality. However, with respect to the broad topics of matter and spirit, body and soul, personal and collective ideas, there is room for growth on both sides. Whereas the secular practice of psychoanalysis is obviously not religion, it is time for Jungian analysts to recognize with greater appreciation the importance of Judaism's emphasis on rules, boundaries, language, and physicality in their practice, while Freudian analysts should open to the therapeutic role of Christianity's focus on love, image, symbol, and spirit. In an optimal analysis both are required.

In my own practice of psychoanalysis, I attempt to combine these two approaches. I rely on Jungian thought in my symbolic interpretation of dreams but also specifically search for oedipal symbology in the dreams of patients. Otherwise, I work primarily from within the transference and try to maintain reasonably strict boundaries. I do not find this approach incongruous nor do my patients report it as confusing. At times I may consciously choose to introduce references to myth, fairy tales, and religion in the treatment, but I am always wary that these topics can be used in the service of defending against addressing painful personal material or feel inappropriate or intrusive.

In my experience, many patients benefit initially from a neo-Freudian analysis; others, and especially those with overly harsh super-egos, or those who are far too tied to the material world, may benefit initially from a Jungian-informed approach, at least until they have enough ego support to begin deconstructing rigid ego defenses in a Freudian analysis.

From my perspective, the approach of the Jewish mystics represents the ideal theoretical approach to psychoanalysis, due to their ability to meld law with spirituality (i.e., structure and freedom), as both are required for mental health and authenticity. From this perspective, the approaches of Freud and Jung should be viewed as complementary, and not exclusive. It may be the case that only when both poles of experience are integrated are states of wholeness and mental health achieved.

Figure Legends

Figure 1. Moses ben Maimon or Maimonides was a twelfth-century rabbinic scholar and Jewish philosopher who compiled the *Mishneh Torah* and authored *Guide of the Perplexed*. His standing as a sage is essentially unrivaled.

Figure 2. Sigmund Freud on his fifty-sixth birthday. Freud was a neuroscientist who went on to develop psychoanalysis.

Figure 3. Carl C. Jung was a Swiss Christian psychiatrist who developed his approach to psychoanalysis after breaking with Freud.

Figure 4. Freud's tripartite structural model of the psyche, which replaced his earlier topographic model, is shown. The dynamic interactions between the parts of the psyche were postulated to determine intrapsychic conflicts.

Figure 5. Jung's model of the psyche was based primarily on symbolic imagery and included a collective unconscious that was the source of the archetypes and the God image or self.

Figure 6. The standard sefirotic kabbalistic diagram includes the ten *sefirot* arranged in triangular form.

Figure 7. The first page of R. Schneur Zalman's classic text of Chabad Hasidism *Likutei Amarim* or the *Tanya* (תניא) based on its first word.

Figure 8. Moses the Lawgiver as portrayed by Charlton Heston in the Cecil B. DeMille blockbuster *The Ten Commandments*.

Figure 9. Avraham Ha Rav Kook, the chief rabbi of Israel during the Palestinian mandate. Kook was a scholar, poet, and a visionary.

References

Aquilo, Eugene and Andrew Newberg. 1999. *Mystical Mind*. Minneapolis: Fortress.

Aristotle. 1984. *Collected Works of Aristotle*. Edited by Jonathan Barnes. Princeton: Bollingen.

Aron, Lewis and Karen Starr. 2013. *A Psychotherapy for the People*. New York: Routledge.

Augustine. 2003. *City of God*. Edited by G. R. Evans and translated by Henry Bettenson. London: Penguin.

Bakan, David. 1958. *Sigmund Freud and the Jewish Mystical Tradition*. Princeton: Van Nostrand.

______. 1991. *Maimonides on Prophecy: A Commentary on Selected Chapters of the Guide of the Perplexed*. Northvale, NJ: Jason Aronson.

Bakan, David, Daniel Merkur, and David Weiss. 2009. *Maimonides' Cure of Souls: Medieval Precursor of Psychoanalysis*. Albany: SUNY Press.

Bartlett, John. 1992. *Familiar Quotations*. Boston: Little Brown.

Batnitzky, Leora. 2013. *How Judaism Became a Religion*. Princeton: Princeton University Press.

Berlin, Adele, et al. 2004. *The Jewish Study Bible*. New York, Oxford: Oxford University Press.

Berlin, Heather. 2011. "The Neural Basis of the Dynamic Unconscious." *Neuropsychoanlysis* 13: 5–71.

Biale, David. 2002. *Cultures of the Jews*. New York: Schocken.

Bion, Wilfred. 1963. *Elements of Psycho-Analysis*. London: Heinemann.

Bohm, David. 2002. *Wholeness and the Implicate Order*. London: Routledge.

Borch-Jacobsen, Mikkeland and Sonu Shamdasani. 2012. *The Freud Files*. Cambridge: Cambridge University Press.

Bowlby, John. 1969. *Attachment and Loss*. New York: Basic Books.

Boyarin, Daniel. 1997. *A Radical Jew: Paul and the Politics of Identity*. Berkeley: University of California.

______. 1999. *Dying for God: Martyrdom and the Making of Christianity and Judaism*. Stanford: Stanford University Press.

______. 2006. *Borderlines: The Partitioning of Judaism and Christianity*. Philadelphia: University of Pennsylvania.

Breuer, Josef and Sigmund Freud. 1895. *Studies on Hysteria*. Vol. 2 of *The Standard Edition of the Complete Psychological Works of Sigmund Freud*, edited by James Strachey, 1–306. London: Hogarth.

Bromberg, Philip. 2001. *Standing in the Spaces*. London: Routledge.

Buber, Martin. 1956. *Tales of the Hasidim*. London: Thames & Hudson.

______. 1958. *Hasidism and Modern Man*. New York: Harper.

Carroll, James. 2001. *Constantine's Sword*. New York: Mariner Books.

Chilton, Bruce. 2002. *Rabbi Jesus*. Colorado Springs, CO: Image.

Cohen, Shaye J. D. 2014. *Maccabees to Mishnah*. Louisville, KY: W. J. Knox.

Crick, Francis and Graeme Mitchison. 1983. "The Function of Dream Sleep." *Nature* 304: 111–114.

Damasio, Anthony. 1994. *Descartes' Error: Emotion, Reason, and the Human Brain*. New York: Putnam.

Darwin, Charles. 2004. *Descent of Man*. New York: Penguin Books.

De Conick, April. 2006. *Paradise Now: Essays on Early Jewish and Christian Mysticism*. Atlanta: Society of Biblical Literature.

Descartes, Rene. 1988. *Selected Philosophical Writings*. Cambridge: Cambridge University Press.

Douglas, Mary. 2002. *Purity and Danger*. London: Taylor.

Dresner, Samuel. 2002. *Heschel, Hasidism, and Halacha*. New York: Fordham University Press.

Drob, Sandor. 2000. *Kabbalah Metaphors*. Northvale, NJ: Jason Aronson.

Edinger, Edward. 1976. *The New God Image*. Wilmette, IL: Chiron.

Ehrman, Bart. 2014. *How Jesus Became God*. New York: Harper.

Eigen, Michael. 2013. *Kabbalah and Psychoanalysis*. London: Karnac.

Eliade, Mircea. 1964. *Shamanism*. Princeton: Bollingen.

Elior, Rachel. 1999. *The Mystical Origins of Hasidism*. Oxford: Littman Library of Jewish Civilization.

Ellenberger, Henri. 1970. *The Discovery of the Unconscious*. New York: Harper & Row.

Erickson, Erik. 1963. *Young Man Luther*. London: W. W. Norton.

Etkes, Immanuel. 1982. *Rabbi Israel Salanter*. Jerusalem: Magnes Press.

______. 2005. *The Besht*. Waltham, MA: Brandeis.

______. 2014. *Schneur Zalman of Lyady*. Waltham, MA: Brandeis.

Eysenck, Hans J. 1994. "The Outcome Problem in Psychotherapy: What Have We Learned?" *Behaviour Research and Therapy* 32 (5): 477–95.

Ferenzci, Sandor. 1994. *Final Contributions to the Problems and Methods of Psychoanalysis*. London: Karnac.

Fine, Lawrence. 2003. *Physician of the Soul, Healer of the Cosmos*. Stanford: Stanford University Press.

Fonagy, Peter. 2001. *Attachment Theory and Psychoanalysis*. New York: Other Press.

Foxbrunner, Roman. 1993. *Habad: The Hasidism of R. Shneuer Zalman of Lyadi*. Northvale, NJ: Jason Aronson.

Frazer, James G. 1922. *The Golden Bough*. New York: McMillan.

Fredricksen, Paula. 2010. *Augustine and the Jews*. New Haven: Yale University Press.

Freud, Sigmund. 1895. *Project for a Scientific Psychology*. Vol. 2 in *Standard Edition of the Works of Sigmund Freud*, edited by James Strachey, 281–392. London: Hogarth.

______. 1900. *The Interpretation of Dreams*. Vol. 4 and 5 in *Standard Edition of the Works of Sigmund Freud*, edited by James Strachey, 1–622. London: Hogarth.

______. 1907. "Obsessive Actions and Religious Practices." Vol 9 in *Standard Edition of the Works of Sigmund Freud*, edited by James Strachey, 115–128. London: Hogarth.

______. 1909. *Notes upon a Case of Obsessional Neurosis*. Vol 9 in *Standard Edition of the Works of Sigmund Freud*, edited by James Strachey, 155–249. London: Hogarth.

______. 1912. "Dynamics of the Transference." Vol 12 in *Standard Edition of the Works of Sigmund Freud*, edited by James Strachey, 97–108. London: Hogarth.

______. 1912a. *Recommendations to Physicians Practicing Psychoanalysis.* Vol. 12 in *Standard Edition of the Works of Sigmund Freud*, edited by James Strachey, 111–120. London: Hogarth.

______. 1913. "On Beginning the Treatment." Vol. 12 in *Standard Edition of the Works of Sigmund Freud*, edited by James Strachey, 121–144. London: Hogarth.

______. 1913a. *Totem and Taboo.* Vol. 13 in *Standard Edition of the Works of Sigmund Freud*, edited by James Strachey, 1–161. London: Hogarth.

______. 1914. "On Narcissism." Vol. 14 in *Standard Edition of the Works of Sigmund Freud*, edited by James Strachey, 67–104. London: Hogarth.

______. 1915. "Observations on Transference Love." Vol. 12 in *Standard Edition of the Works of Sigmund Freud*, edited by James Strachey, 157–171. London: Hogarth.

______. 1916. *Introductory Lectures.* Vol. 16 in *Standard Edition of the Works of Sigmund Freud*, edited by James Strachey, 241–477. London: Hogarth.

______. 1917. "Mourning and Melancholia." Vol. 14 in *Standard Edition of the Works of Sigmund Freud*, edited by James Strachey, 237–258. London: Hogarth.

______. 1920. "Beyond the Pleasure Principle." Vol. 18 in *Standard Edition of the Works of Sigmund Freud*, edited by James Strachey, 1–64. London: Hogarth.

______. 1923. "The Ego and the Id." Vol. 19 in *Standard Edition of the Works of Sigmund Freud*, edited by James Strachey, 115–128. London: Hogarth.

______. 1923a. "A Seventeenth Century Demonological Neurosis." Vol. 19 in *Standard Edition of the Works of Sigmund Freud*, edited by James Strachey, 67–108. London: Hogarth.

______. 1927. *Future of an Illusion.* Vol. 21 in *Standard Edition of the Works of Sigmund Freud*, edited by James Strachey, 1–161. London: Hogarth.

______. 1930. *Civilization and Its Discontents.* Vol. 21 in *Standard Edition of the Works of Sigmund Freud*, edited by James Strachey, 57–146. London: Hogarth.

______. 1939. *Moses and Monotheism*. Vol. 21 in *Standard Edition of the Works of Sigmund Freud*, edited by James Strachey, 1–138. London: Hogarth.

______. 1940. *Outline of Psychoanalysis*. Vol. 23 in *Standard Edition of the Works of Sigmund Freud*, edited by James Strachey, 139–208. London: Hogarth.

______. 1941. "Address to the B'nai B'rith." Vol 20 in *Standard Edition of the Works of Sigmund Freud*, edited by James Strachey, 271–276. London: Hogarth.

Freud, Sigmund and Wilhelm Fliess. 1985. *The Complete Letters of Sigmund Freud to Wilhelm Fliess*. Edited by Jeffrey Masson. Cambridge: Belknap Harvard.

Freud, Sigmund and Karl Abraham. 2002. *The Complete Correspondence of Sigmund Freud and Karl Abraham, 1907–1925*. London: Karnac.

Frosh, Steven. 2009. *Hate and the Jewish Science*. London: Pergamon Macmillan.

Funkenstein, Amos. 1986. *Theology and the Scientific Imagination from the Middle Ages to the Seventeenth Century*. Princeton: Princeton University Press.

Gabbard, Glen and Eva Lester. 2002. *Boundaries and Boundary Violations in Psychoanalysis*. Washington, DC: American Psychiatric Press.

Garb, Jonathan. 2011. *Shamanic Trance in Modern Kabbalah*. Chicago: University of Chicago Press.

Garrett, Don, ed. 1996. *The Cambridge Companion to Spinoza*. Cambridge: Cambridge University Press.

Gaw, Albert. 1993. *Culture, Ethnicity, and Mental Illness*. Washington, DC: American Psychiatry Press.

Gay, Peter. 1978. *Freud, Jews, and Other Germans: Masters and Victims in Modernist Culture*. New York: Oxford University Press.

______. 1985. *Freud for Historians*. New York: Oxford University Press.

______. 1987. *A Godless Jew: Freud, Atheism, and the Making of Psychoanalysis*. New Haven: Yale University Press.

Gay, Volney. 1992. *Freud on Sublimation*. Albany, NY: SUNY Press.

Gilman, Sander. 1993. *Freud, Race, and Gender*. Princeton: Princeton University Press.

Ginsburgh, Yitzchak. 1995. *The Hebrew Letters*. Kfar Chabad: Ganai.

Goethe, Johann. 1810. *A Theory of Color*. Tubingen: J. G. Cotta.

Goetz, Stewart and Charles Taliaferro. 2011. *A Brief History of the Soul*. Oxford: John Wiley-Blackwell.

Goldhagen, David. 2002. *A Moral Reckoning*. New York: Knopf.

______. 2009. *Hitler's Willing Executioners: Ordinary Germans and the Holocaust*. New York: Vintage.

______. 2013. *Anti-Semitism: The Devil that Will Not Die*. Boston: Little, Brown, and Co.

Goldin, Judah. 1990. *The Fathers According to Rabbi Nathan (Avot de Rabbi Nathan)*. New Haven: Yale University Press.

Green, Arthur. 1977. "The Ẓaddiq as Axis Mundi in Later Judaism." *Journal of the American Academy of Religion* 45: 327–347.

______. 2003. *Guide to the Zohar*. Stanford: Stanford University Press.

Gregory, Brad. 2012. *The Unintended Reformation*. Cambridge: Belknap Harvard.

Grosskurth, Phyllis. 1986. *Melanie Klein*. New York: Knopf.

Gunderson, John and Paul Links. 2008. *Borderline Personality Disorder: A Clinical Guide*. 2nd edition. Washington, DC: American Psychiatric Publishers.

Halivni, David. 1998. *Peshat and Derash*. Oxford: Oxford University Press.

Hart, Mitchell, ed. 2011. *Jews and Race*. Waltham, MA: Brandeis.

Haule, John. 1998. *The Love Cure*. Dallas: Spring.

Hegel, George. 1976. *Phenomenology of the Spirit*. Oxford: Oxford University Press.

Heilman, Samuel and Friedman, Menachem. 2012. *The Rebbe: The Life and Afterlife of Menachem Mendel Schneerson*. Princeton: Princeton University Press.

Henderson, David. 2014. *Apophatic Elements in Theory and Practice of Psychoanalysis*. London: Routledge.

Hengel, Martin. 1974. *Judaism and Hellenism: Studies in their Encounter in Palestine During the Early Hellenistic Period*. London: SCM Press.

Herman, Arthur. 2014. *The Cave and the Light*. New York: Random House.

Heschel, Abraham J. 1995. *A Passion for Truth*. New York: Jewish Lights.

Heschel, Abraham J. and David Hartman. 1997. *Between God and Man*. New York: Free Press.

Hillman, James. 1998. *Healing Fictions*. Dallas: Spring.

______. 2014. *In Search: Psychology and Religion*. Dallas: Spring.

Hoffer, Axel. 1991. "The Freud Ferenzci Controversy—A Living Legacy." *International Review of Psychoanalysis* 18: 465–472.

Hoffman, Lawrence. 2012. "From Penitence to Nobility." In *We Have Sinned*, edited by Lawrence Hoffman, 1–38. Woodstock: Jewish Lights.

Homer, Sean. 2004. *Lacan*. London: Routledge.

Horowitz, Aaron. 1987. *Avodat ha Levi*. Lemberg: Hasidic Texts.

Howell, Elizabeth. 2008. *The Dissociative Mind*. London: Routledge.

Idel, Moshe. 1990. *Kabbalah: New Perspectives*. New Haven: Yale University Press.

Jacobs, Louis. 1965. "Honor Thy Father." *Cambridge Opinion* 39: 4–8.

______. 2005. *Their Heads in Heaven*. London: Valentine Mitchell.

______. 2006. *Tractate on Ecstasy*. London: Valentine Mitchell.

James, William. 1902. *The Varieties of Religious Experience: A Study in Human Nature*. New York: Longmans.

______. 1988. "Pragmatism." In the *Collected Works of William James 1902–1910*, 479–624. New York: Library of America.

Janet, Pierre. 1926. *Psychological Healing*. New York: MacMillan.

Jones, James. 2002. *Terror and Transformation*. London: Routledge.

Josephs, Lawrence. 1996. *Balancing Empathy and Interpretation*. Northvale, NJ: Jason Aronson.

Josephus, Flavius. 2003. *Antiquities of the Jews*. New York: Thomas Nelson.

Jung, Carl G. 1911. 1983. *Symbols of Transformation*. Vol. 5 in *The Collected Works of Carl G. Jung*, edited by Sir Herbert Read, Michael Fordham, and Gerhard Adler. Princeton: Princeton University Press.

———. 1916. "The Transcendent Function." Vol. 8 in *The Collected Works of Carl G. Jung*, edited by Sir Herbert Read, Michael Fordham, and Gerhard Adler, 67–91. Princeton: Princeton University Press.

———. 1921. *Psychological Types*. Vol. 6 in *The Collected Works of Carl G. Jung*, edited by Sir Herbert Read, Michael Fordham, and Gerhard Adler. Princeton: Princeton University Press.

———. 1933. "Psychotherapy or Clergy." In *Modern Man in Search of a Soul*, 226–255. London: Kegan Paul.

———. 1934. "The State of Psychotherapy Today." Vol. 10 in *The Collected Works of Carl G. Jung*, edited by Sir Herbert Read, Michael Fordham, and Gerhard Adler, 165–166. Princeton: Princeton University Press.

———. 1942. "Transformation Symbolism in the Mass." Vol. 11 in *The Collected Works of Carl G. Jung*, edited by Sir Herbert Read, Michael Fordham, and Gerhard Adler, 201–298. Princeton: Princeton University Press.

———. 1944. *Psychology and Alchemy*. Vol. 12 in *The Collected Works of Carl G. Jung*, edited by Sir Herbert Read, Michael Fordham, and Gerhard Adler. Princeton: Princeton University Press.

———. 1945. "On the Nature of Dreams." Vol. 8 in *The Collected Works of Carl G. Jung*, edited by Sir Herbert Read, Michael Fordham, and Gerhard Adler, 281–300. Princeton: Princeton University Press.

———. 1946. "The Psychology of the Transference." Vol. 16 in *The Collected Works of Carl G. Jung*, edited by Sir Herbert Read, Michael Fordham, and Gerhard Adler, 163–320. Princeton: Princeton University Press.

———. 1951. "Christ a Symbol of the Self." Vol. 9 in *The Collected Works of Carl G. Jung*, edited by Sir Herbert Read, Michael

Fordham, and Gerhard Adler, 36–71. Princeton: Princeton University Press.

______. 1955. *Mysterium Coniunctionis*. Vol. 14 in *The Collected Works of Carl G. Jung*, edited by Sir Herbert Read, Michael Fordham, and Gerhard Adler. Princeton: Princeton University Press.

______. 1967. "The Structure and Dynamics of the Psyche." Vol. 8 in *The Collected Works of Carl G. Jung*, edited by Sir Herbert Read, Michael Fordham, and Gerhard Adler, 131–158. Princeton: Princeton University Press.

______. 1975. *Letters*. Vol. 18 in *The Collected Works of Carl G. Jung*, edited by Sir Herbert Read, Michael Fordham, and Gerhard Adler. Princeton: Princeton University Press.

______. 1980. *The Archetypes and the Collective Unconscious*. Vol. 9, part 1 in *The Collected Works of Carl G. Jung*, edited by Sir Herbert Read, Michael Fordham, and Gerhard Adler. Princeton: Princeton University Press.

______. 1983. *Zofingia Lectures*. Supplementary Vol. A in *The Collected Works of Carl G. Jung*, edited by Sir Herbert Read, Michael Fordham, and Gerhard Adler. Princeton: Princeton University Press.

______. 1984. *Psychology of Religion: West and East*. Vol. 11 in *The Collected Works of Carl G. Jung*, edited by Sir Herbert Read, Michael Fordham, and Gerhard Adler. Princeton: Princeton University Press.

______. 2009. *The Red Book*. Edited by Sonu Shandasani. London: Philemon/W. Norton.

Jung, Carl G. and Aniella Jaffe. 1989. *Memories, Dreams, Reflections*. New York: Vintage.

Jung, Carl G. and Murray Stein. 1996. *Jung on Evil*. Princeton: Princeton University Press.

Kakar, Sonu. 1991. *Shamans, Mystics and Doctors: A Psychological Inquiry into India and its Healing Traditions*. Chicago: University of Chicago Press.

Kaplan, Aryeh. 2013. *Sefer Ha Bahir*. Northvale, NJ: Jason Aronson.

Katz, Steven T. 1978. *Mysticism and Philosophical Analysis*. New York: Oxford University Press.

______. 2000. *Mysticism and Sacred Scripture*. Oxford: Oxford University Press.

Kaufmann, Yechezkel. 1972. *The Religion of Israel*. New York: Schocken.

Kernberg, Otto. 2000. *Borderline Conditions and Pathological Narcissism*. Northvale, NJ: Jason Aronson.

Kerr, John. 1994. *A Most Dangerous Method*. New York: Vintage.

King, Karen L. 2005. *What is Gnosticism?* Cambridge: Harvard Belknap.

Klawans, Jonathan. 2004. *Impurity and Sin in Ancient Judaism*. Oxford: Oxford University Press.

______. 2005. *Purity, Sacrifice and the Temple*. Oxford, Oxford University Press.

Klein, Melanie. 1958. "Development of Mental Functioning." In *Envy and Gratitude: The Writings of Melanie Klein*, edited by Roger Money-Kyrle, 236–46. New York: Free Press.

______. 1986. *The Selected Melanie Klein*. Edited by Juliet Mitchell. London: Hogarth Press.

Koester, Helmut. 2000. *Introduction to the New Testament*. Amsterdam: De Gruyter.

Koester, Helmut and Thomas Lambdin. 1996. *Gospel of Thomas*. In *The Nag Hammadi Library in English*, edited by James M. Robinson. Leiden: E. J. Brill.

Kohut, Heinz. 1971. *The Analysis of the Self: A Systematic Approach to the Psychoanalytical Treatment of Narcissistic Personality Disorders*. New York: International Universities Press.

______. 1979. "The Two Analyses of Mr. Z." *International Journal of Psychoanalysis* 60: 3–27.

Kradin, Richard. 1997. "The Psychosomatic Symptom and the Self." *Journal of Analytical Psychology* 42: 405–22.

______. 2004. "The Placebo Response Complex." *Journal of Analytical Psychology* 49: 617–34.

______. 2007. "Minding the Gaps: The Role of Informational Encapsulation and Mindful Attention in the Analysis of Transference." *Journal of Jungian Theory and Practice* 9: 1–13.

______. 2008. *The Placebo Response and the Power of Unconscious Healing.* London: Routledge.

______. 2010. "Mysticism and the Healing Ministry of Jesus." Unpublished thesis. Harvard.

______. 2011a. "The Placebo Response: An Attachment Strategy that Counteracts the Effects of Stress-Related Dysfunction." *Perspectives in Biology and Medicine* 54 (4): 438–54.

______. 2011b. "Placebo Response: A Consideration of its Role in Therapeutics." *Current Psychiatry Reports* 13 (1): 37–42.

______. 2012. *Pathologies of the Mind-Body Interface: Exploring the Curious Domain of the Psychosomatic Disorders.* New York: Routledge.

______. 2014. "Converting a Freudian Analysis into a Jungian One: Obsession, Addiction, and An Answer from Job." *Journal of Analytical Psychology* 59: 346–65.

Lasch, Carl. 1991. *The Culture of Narcissism: American Life in an Age of Diminishing Expectations.* London: W. W. Norton.

Lawson, Thomas. 2008. *Jung: Darwin of the Mind.* London: Karnac.

Liebes, Yehuda. 1993. "How the Zohar was Written." In *Studies in the Zohar*, edited by Yehuda Liebes. Albany: State University of New York Press.

Maidenbaum, Aryeh and Stephen Martin. 1991. *Lingering Shadows.* Boston: Shambhala.

Maimon, Moses ben. 1974. *The Guide of the Perplexed.* Chicago: University of Chicago Press.

______. 2007. *Mishneh Torah.* New York: Moznaim.

Majno, Guido. 1975. *The Healing Hand.* Cambridge: Harvard University Press.

Malinen, Tapio. 2010. "Psychotherapy as an Ethical and Spiritual Exercise." *Journal of Family Psychotherapy* 21: 287–298.

Margolese, Howard. 1998. "Engaging in Psychotherapy with the Orthodox Jew: A Critical Review." *American Journal of Psychotherapy* 52: 37–53.

Margolies, Max, trans. 2011. *Tanach*. Philadelphia: Jewish Publication Society.

Martin, Steven and Aryeh Maidenbaum. 1991. *Lingering Shadows: Jung, Freudians, and Anti-Semitism*. Boston: Shambhala.

Matt, Daniel. 1995. "Ayin: The Concept of Nothingness in Jewish Mysticism." In *Essential Papers in Kabbalah*, edited by Lawrence Fine, 67–108. New York: NYU Press.

______. 2015. *The Zohar: Pritzker Edition*. Palo Alto: Stanford University Press.

McGinn, Bernard. 1991. *Foundations of Mysticism*. New York: Crossroad.

______. 2006. *Essential Writings of Christian Mysticism*. New York: Modern Library.

McGinnis, Jon and David C. Reisman. 2007. *Classical Arabic Philosophy: An Anthology of Sources*. Indianapolis: Hackett Publishing Company.

Meeks, Wayne. 2003. *The First Urban Christians: The Social World of the Apostle Paul*. New Haven: Yale.

Meir, John P. 2001. *A Marginal Jew*. New York: Doubleday.

Miller, Chaim. 2014. *Turning Judaism Outward*. New York: Gutnick Library.

Mindel, Nissan. 2002. *Schneur Zalman of Liadi*. New York: Kehot.

Moerman, Donald. 2002. *Meaning, Medicine, and the Placebo Effect*. Cambridge: Cambridge University Press.

Mopsik, Charles. 2005. *Sex and the Soul*. Los Angeles: Cherub Press.

Nachman, Moses ben. 2009. *Ramban's Commentary on the Torah*. New York: Art Scroll.

Neusner, Jacob. 1978. *There We Sat Down: Talmudic Judaism in the Making*. New York: KTAV.

Nirenberg, David. 2013. *Anti-Judaism: The Western Tradition*. London: W. W. Norton.

Ogden, Thomas. 1998. *Reverie and Interpretation*. Northvale, NJ: Jason Aronson.

Otto, Rudolph. 1938. *The Kingdom of God and the Son of Man*. Eugene: Wipf & Stock.

______. 1958. *Idea of the Holy*. Oxford: Oxford University.

Pagels, Elaine. 1989. *The Gnostic Gospels*. New York: Vintage Books.

______. 1995. *The Origin of Satan*. New York: Random House.

Patai, Raphael. 1977. *The Jewish Mind*. Hobart, NY: Hatherleigh Press.

______. 1995. *The Jewish Alchemists*. Princeton: Princeton University Press.

Philo. 1993. *Works of Philo: Complete*. Translated by Charles D. Yonge. Peabody, MA: Hendrickson Press.

Plato. 1999. *Phaedo*. Oxford: Oxford University Press.

Rapaport-Albert, Adele. 1996. "Hasidism after 1772." In *Hasidism Reappraised*, edited by Adele Rapoport-Albert, 76–140. Oxford: Littman Library of Jewish Civilization.

Ratzinger, Joseph. 1969. *Introduction to Christianity*. San Francisco: Iganatius.

______. 2007. *Jesus: From Baptism to Transfiguration*. Rome: Ignatius.

Ricoeur, Paul. 1970. *Freud and Philosophy*. New Haven: Yale University Press.

Rizzuto, Ana-Marie. 1998. *Why Did Freud Reject God? A Psychodynamic Approach*. New Haven: Yale University Press.

Roback, Abraham A. 1929. *Jewish Influence in Modern Thought*. Cambridge: Sci-Art.

Robinson, James. 1990. *The Nag Hamaddi Library*. San Francisco: HarperOne.

Rogers, Carl. 1989. *The Carl Rogers Reader*. New York: Mariner Books.

Rosman, Moshe. 1996. "Social Conflicts in Miedzyboz." In *Hasidism Reappraised*, edited by Adele Rapoport-Albert. Oxford: Litman Library of Jewish Civilization.

Rotenberg, Mordecai. 1997. *The Yetzer*. Northvale, NJ: Jason Aronson.

______. 2003. *Hasidic Psychology: Making Room for Others*. New York: Transaction.

______. 2004. *Rewriting the Self.* New York: Transaction.

Roth, Cecil. 1992. *A History of the Marranos.* New York: Sepher-Hermon Press.

Sacks, Jonathan. "A Stiff Necked People." <rabbisacks.org/covenant-conversation-5768>, accessed Internet site.

Sampson, David and Tzvi Fishman. 1996. *Lights of Orot.* Jerusalem: Eretz Yisroel Publications.

Sanders, Edward P. 1985. *Jesus and Judaism.* Minneapolis: Fortress Press.

______. 1996. *The Historical Figure of Jesus.* New York: Penguin.

Schafer, Peter. 1998. *Judaeophobia: Attitudes towards the Jews in the Ancient World.* Cambridge: Harvard.

______. 2009. *The Origins of Jewish Mysticism.* Princeton: Princeton University Press.

Scheindlen, Raymond. 2000. *A Short History of the Jewish People.* Oxford: Oxford University Press.

Scholem, Gershom. 1969. *The Messianic Idea in Judaism.* New York: Schocken.

______. 1995. *Zohar, the Book of Splendor.* New York: Schocken Books.

______. 1995a. "The Meaning of the Torah in Jewish Mysticism." *Essential Papers on the Kabbalah*, edited by Lawrence Fine, 179–211. New York: NYU Press.

______. 2012. "Jews and Germans." In *The Jews and Judaism in Crisis: Selected Essays by Gershom Scholem*, edited by Werner Dannhauser, 71–92. Philadelphia: Paul Dry Books.

Schottenstein, J. 2004. *The Babylonian Talmud.* New York: Art Scroll.

Schwartz, Daniel. 2012. *The First Modern Jew: Spinoza and the History of an Image.* Princeton: Princeton University Press.

Schwartz, Howard. 2010. *Society Against Itself: Political Correctness and Organizational Self-Destruction.* London: Karnac.

Schweitzer, Albert. 1910. *The Quest for the Historical Jesus.* London: AC & Black.

Sells, Michael. 1994. *Mystical Languages of Unsaying.* Chicago: University of Chicago Press.

Shamdasani, Sonu. 2003. *Jung and the Making of Modern Psychology*. Cambridge: Cambridge University Press.

______. 2012. *Jung: A Biography in Books*. New York: Norton.

Shochet, Immanuel. 1990. *The Maggid*. New York: Kehot.

Shoham, Shlomo. 2013. *The Measure of All Things, Anthropology*. Newcastle: Cambridge Scholars Press.

Shorter, Edward. 1993. *From Paralysis to Fatigue: A History of Psychosomatic Disease in the Modern Era*. New York: Free Press.

Skehan, Patrick and Alexander DiLella. 1995. *The Wisdom of Ben Sirah*. New Haven: Yale University Press.

Siegel, Ronald. 2009. *The Mindfulness Solution*. Boston: Guilford Press.

Smith, Jonathan Riley. 2005. *The Crusades*. New Haven: Yale University Press.

Smith, Morton. 1973. *Clement of Alexandria and a Secret Gospel of Mark*. Cambridge: Harvard.

______. 1981. *Jesus the Magician*. New York: HarperCollins.

Starr, Karen. 2008. *Repair of the Soul*. London: Routledge.

Stein, Murray. 2005. "Individuation: Inner Work." *Journal of Jungian Theory and Practice* 7: 1–13.

______. 2012. *Jung on Christianity*. Princeton: Princeton University Press.

Strauss, Leo. 1988. *Persecution and the Art of Writing*. Chicago: Chicago University Press.

Strozier, Charles. 2001. *Heinz Kohut: The Making of a Psychoanalyst*. New York: Other Press.

Sulloway, Frank. 1979. *Freud: Biologist of the Mind*. New York: Burnett.

Taylor, Charles. 1989. *Sources of the Self*. Cambridge: Harvard.

______. 2007. *A Secular Age*. Cambridge: Belknap Harvard.

Tertullian. 2001. *Christian and Pagan: The Witness of Tertullian*. Edited by Robert Sider. Washington, DC: Catholic University Press.

Uffenheimer, Rivka. 1993. *Hasidism as Mysticism*. Princeton: Princeton University Press.

Van der Kolk, Bessel. 2014. *The Body Keeps the Score: Brain, Mind, and Body in the Healing of Trauma*. New York: Viking.

Vermarseren, Martin. 1959. *Mithras the Great God.* Amsterdam: Elsevier.

Vermes, Geza. 1981. *Jesus the Jew.* Minneapolis: Fortress.

______. 2012. *Complete Dead Sea Scrolls in English.* New York: Penguin.

Vital, Chayim. 2008. *Etz Chayim.* Jerusalem: Arizal.

Voltaire. 1963. *Candide.* Edited by Peter Gay. New York: Saint Martin's Press.

Werblowsky, R. J. Zwi. 1977. *Joseph Karo, Lawyer and Mystic.* Philadelphia: Jewish Publication Society.

Winnicott, Donald W. 1959. "The Fate of the Transitional Object." In *Psychoanalytic Explorations*, edited by Clare Winnicott, Ray Sheperd, and Madeleine Davis, 53–58. Cambridge: Harvard University Press.

______. 1960. *The Maturational Process and the Facilitating Environment.* New York: International Universities Press.

Wolfson, Eliot R. 1995. *Through a Speculum That Shines: Vision and Imagination in Jewish Mysticism.* Princeton: Princeton University Press.

Yaron, Zvi. 1991. *The Philosophy of Rav Kook.* Jerusalem: Eliner Library.

Yerushalmi, Yosef. 1982. *Zachor.* Seattle: University of Washington Press.

______. 1991. *Freud's Moses.* New Haven: Yale University Press.

Zalman, Shneuer. 2012. *Likutei Amarim.* New York: Kehot.

Index

Q

R

S

www.ingramcontent.com/pod-product-compliance
Ingram Content Group UK Ltd.
Pitfield, Milton Keynes, MK11 3LW, UK
UKHW020101210526
471278UK00004B/173

9 781618 114228